Addition

Name ______________________

Total Problems	**40**
Problems Correct	______

1. 6,429 + 5,857
2. 9,247 + 6,938
3. 4,862 + 2,379
4. 8,563 + 4,784
5. 7,437 + 6,829
6. 5,649 + 9,857
7. 7,368 + 8,249
8. 36,483 + 8,279
9. 76,475 + 71,948
10. 95,468 + 32,785
11. 48,263 + 61,178
12. 72,674 + 19,239
13. 74,865 + 94,573
14. 91,768 + 27,347
15. 45,276 + 32,949
16. 39,265 + 94,381
17. 28,394 + 9,158
18. 85,237 + 73,296
19. 64,879 + 82,387
20. 79,365 + 12,847
21. 54,783 + 69,814
22. 88,603 + 43,529
23. 506,486 + 48,237
24. 756,983 + 181,249
25. 926,548 + 297,619
26. 470,869 + 81,473
27. 672,457 + 759,264
28. 946,309 + 717,846
29. 642,038 + 85,297
30. 248,365 + 923,982
31. 743,654 + 7,196
32. 458,964 + 824,395
33. 532,486 + 925,747
34. 810,156 + 364,512
35. 289,547 + 408,968
36. 568,495 + 287,147
37. 723,108 + 298,349
38. 764,258 + 429,169
39. 462,197 + 389,245
40. 265,478 + 396,584

Practice! Practice! Practice!

Addition

Name ____________________

Total Problems 41

Problems Correct ______

1.	3,708 +2,949	**2.**	7,365 +7,482						
3.	4,984 +4,363	**4.**	6,507 +5,824	**5.**	9,234 +4,928	**6.**	5,240 +8,929	**7.**	2,895 +4,927
8.	4,627 +5,248	**9.**	37,241 + 8,469	**10.**	53,209 + 4,648	**11.**	77,241 + 8,679	**12.**	94,216 + 9,867
13.	81,476 + 8,925	**14.**	62,418 + 5,526	**15.**	62,147 +24,928	**16.**	97,612 +26,748	**17.**	45,036 +47,948
18.	27,528 +68,487	**19.**	85,436 +62,795	**20.**	55,326 +27,493	**21.**	93,218 +82,925	**22.**	74,621 +72,943
23.	46,247 +81,964	**24.**	36,219 +48,143	**25.**	50,819 +68,627	**26.**	64,217 +86,946	**27.**	717,402 +816,784
28.	649,217 +432,964	**29.**	824,913 +712,847	**30.**	254,726 +941,645	**31.**	524,613 +452,814	**32.**	968,213 + 84,928
33.	734,216 + 29,832	**34.**	462,519 +589,423	**35.**	643,817 +267,423	**36.**	542,611 +627,498	**37.**	812,436 +419,845
38.	7,240,452 +2,991,829	**39.**	64,615,215 + 8,416,548	**40.**	75,602,527 + 6,519,728	**41.**	45,825,187 +18,742,649		

Addition

Name ____________________

Total Problems 25

Problems Correct ______

1. 764,120
215,328
342,509
56,282
+ 9,164

2. 46,812
527,193
615,739
3,265
+ 434,347

3. 62,102
423,216
4,823
1,169
+ 532,342

4. 47,264
721,436
85,249
2,111
+ 9,327

5. 303,215
24,148
912,325
2,298
+ 56,413

6. 49,325
321,264
723,127
3,836
+ 94,243

7. 624,125
86,257
9,582
323,123
+ 4,448

8. 5,426
625,132
5,588
47,245
+ 123,136

9. 7,778
524,432
7,845
52,136
+ 6,629

10. 706,147
621,542
92,285
346,127
+ 9,325

11. 925,292
32,145
626,327
5,893
+ 8,476

12. 721,625
39,237
61,343
132,183
+ 242,152

13. 3,216
321,423
416,342
8,124
+ 52,306

14. 981,624
724,157
8,216
43,564
+ 132,438

15. 623,415
364,127
251,362
142,125
+ 131,236

16. 743,212
62,193
4,324
8,659
+ 9,924

17. 521,243
162,135
8,262
10,418
+ 63,124

18. 600,000
49,243
123,136
9,419
+ 62,132

19. 2,284
325,721
82,413
56,296
+ 124,132

20. 316,423
47,215
923,134
1,927
+ 6,421

21. 42,146
137,247
8,312
231,436
+ 283,142

22. 132,326
49,123
261,242
96,134
+ 2,808

23. 2,233
85,216
429,463
912,322
+ 83,147

24. 261,342
83,148
9,233
3,892
+ 56,125

25. 4,449
8,426
729,137
4,728
+ 5,213

Practice = Success!

Skill: Addition of Four-, Five- and Six-Digit Numbers

Addition

Name ______________________________

Total Problems	**20**
Problems Correct	______

1.
45,624
305,231
723,715
51,256
+ 2,425

2.
5,201
672,316
1,841
3,462
+ 756,295

3.
840,316
3,723
56,104
92,457
+ 295,262

4.
35,206
742,527
1,282
74,653
+ 5,474

5.
642,563
51,284
549,326
74,419
+ 638,247

6.
364,218
3,423
542,852
84,336
+ 92,574

7.
46,359
862,432
8,274
434,648
+ 2,423

8.
4,682
56,243
81,425
563,839
+ 845,158

9.
546,523
852,196
2,465
65,287
+ 473,324

10.
642,394
1,237
36,248
3,855
+ 3,464

11.
365,496
246,278
121,362
384,629
+ 937,845

12.
6,514
362,825
58,283
823,647
+ 634,739

13.
350,002
86,247
932,351
8,963
+ 4,688

14.
816,243
42,686
924,312
8,197
+ 539,438

15.
56,421
962,536
8,923
84,368
+ 547,827

16.
6,764
826,283
9,436
58,149
+ 932,527

17.
463,192
6,824
732,648
37,352
+ 546,475

18.
843,619
65,243
924,306
1,896
+ 347,247

19.
362,485
925,247
36,523
922,587
+ 364,254

20.
625,143
463,258
142,324
368,432
+ 724,897

Practice takes you to the top!

Subtraction

Name ____________________

Total Problems	**40**
Problems Correct	______

1. 8,913 − 6,346
2. 5,137 − 2,986
3. 4,876 − 1,989
4. 7,348 − 2,479
5. 9,600 − 3,834
6. 6,524 − 4,259
7. 3,726 − 1,958
8. 8,432 − 5,649
9. 2,986 − 1,498
10. 7,543 − 2,798
11. 5,849 − 4,967
12. 8,643 − 4,857
13. 48,362 − 9,625
14. 84,758 − 61,269
15. 57,648 − 8,729
16. 74,682 − 52,797
17. 96,200 − 57,456
18. 74,649 − 15,783
19. 65,428 − 8,279
20. 88,427 − 49,383
21. 57,436 − 13,683
22. 96,425 − 67,248
23. 48,615 − 29,784
24. 72,106 − 41,728
25. 25,423 − 19,146
26. 63,289 − 46,195
27. 58,314 − 9,426
28. 76,249 − 27,413
29. 43,628 − 28,349
30. 94,562 − 5,728
31. 87,658 − 52,879
32. 53,628 − 38,249
33. 62,495 − 35,718
34. 79,645 − 63,257
35. 43,625 − 16,476
36. 89,235 − 32,487
37. 46,387 − 31,824
38. 29,357 − 14,189
39. 58,437 − 29,148
40. 35,428 − 26,139

Practice brings success!

Subtraction

Name ____________________

Total Problems	**42**
Problems Correct	______

1. 76,004 − 9,212

2. 7,421 − 1,546

3. 8,914 − 2,389

4. 73,125 − 24,314

5. 6,143 − 2,684

6. 42,156 − 8,219

7. 476,214 − 28,156

8. 62,146 − 8,527

9. 74,216 − 29,348

10. 9,215 − 2,647

11. 264,319 − 125,123

12. 4,000 − 2,184

13. 70,547 − 9,262

14. 524,615 − 241,328

15. 5,016 − 2,428

16. 41,646 − 8,293

17. 842,196 − 8,049

18. 92,004 − 27,123

19. 4,215,302 − 804,921

20. 7,006 − 2,439

21. 65,214 − 27,183

22. 47,215 − 28,306

23. 82,147 − 27,328

24. 726,154 − 8,239

25. 42,156,142 − 21,327,027

26. 8,147 − 2,473

27. 31,426 − 28,248

28. 91,346 − 28,127

29. 502,142 − 84,261

30. 4,312,006 − 916,124

31. 28,416 − 14,249

32. 27,416,545 − 8,312,287

33. 43,216 − 28,409

34. 71,000 − 25,242

35. 347,214 − 152,148

36. 5,614 − 2,852

37. 9,214,685 − 826,248

38. 5,214,599 − 2,843,288

39. 3,008 − 1,764

40. 4,020 − 2,452

41. 56,413,219 − 24,246,143

42. 76,423 − 4,247

Practice = Success!

Subtraction

Name ____________________

Total Problems	**41**
Problems Correct	______

1. 621,435 − 340,829
2. 924,365 − 742,826
3. 7,645,124 − 824,539
4. 4,620,000 − 341,362
5. 9,245,156 − 316,249
6. 807,421 − 324,618
7. 436,124 − 89,365
8. 29,006 − 22,438
9. 743,615 − 361,784
10. 9,432,106 − 521,817
11. 56,418 − 27,243
12. 762,415 − 215,423
13. 924,065 − 18,472
14. 5,000,462 − 326,248
15. 425,147 − 216,083
16. 7,624,508 − 815,142
17. 3,201,426 − 614,819
18. 5,421,879 − 210,342
19. 8,641,526 − 88,249
20. 46,517 − 29,284
21. 9,246,132 − 652,824
22. 812,456 − 19,582
23. 38,614 − 22,927
24. 462,517 − 324,618
25. 3,214,684 − 815,742
26. 6,421,007 − 614,143
27. 5,142,542 − 3,164,231
28. 8,401,624 − 3,216,418
29. 7,642,145 − 86,589
30. 89,654 − 77,497
31. 9,614,506 − 718,247
32. 5,432,187 − 4,286,324
33. 52,146,513 − 27,423,241
34. 32,146,892 − 4,382,971
35. 8,324,695 − 683,742
36. 92,436,149 − 825,426
37. 57,243,615 − 9,621,242
38. 25,408 − 12,629
39. 66,421,547 − 8,342,125
40. 7,615,243 − 3,246,318
41. 3,892,146 − 1,941,183

Practice! Practice! Practice!

Skill: Subtraction of Six-, Seven- and Eight-Digit Numbers

Subtraction

Name ____________________

Total Problems	**34**
Problems Correct	______

1. 305,628 − 187,849
2. 743,629 − 281,783
3. 640,321 − 192,846
4. 843,216 − 372,642
5. 462,317 − 281,548
6. 964,374 − 172,846
7. 465,389 − 127,694
8. 864,397 − 671,648
9. 843,108 − 381,423
10. 462,009 − 185,236
11. 565,432 − 279,247
12. 646,374 − 493,189
13. 762,348 − 531,459
14. 926,348 − 345,653
15. 463,899 − 285,946
16. 964,302 − 481,428
17. 762,498 − 478,824
18. 784,537 − 396,846
19. 463,402 − 234,761
20. 648,514 − 529,348
21. 385,387 − 191,298
22. 524,318 − 341,846
23. 829,416 − 435,824
24. 475,234 − 387,613
25. 629,432 − 436,829
26. 928,316 − 731,264
27. 8,462,103 − 741,316
28. 5,432,148 − 3,651,829
29. 7,431,645 − 2,640,859
30. 3,218,643 − 809,751
31. 6,257,431 − 4,319,614
32. 5,642,918 − 1,853,486
33. 78,430,615 − 9,511,283
34. 96,431,265 − 48,514,391

Practice takes you to the top!

Multiplication

Name ____________________

Total Problems	**40**
Problems Correct	______

1. 649 × 8
2. 858 × 7
3. 7,642 × 5
4. 8,219 × 3
5. 5,238 × 6
6. 4,623 × 9
7. 8,249 × 4
8. 6,518 × 7
9. 8,943 × 9
10. 3,268 × 5
11. 4,637 × 8
12. 8,924 × 6
13. 5,387 × 4
14. 8,264 × 9
15. 4,875 × 7
16. 5,689 × 8
17. 9,243 × 4
18. 7,643 × 9
19. 8,540 × 6
20. 3,726 × 5
21. 83,243 × 6
22. 74,254 × 7
23. 62,435 × 9
24. 95,201 × 5
25. 73,643 × 8
26. 51,476 × 4
27. 73,629 × 5
28. 87,642 × 7
29. 25,624 × 4
30. 63,928 × 8
31. 98,215 × 6
32. 41,826 × 9
33. 53,214 × 8
34. 83,265 × 4
35. 65,429 × 5
36. 79,267 × 3
37. 46,254 × 7
38. 91,242 × 8
39. 73,263 × 6
40. 35,584 × 2

Anything's possible with practice!

Skill: Multiplying by Two-Digit Numbers

Multiplication

Name ______________________

Show your work on another sheet. Write your answers here.

Total Problems	40
Problems Correct	______

1. 467 × 35

2. 538 × 47

3. 393 × 82

4. 724 × 56

5. 821 × 75

6. 463 × 43

7. 522 × 68

8. 326 × 92

9. 735 × 45

10. 268 × 39

11. 534 × 76

12. 232 × 98

13. 845 × 63

14. 928 × 81

15. 625 × 33

16. 856 × 42

17. 932 × 58

18. 734 × 54

19. 487 × 72

20. 289 × 79

21. 824 × 75

22. 936 × 47

23. 365 × 28

24. 573 × 65

25. 792 × 34

26. 476 × 83

27. 468 × 57

28. 323 × 92

29. 645 × 73

30. 765 × 48

31. 859 × 63

32. 368 × 87

33. 428 × 61

34. 537 × 44

35. 804 × 87

36. 348 × 29

Practice makes perfect!

37. 437 × 73

38. 725 × 52

39. 639 × 38

40. 457 × 86

Multiplication

Name ____________________

Total Problems 48

Problems Correct ______

Show your work on another sheet. Write your answers here.

1. 6,142 × 3
2. 4,921 × 5
3. 3,168 × 8
4. 2,482 × 9
5. 8,142 × 3
6. 4,628 × 7
7. 9,874 × 2
8. 7,425 × 6
9. 5,487 × 4
10. 6,849 × 7
11. 9,240 × 8
12. 7,645 × 4
13. 4,208 × 9
14. 8,004 × 2
15. 43,619 × 6
16. 54,613 × 4
17. 86,423 × 9
18. 56,984 × 7
19. 82,412 × 3
20. 46,304 × 8
21. 82,425 × 5
22. 51,403 × 9
23. 413,642 × 3
24. 549,627 × 8
25. 840,205 × 7
26. 1,364 × 42
27. 2,423 × 57
28. 3,920 × 84
29. 5,549 × 30
30. 6,847 × 27
31. 2,925 × 56
32. 2,427 × 93
33. 3,240 × 64
34. 5,149 × 80
35. 6,847 × 92
36. 5,148 × 24
37. 5,492 × 76
38. 6,284 × 33
39. 62,003 × 34
40. 82,413 × 47
41. 81,404 × 76
42. 38,243 × 91
43. 54,128 × 24
44. 24,136 × 58
45. 76,132 × 49
46. 59,149 × 26
47. 62,427 × 78
48. 51,264 × 32

Practice hard. You'll win.

Multiplication

Name ____________________

Total Problems	**40**
Problems Correct	______

Show your work on another sheet. Write your answers here.

1. 325 ×614	**2.** 463 ×527				
3. 265 ×921	**4.** 429 ×304	**5.** 724 ×630	**6.** 512 ×825	**7.** 189 ×432	**8.** 382 ×265
9. 361 ×543	**10.** 465 ×734	**11.** 412 ×398	**12.** 252 ×726	**13.** 736 ×413	**14.** 425 ×817
15. 832 ×625	**16.** 923 ×542	**17.** 234 ×489	**18.** 564 ×820	**19.** 713 ×256	**20.** 468 ×375
21. 568 ×943	**22.** 726 ×245	**23.** 364 ×545	**24.** 463 ×982	**25.** 523 ×764	**26.** 624 ×846
27. 821 ×265	**28.** 486 ×631	**29.** 824 ×532	**30.** 842 ×701	**31.** 523 ×438	**32.** 265 ×835
33. 547 ×325	**34.** 406 ×982	**35.** 397 ×768	**36.** 725 ×424		
37. 481 ×632	**38.** 254 ×825	**39.** 932 ×364	**40.** 589 ×746		

With practice, you can do it!

Multiplication

Name ____________________

Total Problems	**48**
Problems Correct	______

Show your work on another sheet. Write your answers here.

1. 628 × 403	**2.** 531 × 724				
3. 248 × 265	**4.** 304 × 529	**5.** 246 × 824	**6.** 146 × 532	**7.** 308 × 236	**8.** 813 × 432
9. 385 × 274	**10.** 284 × 621	**11.** 486 × 513	**12.** 314 × 249	**13.** 485 × 613	**14.** 461 × 920
15. 212 × 685	**16.** 329 × 400	**17.** 215 × 548	**18.** 243 × 824	**19.** 149 × 632	**20.** 475 × 362
21. 140 × 523	**22.** 147 × 250	**23.** 827 × 342	**24.** 389 × 921	**25.** 142 × 265	**26.** 527 × 462
27. 3,615 × 204	**28.** 4,014 × 325	**29.** 3,614 × 827	**30.** 1,464 × 532	**31.** 5,621 × 764	**32.** 2,619 × 483
33. 5,762 × 728	**34.** 3,147 × 482	**35.** 2,418 × 625	**36.** 8,145 × 327	**37.** 5,134 × 842	**38.** 8,040 × 532
39. 3,015 × 604	**40.** 3,802 × 824	**41.** 5,124 × 324	**42.** 7,241 × 530	**43.** 6,030 × 724	**44.** 2,043 × 821
45. 5,341 × 231	**46.** 7,624 × 342	**47.** 3,146 × 620	**48.** 4,252 × 482		

Success ahoy! Just practice!

Multiplication

Name ______________________

Total Problems	48
Problems Correct	______

Show your work on another sheet. Write your answers here.

1. 5,406 × 2,142	**2.** 2,482 × 4,321				
3. 2,042 × 9,123	**4.** 2,489 × 4,300	**5.** 4,364 × 5,127	**6.** 1,481 × 6,824	**7.** 1,348 × 3,421	**8.** 3,901 × 4,612
9. 3,842 × 3,615	**10.** 3,246 × 1,482	**11.** 1,498 × 8,003	**12.** 2,514 × 3,486	**13.** 3,628 × 2,749	**14.** 4,215 × 1,321
15. 1,347 × 5,621	**16.** 1,541 × 2,824	**17.** 3,045 × 9,120	**18.** 1,423 × 6,215	**19.** 2,653 × 5,214	**20.** 1,434 × 8,172
21. 1,545 × 8,432	**22.** 9,242 × 6,132	**23.** 1,356 × 3,642	**24.** 2,405 × 9,163	**25.** 2,348 × 1,405	**26.** 1,450 × 3,642
27. 1,456 × 7,214	**28.** 3,014 × 6,215	**29.** 8,042 × 3,217	**30.** 3,289 × 5,116	**31.** 8,649 × 5,472	**32.** 5,892 × 3,246
33. 3,264 × 7,132	**34.** 1,327 × 4,263	**35.** 1,283 × 6,245	**36.** 3,415 × 1,200	**37.** 1,523 × 3,649	**38.** 1,629 × 4,725
39. 5,412 × 2,743	**40.** 2,341 × 8,649	**41.** 1,006 × 3,215	**42.** 3,012 × 1,264	**43.** 1,262 × 5,215	**44.** 1,423 × 4,201
45. 2,512 × 2,642	**46.** 8,132 × 3,614	**47.** 1,482 × 9,125	**48.** 8,541 × 3,264		

Anything's possible with practice!

Multiplication

Name ____________________

Total Problems	**50**
Problems Correct	______

Show your work on another sheet. Write your answers here.

1. $3 \times (2 \times 2) =$

2. $4 \times (1 \times 6) =$

3. $7 \times (3 \times 2) =$

4. $(2 \times 2) \times 6 =$

5. $(6 \times 2) \times 4 =$

6. $(4 \times 2) \times 3 =$

7. $5 \times (2 \times 3) =$

8. $9 \times (2 \times 3) =$

9. $7 \times (2 \times 4) =$

10. $(3 \times 2) \times 4 =$

11. $3 \times (3 \times 2) =$

12. $2 \times (4 \times 3) =$

13. $5 \times (4 + 2) =$

14. $(8 \times 1) \times 5 =$

15. $3 \times (4 + 4) =$

16. $9 \times (6 \times 2) =$

17. $(3 \times 2) + (4 \times 2) =$

18. $8 \times (3 + 1) =$

19. $(4 \times 2) + (6 \times 3) =$

20. $(7 \times 1) \times 6 =$

21. $(5 + 5) \times 3 =$

22. $6 \times (3 \times 3) =$

23. $(5 \times 5) + 8 =$

24. $(2 \times 3) \times 8 =$

25. $(4 \times 2) + (3 \times 4) =$

26. $(3 \times 3) \times 6 =$

27. $(3 + 4) \times (2 + 5) =$

28. $(6 \times 2) \times 5 =$

29. $(6 \times 1) \times (2 \times 3) =$

30. $(9 \times 1) \times 7 =$

31. $(3 \times 2) \times 8 =$

32. $(5 + 3) \times 8 =$

33. $(4 \times 3) \times 4 =$

34. $(3 \times 2) \times 5 =$

35. $(3 \times 4) + 9 =$

36. $3 \times (5 \times 2) =$

37. $5 \times (3 \times 3) =$

38. $(3 \times 3) + (4 \times 2) =$

39. $6 \times (3 \times 4) =$

40. $7 \times (3 + 5) =$

41. $(6 + 2) \times (2 + 2) =$

42. $(7 \times 3) + 6 =$

43. $8 + (9 \times 12) =$

44. $6 \times (6 \times 2) =$

45. $(3 \times 8) + (4 \times 9) =$

46. $9 \times (3 \times 4) =$

47. $5 \times (2 \times 5) =$

48. $(6 \times 3) + 8 =$

49. $(4 + 5) \times (2 \times 4) =$

50. $(7 \times 6) + (5 \times 12) =$

With practice, you can do it!

Skill: One-Digit Divisors

Division

Name ______________________________

Show your work on another sheet. Write your answers here.

Total Problems	**40**
Problems Correct	______

1. 8 | 3,216

2. 4 | 1,272

3. 7 | 1,502

4. 3 | 296

5. 6 | 4,811

6. 9 | 788

7. 5 | 554

8. 8 | 1,143

9. 4 | 362

10. 3 | 1,553

11. 6 | 5,554

12. 7 | 487

13. 2 | 1,694

14. 4 | 1,550

15. 9 | 7,155

16. 5 | 2,093

17. 7 | 4,778

18. 3 | 316

19. 6 | 483

20. 4 | 515

21. 5 | 2,013

22. 8 | 1,886

23. 9 | 2,591

24. 7 | 3,330

25. 2 | 219

26. 3 | 632

27. 5 | 1,835

28. 8 | 567

29. 6 | 6,150

30. 4 | 1,278

31. 5 | 4,250

32. 2 | 819

33. 9 | 11,232

34. 7 | 22,734

35. 8 | 11,269

36. 3 | 8,693

37. 4 | 20,868

38. 6 | 24,645

39. 9 | 10,889

40. 8 | 9,198

With practice, you can do it!

Division

Name ____________________

Total Problems	**43**
Problems Correct	______

Show your work on another sheet. Write your answers here.

1. 27 ⟌ 216
2. 48 ⟌ 432
3. 35 ⟌ 245
4. 81 ⟌ 729
5. 32 ⟌ 192
6. 21 ⟌ 168
7. 84 ⟌ 588
8. 74 ⟌ 444
9. 65 ⟌ 520
10. 25 ⟌ 225
11. 92 ⟌ 644
12. 75 ⟌ 450
13. 24 ⟌ 192
14. 58 ⟌ 464
15. 42 ⟌ 252
16. 65 ⟌ 455
17. 86 ⟌ 278
18. 29 ⟌ 128
19. 36 ⟌ 302
20. 43 ⟌ 265
21. 82 ⟌ 427
22. 95 ⟌ 596
23. 61 ⟌ 594
24. 49 ⟌ 126
25. 82 ⟌ 753
26. 91 ⟌ 366
27. 56 ⟌ 420
28. 43 ⟌ 270
29. 68 ⟌ 662
30. 51 ⟌ 323
31. 37 ⟌ 310
32. 88 ⟌ 547
33. 48 ⟌ 359
34. 37 ⟌ 228
35. 67 ⟌ 362
36. 92 ⟌ 742
37. 73 ⟌ 687
38. 89 ⟌ 541
39. 25 ⟌ 188
40. 46 ⟌ 239
41. 73 ⟌ 646
42. 38 ⟌ 292
43. 63 ⟌ 552

Practice makes perfect!

Division

Name ______________________

Total Problems	**45**
Problems Correct	______

Show your work on another sheet. Write your answers here.

1. 14)326	**2.** 34)888			
3. 21)298	**4.** 46)690	**5.** 31)843	**6.** 17)578	**7.** 54)918
8. 62)1,143	**9.** 20)706	**10.** 42)675	**11.** 23)653	**12.** 81)2,195
13. 71)3,550	**14.** 24)872	**15.** 19)825	**16.** 32)1,997	**17.** 44)1,678
18. 38)2,482	**19.** 15)398	**20.** 82)2,952	**21.** 11)996	**22.** 27)432
23. 64)1,988	**24.** 45)1,292	**25.** 33)462	**26.** 22)933	**27.** 30)2,467
28. 43)989	**29.** 37)976	**30.** 28)1,576	**31.** 84)2,304	**32.** 16)304
33. 92)4,356	**34.** 40)1,573	**35.** 75)3,756	**36.** 13)1,101	**37.** 41)2,583
38. 61)1,731	**39.** 73)1,799	**40.** 80)1,360	**41.** 32)1,946	**42.** 20)1,047
43. 18)1,248	**44.** 26)1,932	**45.** 35)634		

Practice = Success!

Division

Name ____________________

Show your work on another sheet. Write your answers here.

Total Problems	**43**
Problems Correct	______

1. $35\overline{)2{,}170}$

2. $42\overline{)4{,}032}$

3. $64\overline{)5{,}443}$

4. $81\overline{)5{,}200}$

5. $73\overline{)1{,}254}$

6. $94\overline{)2{,}553}$

7. $62\overline{)4{,}426}$

8. $96\overline{)4{,}044}$

9. $46\overline{)3{,}889}$

10. $31\overline{)1{,}705}$

11. $75\overline{)3{,}635}$

12. $48\overline{)3{,}861}$

13. $86\overline{)2{,}336}$

14. $37\overline{)3{,}451}$

15. $28\overline{)1{,}834}$

16. $97\overline{)7{,}979}$

17. $63\overline{)2{,}990}$

18. $74\overline{)4{,}993}$

19. $68\overline{)3{,}234}$

20. $96\overline{)7{,}358}$

21. $45\overline{)3{,}702}$

22. $26\overline{)2{,}494}$

23. $38\overline{)2{,}636}$

24. $49\overline{)3{,}514}$

25. $74\overline{)4{,}476}$

26. $96\overline{)5{,}585}$

27. $82\overline{)6{,}074}$

28. $43\overline{)3{,}637}$

29. $87\overline{)5{,}509}$

30. $56\overline{)4{,}402}$

31. $27\overline{)2{,}307}$

32. $47\overline{)3{,}543}$

33. $95\overline{)7{,}921}$

34. $28\overline{)2{,}645}$

35. $78\overline{)3{,}886}$

36. $46\overline{)3{,}246}$

37. $83\overline{)3{,}908}$

38. $92\overline{)6{,}288}$

39. $27\overline{)1{,}875}$

40. $48\overline{)3{,}673}$

41. $37\overline{)3{,}581}$

42. $62\overline{)5{,}371}$

43. $88\overline{)5{,}045}$

With practice, you can do it!

Division

Name ____________________

Total Problems	43
Problems Correct	______

Show your work on another sheet. Write your answers here.

1. $14\overline{)1,170}$
2. $82\overline{)5,539}$
3. $43\overline{)3,905}$
4. $65\overline{)1,899}$
5. $27\overline{)1,450}$
6. $32\overline{)3,018}$
7. $54\overline{)3,846}$
8. $75\overline{)3,699}$
9. $48\overline{)3,972}$
10. $21\overline{)1,611}$
11. $25\overline{)1,521}$
12. $48\overline{)4,015}$
13. $39\overline{)3,574}$
14. $86\overline{)6,169}$
15. $94\overline{)2,174}$
16. $75\overline{)5,876}$
17. $55\overline{)4,909}$
18. $71\overline{)3,592}$
19. $48\overline{)3,243}$
20. $62\overline{)5,236}$
21. $39\overline{)2,390}$
22. $21\overline{)1,966}$
23. $59\overline{)4,523}$
24. $28\overline{)1,926}$
25. $47\overline{)2,796}$
26. $87\overline{)8,147}$
27. $65\overline{)4,506}$
28. $43\overline{)3,644}$
29. $72\overline{)6,523}$
30. $51\overline{)3,236}$
31. $96\overline{)4,597}$
32. $58\overline{)4,085}$
33. $63\overline{)5,178}$
34. $49\overline{)4,583}$
35. $83\overline{)3,962}$
36. $74\overline{)5,142}$
37. $29\overline{)2,334}$
38. $59\overline{)4,456}$
39. $23\overline{)1,830}$
40. $95\overline{)8,197}$
41. $72\overline{)6,023}$
42. $46\overline{)3,287}$
43. $28\overline{)2,646}$

Anything's possible with practice!

Skill: Division With Three-Digit Quotients

Division

Name ______________________

Show your work on another sheet. Write your answers here.

Total Problems	40
Problems Correct	______

1. $12\overline{)7{,}620}$

2. $23\overline{)9{,}476}$

3. $14\overline{)5{,}166}$

4. $18\overline{)8{,}802}$

5. $16\overline{)8{,}000}$

6. $19\overline{)7{,}885}$

7. $21\overline{)4{,}914}$

8. $25\overline{)7{,}875}$

9. $32\overline{)7{,}520}$

10. $15\overline{)9{,}375}$

11. $11\overline{)8{,}679}$

12. $22\overline{)6{,}732}$

13. $35\overline{)9{,}275}$

14. $17\overline{)7{,}854}$

15. $23\overline{)6{,}647}$

16. $42\overline{)6{,}216}$

17. $65\overline{)6{,}630}$

18. $24\overline{)7{,}800}$

19. $18\overline{)7{,}164}$

20. $13\overline{)8{,}554}$

21. $16\overline{)7{,}648}$

22. $25\overline{)8{,}525}$

23. $13\overline{)7{,}657}$

24. $40\overline{)9{,}400}$

25. $31\overline{)8{,}494}$

26. $17\overline{)6{,}273}$

27. $20\overline{)9{,}360}$

28. $52\overline{)7{,}407}$

29. $86\overline{)8{,}900}$

30. $14\overline{)7{,}371}$

31. $33\overline{)8{,}889}$

32. $24\overline{)8{,}366}$

33. $15\overline{)7{,}298}$

34. $17\overline{)8{,}030}$

35. $89\overline{)9{,}282}$

36. $94\overline{)9{,}494}$

37. $27\overline{)6{,}954}$

38. $74\overline{)8{,}324}$

39. $32\overline{)9{,}628}$

40. $22\overline{)7{,}916}$

Practice! Practice! Practice!

Division

Name ____________________

Show your work on another sheet. Write your answers here.

Total Problems	43
Problems Correct	______

1. $14\overline{)7{,}415}$

2. $22\overline{)6{,}750}$

3. $16\overline{)7{,}672}$

4. $19\overline{)5{,}640}$

5. $51\overline{)7{,}749}$

6. $32\overline{)8{,}558}$

7. $12\overline{)7{,}543}$

8. $15\overline{)5{,}856}$

9. $24\overline{)8{,}757}$

10. $31\overline{)7{,}991}$

11. $23\overline{)8{,}314}$

12. $13\overline{)4{,}536}$

13. $17\overline{)4{,}872}$

14. $25\overline{)9{,}240}$

15. $33\overline{)7{,}085}$

16. $20\overline{)9{,}657}$

17. $14\overline{)7{,}244}$

18. $48\overline{)6{,}960}$

19. $27\overline{)8{,}617}$

20. $13\overline{)8{,}133}$

21. $29\overline{)8{,}340}$

22. $32\overline{)8{,}275}$

23. $16\overline{)7{,}577}$

24. $21\overline{)8{,}316}$

25. $18\overline{)5{,}400}$

26. $34\overline{)4{,}279}$

27. $52\overline{)5{,}559}$

28. $13\overline{)3{,}529}$

29. $27\overline{)7{,}227}$

30. $36\overline{)5{,}391}$

31. $40\overline{)5{,}112}$

32. $16\overline{)7{,}655}$

33. $82\overline{)8{,}276}$

34. $50\overline{)7{,}628}$

35. $63\overline{)8{,}568}$

36. $91\overline{)9{,}305}$

37. $24\overline{)6{,}205}$

38. $16\overline{)7{,}719}$

39. $12\overline{)9{,}471}$

40. $86\overline{)8{,}930}$

41. $53\overline{)5{,}972}$

42. $47\overline{)8{,}249}$

43. $28\overline{)4{,}282}$

With practice, you can do it!

Division

Name ______________________

Total Problems	**44**
Problems Correct	______

Show your work on another sheet. Write your answers here.

1. $14\overline{)3,010}$

2. $25\overline{)8,130}$

3. $32\overline{)5,696}$

4. $41\overline{)15,100}$

5. $20\overline{)2,900}$

6. $53\overline{)5,565}$

7. $27\overline{)6,943}$

8. $71\overline{)9,111}$

9. $82\overline{)11,361}$

10. $43\overline{)13,510}$

11. $23\overline{)9,568}$

12. $62\overline{)14,942}$

13. $19\overline{)6,620}$

14. $36\overline{)11,346}$

15. $52\overline{)11,336}$

16. $21\overline{)7,763}$

17. $73\overline{)7,379}$

18. $40\overline{)10,333}$

19. $84\overline{)12,542}$

20. $15\overline{)9,384}$

21. $34\overline{)15,389}$

22. $45\overline{)8,433}$

23. $72\overline{)7,812}$

24. $22\overline{)16,031}$

25. $42\overline{)10,812}$

26. $64\overline{)15,552}$

27. $54\overline{)7,304}$

28. $47\overline{)24,839}$

29. $33\overline{)20,394}$

30. $86\overline{)12,687}$

31. $50\overline{)15,700}$

32. $17\overline{)11,875}$

33. $30\overline{)3,614}$

34. $16\overline{)14,743}$

35. $24\overline{)5,160}$

36. $74\overline{)11,715}$

37. $46\overline{)7,291}$

38. $91\overline{)9,671}$

39. $78\overline{)24,851}$

40. $92\overline{)12,052}$

41. $35\overline{)9,954}$

42. $84\overline{)35,148}$

43. $44\overline{)10,220}$

44. $26\overline{)6,370}$

Practice makes perfect!

Division

Name ____________________

Total Problems	**33**
Problems Correct	______

Show your work on another sheet. Write your answers here.

1. 24) 16,440

2. 52) 50,128

3. 36) 31,536

4. 48) 44,496

5. 72) 53,856

6. 58) 39,672

7. 64) 58,112

8. 92) 72,354

9. 43) 38,478

10. 21) 15,724

11. 86) 82,599

12. 76) 63,051

13. 48) 45,495

14. 97) 84,380

15. 54) 31,698

16. 31) 28,978

17. 27) 24,314

18. 42) 35,602

19. 39) 24,960

20. 84) 81,051

21. 57) 49,275

22. 95) 73,093

23. 17) 15,436

24. 70) 58,425

25. 53) 36,882

26. 23) 21,798

27. 59) 38,291

28. 37) 22,484

29. 81) 54,729

30. 93) 69,313

31. 73) 69,934

32. 29) 11,223

33. 50) 33,999

Practice and anything's possible!

Division

Name ____________________

Total Problems	**45**
Problems Correct	______

Show your work on another sheet. Write your answers here.

1. 21 ⟌ 852
2. 14 ⟌ 784
3. 12 ⟌ 1,016
4. 31 ⟌ 730
5. 40 ⟌ 386
6. 74 ⟌ 2,085
7. 25 ⟌ 1,950
8. 16 ⟌ 569
9. 26 ⟌ 1,222
10. 78 ⟌ 1,652
11. 51 ⟌ 1,339
12. 32 ⟌ 1,616
13. 93 ⟌ 2,567
14. 18 ⟌ 291
15. 22 ⟌ 897
16. 43 ⟌ 669
17. 53 ⟌ 1,500
18. 50 ⟌ 462
19. 41 ⟌ 1,163
20. 36 ⟌ 658
21. 20 ⟌ 1,054
22. 97 ⟌ 4,658
23. 66 ⟌ 663
24. 62 ⟌ 3,732
25. 42 ⟌ 466
26. 54 ⟌ 3,888
27. 35 ⟌ 551
28. 95 ⟌ 783
29. 23 ⟌ 328
30. 77 ⟌ 6,935
31. 44 ⟌ 1,240
32. 68 ⟌ 2,085
33. 81 ⟌ 8,505
34. 61 ⟌ 13,063
35. 39 ⟌ 4,615
36. 52 ⟌ 16,640
37. 47 ⟌ 8,402
38. 10 ⟌ 8,428
39. 45 ⟌ 9,872
40. 27 ⟌ 4,039
41. 82 ⟌ 8,739
42. 33 ⟌ 6,849
43. 13 ⟌ 6,851
44. 24 ⟌ 19,812
45. 34 ⟌ 21,243

Practice!
Practice!
Practice!

Skill: Three-Digit Divisors

Division

Name ____________________

Total Problems	45
Problems Correct	______

Show your work on another sheet. Write your answers here.

1. 143) 1,287

2. 623) 12,460

3. 431) 3,448

4. 264) 2,376

5. 172) 2,064

6. 532) 3,747

7. 803) 12,090

8. 515) 3,138

9. 634) 17,443

10. 572) 8,033

11. 145) 5,539

12. 924) 7,448

13. 232) 4,908

14. 297) 3,888

15. 128) 2,304

16. 400) 9,249

17. 103) 2,101

18. 745) 12,693

19. 312) 3,149

20. 692) 5,578

21. 154) 2,950

22. 265) 3,236

23. 857) 12,027

24. 657) 15,111

25. 746) 21,013

26. 114) 4,123

27. 256) 13,824

28. 789) 32,388

29. 364) 17,472

30. 205) 12,963

31. 108) 4,052

32. 693) 29,106

33. 624) 5,361

34. 126) 7,850

35. 642) 17,976

36. 283) 7,766

37. 456) 10,488

38. 982) 34,102

39. 537) 26,886

40. 134) 8,308

41. 224) 8,551

42. 238) 19,540

43. 842) 62,308

44. 427) 38,430

45. 216) 67,824

Practice brings success!

Decimals

Name ____________________

Total Problems	**40**
Problems Correct	______

1. 3.85 + 2.46	**2.** 6.08 + 9.23				
3. 39.8 + 56.7	**4.** 4.32 + 0.89	**5.** 98.6 + 43.5	**6.** 0.68 + 3.47	**7.** 78.6 + 83.9	**8.** 43.7 + 98.2
9. 42.37 + 34.85	**10.** 92.65 + 82.83	**11.** 27.36 + 90.24	**12.** 47.32 + 71.83	**13.** 56.34 + 92.43	**14.** 9.326 + 3.417
15. 643.2 + 481.9	**16.** 37.48 + 42.32	**17.** 964.3 + 382.4	**18.** 426.3 + 442.3	**19.** 87.43 + 42.74	**20.** 7.306 + 4.037
21. 9.234 + 2.641	**22.** 49.83 + 52.57	**23.** 56.27 + 83.53	**24.** 362.5 + 243.9	**25.** 76.38 + 35.24	**26.** 62.85 + 43.46
27. 482.51 + 801.03	**28.** 36.059 + 42.482	**29.** 924.38 + 643.92	**30.** 623.42 + 85.36	**31.** 83.04 + 9.28	**32.** 0.38 + 9.43
33. 564.32 + 9.08	**34.** 68.42 + 924.39	**35.** 836.40 + 93.84	**36.** 4.65 + 859.23		
37. 364.94 + 725.38	**38.** 629.38 + 842.45	**39.** 89.006 + 92.848	**40.** 4.6258 + 5.2923		

Practice hard. You'll win.

Skill: Addition of Decimals

Decimals

Name ____________________

Total Problems	**42**
Problems Correct	______

1. 26.9 +427.22	**2.** 324.05 + 48.94				
3. 82.495 +49.28	**4.** 3,245.6 + 89.5	**5.** 4.804 +3.29	**6.** 9.62 +39.407	**7.** 84.005 +746.92	**8.** 76.09 +384.87
9. 5.72 +87.479	**10.** 89.8 +786.92	**11.** 346.08 + 79.96	**12.** 2.02 +49.869	**13.** 94.568 +487.8	**14.** 700.08 + 98.89
15. 4.8469 +0.7889	**16.** 8.92 +768.724	**17.** 4.06 +765.976	**18.** 604.72 + 87.99	**19.** 8,462.9 + 97.09	**20.** 76.46 +497.9
21. 86.479 + 9.36	**22.** 7.04 +86.798	**23.** 4.897 +8.24	**24.** 80.46 + 9.87	**25.** 8.496 +0.897	**26.** 9.71 +87.642
27. 4.06 +87.8	**28.** 8.465 +7.008	**29.** 645.176 +787.846	**30.** 46.07 +878.787	**31.** 8.76 +79.878	**32.** 8.91 +78.489
33. 897.4 43.62 + 0.97	**34.** 9.7 62.46 +423.09	**35.** 0.406 7.009 +6.89	**36.** 84.076 2.89 +25.8	**37.** 764.25 42.146 + 9.352	**38.** 6.2 847.09 + 24.76
39. 7.9 82.46 + 9.476	**40.** 0.476 46.219 + 7.4821	**41.** 23.462 6.248 + 2.689	**42.** 0.215 236.89 + 4.234		

Practice puts you on top!

Decimals

Name ______________________

Total Problems	40
Problems Correct	______

1. 32.50 0.89 +46.27	**2.** 842.9 56.32 +912.8				
3. 362.54 3.85 + 46.39	**4.** 200.69 463.2 + 8.56	**5.** 0.87 6.42 +8.965	**6.** 642.36 58.29 + 0.37	**7.** 845.236 32.873 + 0.46	**8.** 27.5 34.62 + 5.38
9. 7.64 37.46 +29.583	**10.** 526.9 38.62 +300.18	**11.** 9642.31 821.24 + 9.56	**12.** 47.312 314.25 + 82.74	**13.** 602.45 86.37 + 2.48	**14.** 68.75 214.23 + 9.462
15. 312.46 46.231 + 0.59	**16.** 84.06 246.23 + 38.4	**17.** 918.06 54.08 +312.04	**18.** 0.75 28.14 + 7.32	**19.** 4.72 32.25 + 6.9	**20.** 602.43 35.26 +432.52
21. 426.08 62.32 +513.23	**22.** 22.31 624.15 + 8.04	**23.** 856.24 0.89 + 46.03	**24.** 0.96 123.14 + 84.03	**25.** 4.15 36.124 +82.354	**26.** 362.45 121.32 +143.65
27. 42.395 6.25 + 4.8	**28.** 62.46 3.821 +543.4	**29.** 365.1 2.326 + 28.45	**30.** 430.65 84.32 +312.46	**31.** 842.34 26.15 + 8.56	**32.** 64.59 302.152 + 8.71
33. 546.09 52.43 + 3.43	**34.** 782.08 96.23 +214.41	**35.** 20.415 4.28 +321.14	**36.** 643.38 51.412 + 0.32		
37. 364.25 8.46 + 45.25	**38.** 920.04 36.4 + 24.25	**39.** 0.64 321.02 + 8.5	**40.** 462.98 0.55 + 48.21		

Success ahoy!
Just practice!

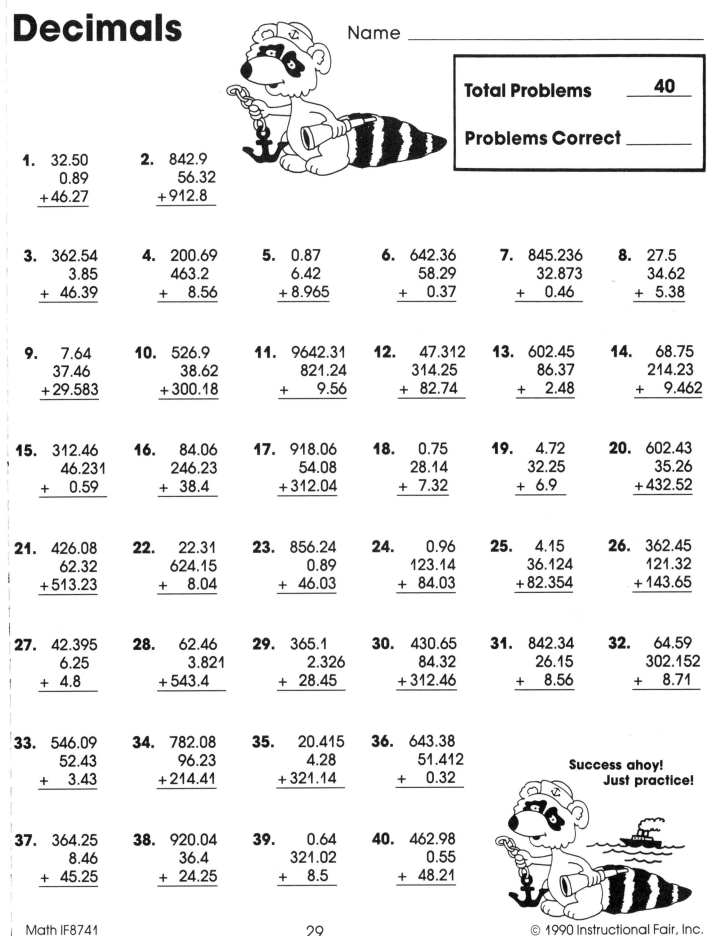

Decimals

Name ______________________

Total Problems	36
Problems Correct	______

1.
6.042
8.253
+4.628

2.
6.54
58.47
+ 9.384

3.
94.025
3.684
+ 9.74

4.
654.207
6.87
+ 92.5

5.
76.8
842.78
+ 8.43

6.
562.43
94.2
+ 3.57

7.
29.43
37.52
+48.25

8.
64.57
2.76
+85.218

9.
6.51
82.43
+ 9.25

10.
3.26
46.38
+ 8.79

11.
5.214
0.36
+2.582

12.
76.002
321.4
+ 8.65

13.
0.572
82.41
+ 5.743

14.
643.5
26.43
+ 52.86

15.
64.316
2.465
31.21
+ 5.562

16.
748.21
36.48
7.24
+ 2.53

17.
76.21
8.36
4.01
+52.14

18.
852.15
4215.3
82.7
+ 3.64

19.
464.06
35.12
6.94
+ 57.23

20.
312.24
63.45
92.37
+654.52

21.
24.32
65.27
48.51
+23.49

22.
5.163
2.413
3.242
+5.161

23.
36.215
8.46
21.15
+ 3.271

24.
851.2
46.35
912.5
+ 9.21

25.
342.3
26.5
68.42
+521.35

26.
62.4
572.52
24.08
+345.21

27.
501.26
46.87
24.35
+ 59.23

28.
43.215
1.486
5.143
+68.472

29.
92.54
324.21
65.148
+ 28.352

30.
542.6
28.45
3.215
+ 34.52

31.
3521.3
264.56
486.1
+5124.3

32.
69.24
524.03
51.36
+ 48.13

33.
2.15
4.82
16.51
+ 9.72

34.
36.22
41.52
8.21
+ 3.46

35.
38.472
3.21
5.481
+ 2.124

36.
5.2105
0.465
2.724
+0.8131

Practice takes you to the top!

Decimals

Name ________________________

Total Problems	**40**
Problems Correct	______

1. 62.42 − 24.23

2. 93.56 − 42.38

3. 47.32 − 14.28

4. 3.25 − 2.67

5. 40.05 − 23.28

6. 8.621 − 3.248

7. 90.5 − 62.9

8. 583.7 − 392.4

9. 7.642 − 5.269

10. 36.49 − 29.82

11. 500.6 − 341.2

12. 80.94 − 28.23

13. 69.48 − 42.93

14. 9.302 − 7.281

15. 6.94 − 4.83

16. 76.4 − 52.8

17. 94.53 − 42.82

18. 64.07 − 52.82

19. 300.2 − 225.4

20. 500.5 − 432.2

21. 85.245 − 43.462

22. 300.24 − 142.48

23. 38.325 − 13.146

24. 564.02 − 325.24

25. 306.95 − 212.28

26. 762.14 − 341.25

27. 52.432 − 26.514

28. 746.34 − 482.16

29. 241.36 − 118.18

30. 462.5 − 293.8

31. 5.206 − 3.642

32. 842.36 − 381.64

33. 745.32 − 382.64

34. 546.07 − 327.18

35. 8.4162 − 5.5216

36. 7.6241 − 6.8413

Success ahoy! Just practice!

37. 632.45 − 424.27

38. 82.611 − 41.802

39. 3642.5 − 1861.9

40. 700.45 − 346.26

Skill: Subtraction of Decimals

Decimals

Name ____________________

Total Problems	40
Problems Correct	

1. 324.6 − 52.41
2. 26.39 − 8.246
3. 642.51 − 58.3
4. 742.8 − 6.35
5. 89.625 − 3.84
6. 4.006 − 2.85
7. 524.06 − 62.952
8. 62.05 − 8.226
9. 58.214 − 9.64
10. 8.11 − 2.325
11. 64.04 − 9.8
12. 462.51 − 38.823
13. 84.006 − 2.439
14. 4.625 − 0.259
15. 584.0 − 32.45
16. 364.25 − 8.364
17. 18.01 − 4.743
18. 392.1 − 246.81
19. 762.4 − 5.264
20. 564.7 − 58.65
21. 30.615 − 8.28
22. 716.8 − 47.28
23. 46.02 − 2.307
24. 6354.2 − 87.19
25. 532.4 − 8.245
26. 574.04 − 0.321
27. 47.321 − 3.845
28. 26.001 − 3.245
29. 8.4182 − 0.2328
30. 376.06 − 8.239
31. 6.32 − 0.489
32. 764.2 − 8.465
33. 57.018 − 6.14
34. 84.03 − 0.645
35. 916.2 − 82.9
36. 3642.9 − 3.625
37. 478.1 − 7.25
38. 600.14 − 84.36
39. 723.8 − 64.35
40. 21.3 − 8.4365

Anything's possible with practice!

Decimals

Name ______________________

Total Problems 46

Problems Correct ______

1. 4.51 − 3.247	**2.** 36.2 − 18.416			
3. 754.21 − 8.462	**4.** 17.1 − 2.145	**5.** 36.1 − 0.362	**6.** 6421.15 − 36.438	**7.** 85.413 − 2.245
8. 92.5 − 3.462	**9.** 27.348 − 0.419	**10.** 32.147 − 8.56	**11.** 0.416 − 0.145	**12.** 54.007 − 3.12
13. 584.215 − 8.324	**14.** 852.4 − 0.146	**15.** 74.2 − 5.165	**16.** 9.22 − 1.248	**17.** 47.215 − 8.64
18. 946.01 − 57.16	**19.** 83.012 − 4.16	**20.** 3.14625 − 1.463	**21.** 764.08 − 246.26	**22.** 59.16 − 8.425
23. 762.15 − 248.9	**24.** 46.21 − 28.5	**25.** 5421.7 − 0.3472	**26.** 10.5 − 0.465	**27.** 572.6 − 0.464
28. 854.216 − 81.9	**29.** 50.41 − 8.562	**30.** 900.001 − 46.14	**31.** 842.15 − 56.47	**32.** 542.16 − 58.72
33. 856.19 − 4.247	**34.** 345.1 − 6.527	**35.** 564.21 − 86.541	**36.** 6724.2 − 2.149	**37.** 48.12 − 4.564
38. 89.142 − 3.86	**39.** 52.73 − 0.4234	**40.** 9.45 − 0.24	**41.** 623.46 − 248.1	**42.** 5424.16 − 365.24
43. 847.145 − 8.95	**44.** 3745.2 − 8.84			
45. 6241.6 − 5.3215	**46.** 584.1 − 2.51642			

Practice brings success!

Decimals

Name ____________________

Total Problems 48

Problems Correct ________

1. 8.98 − 4.73
2. 7.88 − 0.465
3. 600.42 − 49.81
4. 72.465 − 8.79
5. 80.004 − 7.492
6. 5.245 − 0.869
7. 72.462 − 8.294
8. 602.47 − 47.09
9. 4,674.98 − 8.321
10. 764.217 − 89.148
11. 4.009 − 0.872
12. 82.476 − 4.088
13. 27.8 − 2.432
14. 800.08 − 32.42
15. 0.369 − 0.281
16. 874.9 − 288.3
17. 3.4169 − 0.8423
18. 7.03 − 2.89
19. 43.4107 − 8.2619
20. 6.98 − 2.4694
21. 34.007 − 2.43
22. 600.08 − 23.12
23. 3,214.8 − 2,187.3
24. 84.329 − 8.46
25. 7.87 − 0.3294
26. 47.463 − 6.872
27. 20.006 − 8.43
28. 6,489.3 − 2.468
29. 46.24 − 8.265
30. 7.69 − 2.96
31. 36.423 − 2.894
32. 6.047 − 2.89
33. 642.98 − 0.432
34. 8.99 − 0.4657
35. 72.09 − 8.462
36. 16.19 − 4.764
37. 40.07 − 8.325
38. 67.46 − 2.897
39. 0.399 − 0.276
40. 92.463 − 8.272
41. 8.39 − 2.598
42. 6,742.8 − 86.42
43. 27.6 − 4.6321
44. 76.45 − 8.3264
45. 9.96 − 2.145
46. 464.25 − 85.472
47. 76.59 − 8.432
48. 464.98 − 0.3264

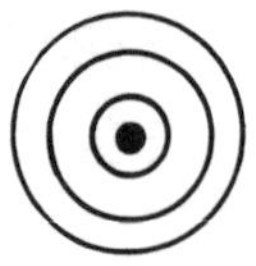

Practice hard.
You'll win!

Skill: Multiplication of Decimals by Whole Numbers

Decimals

Name ______________________

Total Problems 40

Problems Correct ______

1. 3.64 × 4	**2.** 7.8 × 6				
3. 26.5 × 9	**4.** 3.89 × 7	**5.** 0.24 × 5	**6.** 7.9 × 8	**7.** 0.65 × 9	**8.** 3.97 × 5
9. 12.63 × 6	**10.** 143.8 × 8	**11.** 158.4 × 5	**12.** 98.62 × 8	**13.** 4.613 × 7	**14.** 0.146 × 4
15. 0.516 × 9	**16.** 0.849 × 7	**17.** 0.326 × 5	**18.** 12.89 × 6	**19.** 0.54 × 9	**20.** 421.5 × 7
21. 0.8 × 6	**22.** 3.87 × 9	**23.** 3.338 × 2	**24.** 4.31 × 8	**25.** 0.895 × 6	**26.** 7.362 × 9
27. 3.3156 × 8	**28.** 32.416 × 7	**29.** 642.17 × 9	**30.** 78.148 × 3	**31.** 9465.3 × 5	**32.** 46.418 × 3
33. 0.15426 × 8	**34.** 62.517 × 4	**35.** 56.58 × 9	**36.** 3.618 × 7		
37. 8.7154 × 4	**38.** 0.1578 × 7	**39.** 476.24 × 8	**40.** 74.389 × 2		

With practice, you can do it!

Skill: Multiplication of Tenths and Hundredths

Decimals

Name ____________________

Total Problems	40
Problems Correct	______

Show your work on another sheet. Write your answers here.

1. 0.9 × 0.7

2. 0.7 × 0.4

3. 0.8 × 0.3

4. 1.9 × 0.6

5. 1.45 × 0.7

6. 4.8 × 1.6

7. 4.3 × 3.6

8. 5.87 × 3.6

9. 7.9 × 0.86

10. 12.3 × 0.45

11. 3.14 × 2.7

12. 7.46 × 3.8

13. 84.6 × 0.27

14. 24.5 × 8.2

15. 23.6 × 0.49

16. 0.8 × 0.4

17. 0.6 × 0.5

18. 21.4 × 0.94

19. 31.2 × 0.64

20. 46.9 × 0.85

21. 1.59 × 0.4

22. 12.8 × 3.7

23. 14.5 × 0.57

24. 94.6 × 0.24

25. 51.2 × 5.6

26. 14.9 × 0.76

27. 46.2 × 0.23

28. 7.25 × 3.9

29. 33.2 × 6.8

30. 61.6 × 0.73

31. 31.5 × 0.34

32. 14.5 × 0.56

33. 41.5 × 0.89

34. 13.2 × 0.34

35. 14.6 × 0.86

36. 1.6 × 0.54

37. 21.4 × 0.36

38. 14.6 × 3.7

39. 9.25 × 7.6

40. 8.16 × 5.6

Practice! Practice! Practice!

Decimals

Name ____________________

Show your work on another sheet. Write your answers here.

Total Problems	**40**
Problems Correct	______

1. 0.2×0.2
2. 0.9×0.1
3. 1.7×0.03
4. 1.6×0.04
5. 0.39×0.2
6. 1.6×0.02
7. 2.3×0.04
8. 0.33×0.3
9. 0.08×0.8
10. 0.03×0.7
11. 0.15×0.04
12. 0.13×0.7
13. 4.3×0.02
14. 0.07×0.6
15. 0.35×0.2
16. 0.17×0.3
17. 0.09×0.4
18. 0.36×0.2
19. 0.07×0.2
20. 0.006×3
21. 0.01×5
22. 0.03×2
23. 0.03×0.4
24. 0.028×3
25. 0.02×4
26. 0.049×2
27. 0.4×0.1
28. 0.01×9
29. 0.08×1
30. 0.002×7
31. 0.09×0.3
32. 0.03×0.5
33. 0.1×0.8
34. 0.3×0.3
35. 0.05×0.6
36. 0.51×0.01
37. 0.024×3
38. 0.01×6
39. 0.005×5
40. 0.3×0.2

Practice brings success!

Skill: Multiplication of Decimals

Decimals

Name ______________________

Total Problems	**42**
Problems Correct	______

Show your work on another sheet.
Write your answers here.

1. 36.5 ×8.4	**2.** 516.24 ×0.3				
3. 3.614 ×0.57	**4.** 516.4 ×0.04	**5.** 462.3 ×7.1	**6.** 742.01 ×3.4	**7.** 0.316 ×1.7	**8.** 486.1 ×5.6
9. 56.01 ×0.8	**10.** 20.147 ×3.8	**11.** 43.4 ×0.67	**12.** 64.8 ×3.2	**13.** 1.015 ×0.3	**14.** 61.3 ×5.4
15. 4621.4 ×0.42	**16.** 874.7 ×4.3	**17.** 0.148 ×0.7	**18.** 23.52 ×7.8	**19.** 51.6 ×4.9	**20.** 8.64 ×3.4
21. 6.454 ×5.6	**22.** 1.462 ×0.83	**23.** 21.362 ×5.7	**24.** 7.218 ×0.68	**25.** 6.145 ×7.4	**26.** 92.32 ×0.94
27. 314.6 ×0.7	**28.** 864.25 ×8.5	**29.** 57.328 ×0.64	**30.** 74.25 ×0.8	**31.** 3.145 ×9.6	**32.** 2.145 ×0.4
33. 624.9 ×8.5	**34.** 326.1 ×9.2	**35.** 43.15 ×0.08	**36.** 59.46 ×8.2	**37.** 926.8 ×3.7	**38.** 8.41 ×0.7
39. 4.361 ×0.7	**40.** 5.004 ×0.65	**41.** 37.48 ×0.21	**42.** 214.61 ×.08		

Practice hard. You'll win!

Skill: Multiplication of Decimals

Decimals

Name ____________________

Total Problems	**50**
Problems Correct	______

Show your work on another sheet. Write your answers here.

1. 48.8 ×7.4

2. 5.184 ×2.7

3. 321.4 ×5.6

4. 7.8 ×52.02

5. 21.09 ×9.26

6. 843.1 ×0.2

7. 61.4 ×9.2

8. 7.612 ×5.143

9. 8.12 ×0.04

10. 9.14 ×3.6

11. 84.36 ×7.2

12. 7.04 ×4.65

13. 84.98 ×6.2

14. 6.40 ×5.8

15. 8.43 ×0.146

16. 64.2 ×5.9

17. 0.14 ×8.35

18. 7.006 ×9.4

19. 0.45 ×7.321

20. 6.05 ×0.24

21. 7.106 ×0.9

22. 64.2 ×3.02

23. 214.6 ×3.4

24. 41.254 ×6.1

25. 51.6 ×8.43

26. 0.007 ×3.6

27. 4.643 ×5.8

28. 3.26 ×0.47

29. 8.094 ×3.6

30. 41.3 ×0.05

31. 392.6 ×50.4

32. 24.09 ×7.24

33. 43.6 ×7.4

34. 3,214.9 ×8.1

35. 5.012 ×8.32

36. 8.2 ×0.003

37. 843.4 ×41.3

38. 8.64 ×9.2

39. 0.145 ×0.1342

40. 1.368 ×0.03

41. 49.7 ×3.64

42. 142.6 ×4.54

43. 64.8 ×0.004

44. 564.9 ×38.2

45. 59.006 ×3.2

46. 6,143.6 ×6.5

47. 3.0062 ×2.42

48. 8.4 ×354.2

49. 0.43 ×0.2102

50. 8.14 ×2.03

Success ahoy! Just practice!

Decimals

Name ______________________________

Total Problems	40
Problems Correct	______

Show your work on another sheet. Write your answers here.

1. $6\overline{)7.5}$
2. $4\overline{)9.2}$
3. $3\overline{)8.7}$
4. $9\overline{)3.6}$
5. $7\overline{)6.3}$
6. $5\overline{)10.5}$
7. $2\overline{)32.6}$
8. $8\overline{)4.16}$
9. $4\overline{)5.24}$
10. $9\overline{)8.82}$
11. $3\overline{)7.68}$
12. $6\overline{)5.34}$
13. $4\overline{)8.68}$
14. $7\overline{)4.83}$
15. $5\overline{)15.5}$
16. $2\overline{)16.4}$
17. $7\overline{)4.76}$
18. $3\overline{)13.5}$
19. $8\overline{)24.8}$
20. $9\overline{)30.6}$
21. $4\overline{)24.8}$
22. $6\overline{)0.528}$
23. $8\overline{)25.92}$
24. $7\overline{)6.72}$
25. $3\overline{)21.42}$
26. $2\overline{)13.16}$
27. $4\overline{)36.56}$
28. $6\overline{)32.82}$
29. $5\overline{)4.25}$
30. $4\overline{)12.8}$
31. $8\overline{)32.8}$
32. $3\overline{)14.4}$
33. $5\overline{)30.5}$
34. $9\overline{)211.5}$
35. $7\overline{)442.4}$
36. $4\overline{)0.848}$
37. $6\overline{)2.34}$
38. $3\overline{)0.294}$
39. $2\overline{)0.18}$
40. $8\overline{)23.84}$

Practice puts you on top!

Decimals

Name ______________________

Total Problems	40
Problems Correct	____

Show your work on another sheet. Write your answers here.

1. $23\overline{)94.76}$
2. $48\overline{)28.32}$
3. $13\overline{)74.62}$
4. $17\overline{)88.4}$
5. $52\overline{)35.88}$
6. $14\overline{)8.12}$
7. $12\overline{)40.8}$
8. $34\overline{)84.32}$
9. $23\overline{)98.21}$
10. $38\overline{)9.766}$
11. $45\overline{)135.45}$
12. $28\overline{)97.16}$
13. $43\overline{)24.51}$
14. $62\overline{)22.32}$
15. $27\overline{)6.75}$
16. $13\overline{)10.4}$
17. $24\overline{)88.56}$
18. $37\overline{)7.881}$
19. $84\overline{)100.8}$
20. $35\overline{)80.5}$
21. $22\overline{)7.832}$
22. $15\overline{)7.05}$
23. $39\overline{)93.6}$
24. $12\overline{)6.96}$
25. $16\overline{)55.52}$
26. $42\overline{)19.74}$
27. $94\overline{)122.2}$
28. $33\overline{)1.65}$
29. $47\overline{)58.75}$
30. $52\overline{)13.52}$
31. $62\overline{)74.4}$
32. $81\overline{)11.34}$
33. $25\overline{)9.75}$
34. $32\overline{)41.6}$
35. $17\overline{)49.13}$
36. $13\overline{)11.57}$
37. $45\overline{)157.05}$
38. $72\overline{)2.88}$
39. $57\overline{)236.55}$
40. $74\overline{)17.76}$

Success ahoy! Just practice!

Skill: Division of Decimals by Whole Numbers

Decimals

Name ____________________

Show your work on another sheet. Write your answers here.

Total Problems	45
Problems Correct	______

1. $4\overline{)10.32}$

2. $6\overline{)8.34}$

3. $8\overline{)5.44}$

4. $2\overline{)13.74}$

5. $9\overline{)7.02}$

6. $7\overline{)10.22}$

7. $6\overline{)23.7}$

8. $3\overline{)1.962}$

9. $5\overline{)40.7}$

10. $8\overline{)34.24}$

11. $4\overline{)29.56}$

12. $2\overline{)18.74}$

13. $5\overline{)4.735}$

14. $7\overline{)48.79}$

15. $9\overline{)0.783}$

16. $8\overline{)20.32}$

17. $3\overline{)4.107}$

18. $6\overline{)1.188}$

19. $4\overline{)3.416}$

20. $7\overline{)17.29}$

21. $5\overline{)0.89}$

22. $3\overline{)2.622}$

23. $8\overline{)52.72}$

24. $9\overline{)110.7}$

25. $6\overline{)0.42}$

26. $4\overline{)37.08}$

27. $7\overline{)177.8}$

28. $3\overline{)13.17}$

29. $9\overline{)292.5}$

30. $8\overline{)25.36}$

31. $2\overline{)6.516}$

32. $6\overline{)2.19}$

33. $4\overline{)0.396}$

34. $8\overline{)190.4}$

35. $7\overline{)2.779}$

36. $4\overline{)26.28}$

37. $3\overline{)109.5}$

38. $6\overline{)0.54}$

39. $8\overline{)58.08}$

40. $2\overline{)15.78}$

41. $5\overline{)0.73}$

42. $7\overline{)24.36}$

43. $6\overline{)325.26}$

44. $4\overline{)148.56}$

45. $2\overline{)0.316}$

Practice! Practice! Practice!

Decimals

Name ______________________

Show your work on another sheet. Write your answers here.

Total Problems	43
Problems Correct	______

1. 0.7)2.198

2. 0.4)8.8

3. 0.5)3.2

4. 0.9)37.08

5. 1.2)8.46

6. 3.4)174.08

7. 0.8)3.92

8. 0.9)2.16

9. 1.6)11.776

10. 4.2)36.54

11. 4.4)33.44

12. 21.1)50.64

13. 0.2)12.428

14. 0.5)3.02

15. 1.3)11.05

16. 2.6)14.56

17. 3.2)250.88

18. 5.1)49.98

19. 0.2)6.4

20. 0.4)1.472

21. 0.8)7.52

22. 1.7)60.86

23. 3.4)21.998

24. 2.7)19.062

25. 1.3)7.02

26. 2.1)7.539

27. 0.7)6.23

28. 2.7)11.286

29. 1.4)8.96

30. 0.3)1.248

31. 0.6)0.249

32. 1.4)5.32

33. 2.3)17.02

34. 5.2)34.84

35. 0.5)2.5

36. 0.8)3.68

37. 1.8)17.1

38. 3.8)18.24

39. 5.6)17.024

40. 2.9)19.72

41. 3.4)10.778

42. 0.7)0.0896

43. 0.6)3.48

Practice makes perfect!

Skill: Division of Decimals by Hundredths

Decimals

Name ____________________

Show your work on another sheet. Write your answers here.

Total Problems 45

Problems Correct ______

1. $0.14\overline{)3.276}$
2. $0.04\overline{)0.1032}$
3. $1.22\overline{)8.418}$
4. $0.06\overline{)0.1944}$
5. $0.36\overline{)3.024}$
6. $0.17\overline{)0.646}$
7. $0.26\overline{)2.34}$
8. $0.47\overline{)3.854}$
9. $0.32\overline{)0.6848}$
10. $0.22\overline{)5.588}$
11. $0.29\overline{)18.85}$
12. $0.03\overline{)2.526}$
13. $0.54\overline{)14.418}$
14. $0.35\overline{)30.87}$
15. $0.09\overline{)5.715}$
16. $1.24\overline{)11.036}$
17. $0.16\overline{)1.248}$
18. $5.03\overline{)23.641}$
19. $0.21\overline{)0.5565}$
20. $0.13\overline{)11.102}$
21. $0.07\overline{)5.502}$
22. $0.37\overline{)35.52}$
23. $0.11\overline{)6.6}$
24. $0.46\overline{)1.794}$
25. $0.18\overline{)64.8}$
26. $0.39\overline{)25.233}$
27. $0.25\overline{)22.25}$
28. $0.24\overline{)18.84}$
29. $0.12\overline{)0.624}$
30. $0.08\overline{)6.368}$
31. $0.38\overline{)24.51}$
32. $3.92\overline{)18.032}$
33. $2.53\overline{)9.108}$
34. $0.57\overline{)47.88}$
35. $0.43\overline{)10.277}$
36. $0.02\overline{)0.178}$
37. $0.24\overline{)1.632}$
38. $1.21\overline{)78.65}$
39. $0.23\overline{)17.204}$
40. $0.05\overline{)4.35}$
41. $6.04\overline{)54.36}$
42. $0.62\overline{)2.914}$
43. $0.15\overline{)9.555}$
44. $0.33\overline{)3.267}$
45. $0.29\overline{)2.03}$

Practice puts you on top!

Decimals

Name ______________________

Show your work on another sheet. Write your answers here.

Total Problems 43

Problems Correct ______

1. $0.12\overline{)10.68}$

2. $4.14\overline{)28.152}$

3. $0.62\overline{)4.154}$

4. $0.07\overline{)0.6552}$

5. $0.42\overline{)1.554}$

6. $0.17\overline{)13.634}$

7. $0.67\overline{)5.762}$

8. $0.05\overline{)4.93}$

9. $0.03\overline{)223.59}$

10. $0.15\overline{)13.05}$

11. $0.31\overline{)19.592}$

12. $0.24\overline{)2.544}$

13. $6.54\overline{)30.084}$

14. $0.26\overline{)14.56}$

15. $0.41\overline{)1.148}$

16. $0.18\overline{)3.852}$

17. $0.84\overline{)34.692}$

18. $0.19\overline{)3.857}$

19. $0.92\overline{)3.6984}$

20. $0.04\overline{)3.72}$

21. $0.28\overline{)0.756}$

22. $0.68\overline{)9.86}$

23. $0.39\overline{)2.262}$

24. $0.21\overline{)1.407}$

25. $0.08\overline{)50.4}$

26. $0.42\overline{)7.518}$

27. $0.74\overline{)5.18}$

28. $0.98\overline{)7.84}$

29. $0.17\overline{)0.816}$

30. $0.24\overline{)1.368}$

31. $0.14\overline{)0.476}$

32. $0.09\overline{)0.0027}$

33. $0.39\overline{)4.875}$

34. $0.64\overline{)4.864}$

35. $1.26\overline{)4.536}$

36. $5.03\overline{)24.144}$

37. $0.65\overline{)5.252}$

38. $0.38\overline{)1.14}$

39. $2.04\overline{)6.936}$

40. $2.94\overline{)14.406}$

41. $0.69\overline{)55.338}$

42. $3.02\overline{)175.16}$

43. $0.54\overline{)2.052}$

Practice brings success!

Skill: Division of Decimals by Thousandths

Decimals

Name ____________________

Show your work on another sheet. Write your answers here.

Total Problems **40**

Problems Correct ______

1. $0.002\overline{)0.17}$

2. $0.415\overline{)3.735}$

3. $0.314\overline{)0.157}$

4. $0.006\overline{)0.282}$

5. $0.028\overline{)14.112}$

6. $0.054\overline{)0.3726}$

7. $0.329\overline{)2.632}$

8. $0.712\overline{)32.04}$

9. $0.742\overline{)471.17}$

10. $0.092\overline{)0.552}$

11. $0.184\overline{)0.6624}$

12. $0.003\overline{)0.2358}$

13. $0.246\overline{)11.808}$

14. $0.008\overline{)7.12}$

15. $0.623\overline{)34.888}$

16. $0.037\overline{)0.3552}$

17. $0.624\overline{)4.368}$

18. $0.108\overline{)6.804}$

19. $0.146\overline{)3.431}$

20. $0.609\overline{)4.872}$

21. $0.005\overline{)4.92}$

22. $0.424\overline{)22.896}$

23. $0.507\overline{)3.549}$

24. $0.319\overline{)6.38}$

25. $0.006\overline{)0.27}$

26. $0.031\overline{)2.3653}$

27. $0.506\overline{)376.97}$

28. $0.085\overline{)0.51}$

29. $0.046\overline{)24.104}$

30. $0.007\overline{)6.132}$

31. $0.024\overline{)2.304}$

32. $0.427\overline{)1.5372}$

33. $0.218\overline{)7.848}$

34. $0.611\overline{)5.499}$

35. $0.048\overline{)0.672}$

36. $0.009\overline{)6.705}$

37. $0.247\overline{)1.235}$

38. $0.329\overline{)29.281}$

39. $0.704\overline{)2.816}$

40. $0.162\overline{)3.4668}$

Practice brings success!

Fractions

Name ____________________

Total Problems	**40**
Problems Correct	______

Show your work on another sheet. Write your answers here.

1. $\frac{1}{4} = \frac{\quad}{16}$
2. $\frac{3}{8} = \frac{\quad}{24}$
3. $\frac{1}{2} = \frac{\quad}{8}$
4. $\frac{2}{5} = \frac{\quad}{10}$
5. $\frac{3}{6} = \frac{\quad}{12}$
6. $\frac{2}{6} = \frac{\quad}{18}$
7. $\frac{3}{\quad} = \frac{6}{18}$
8. $\frac{1}{5} = \frac{3}{\quad}$
9. $\frac{2}{\quad} = \frac{4}{6}$
10. $\frac{7}{8} = \frac{\quad}{16}$
11. $\frac{\quad}{5} = \frac{4}{20}$
12. $\frac{1}{3} = \frac{\quad}{15}$
13. $\frac{2}{4} = \frac{4}{\quad}$
14. $\frac{3}{4} = \frac{21}{\quad}$
15. $\frac{3}{6} = \frac{\quad}{18}$
16. $\frac{4}{5} = \frac{\quad}{20}$
17. $\frac{\quad}{7} = \frac{12}{14}$
18. $\frac{2}{6} = \frac{\quad}{24}$
19. $\frac{\quad}{4} = \frac{6}{12}$
20. $\frac{\quad}{3} = \frac{9}{27}$
21. $\frac{2}{8} = \frac{6}{\quad}$
22. $\frac{1}{9} = \frac{\quad}{18}$
23. $\frac{2}{\quad} = \frac{4}{20}$
24. $\frac{3}{6} = \frac{12}{\quad}$
25. $\frac{9}{10} = \frac{\quad}{30}$
26. $\frac{\quad}{6} = \frac{10}{30}$
27. $\frac{3}{7} = \frac{21}{\quad}$
28. $\frac{11}{12} = \frac{110}{\quad}$
29. $\frac{4}{9} = \frac{16}{\quad}$
30. $\frac{3}{4} = \frac{\quad}{32}$
31. $\frac{2}{6} = \frac{\quad}{36}$
32. $\frac{8}{9} = \frac{16}{\quad}$
33. $\frac{\quad}{5} = \frac{14}{35}$
34. $\frac{2}{7} = \frac{\quad}{42}$
35. $\frac{3}{12} = \frac{9}{\quad}$
36. $\frac{6}{11} = \frac{\quad}{132}$
37. $\frac{\quad}{8} = \frac{12}{96}$
38. $\frac{5}{10} = \frac{\quad}{120}$
39. $\frac{2}{\quad} = \frac{8}{24}$
40. $\frac{6}{9} = \frac{\quad}{72}$

Practice brings success!

Fractions

Name ________________________

Total Problems 50

Problems Correct ________

Reduce these fractions to lowest terms. Show your work on another sheet. Write your answers here.

1. $\frac{4}{8} =$
2. $\frac{6}{12} =$
3. $\frac{3}{9} =$
4. $\frac{8}{12} =$
5. $\frac{4}{16} =$
6. $\frac{5}{15} =$
7. $\frac{3}{12} =$
8. $\frac{5}{10} =$
9. $\frac{9}{18} =$
10. $\frac{2}{6} =$
11. $\frac{2}{10} =$
12. $\frac{16}{18} =$
13. $\frac{6}{9} =$
14. $\frac{10}{25} =$
15. $\frac{2}{4} =$
16. $\frac{2}{14} =$
17. $\frac{8}{16} =$
18. $\frac{6}{10} =$
19. $\frac{3}{6} =$
20. $\frac{10}{20} =$
21. $\frac{10}{12} =$
22. $\frac{6}{30} =$
23. $\frac{4}{24} =$
24. $\frac{14}{16} =$
25. $\frac{4}{20} =$
26. $\frac{7}{14} =$
27. $\frac{8}{8} =$
28. $\frac{5}{20} =$
29. $\frac{2}{8} =$
30. $\frac{4}{10} =$
31. $\frac{14}{20} =$
32. $\frac{8}{10} =$
33. $\frac{4}{6} =$
34. $\frac{8}{24} =$
35. $\frac{3}{18} =$
36. $\frac{20}{25} =$
37. $\frac{6}{8} =$
38. $\frac{10}{16} =$
39. $\frac{10}{22} =$
40. $\frac{6}{18} =$
41. $\frac{12}{20} =$
42. $\frac{5}{30} =$
43. $\frac{4}{12} =$
44. $\frac{12}{24} =$
45. $\frac{16}{20} =$
46. $\frac{3}{24} =$
47. $\frac{5}{25} =$
48. $\frac{18}{20} =$
49. $\frac{13}{26} =$
50. $\frac{12}{16} =$

Practice and anything's possible!

Skill: Changing Improper Fractions to Mixed Numbers

Fractions

Name ______________________________

Total Problems 42

Problems Correct ________

Change these fractions to mixed numbers in lowest terms. Show your work on another sheet. Write your answers here.

1. $\frac{10}{3} =$ **2.** $\frac{14}{6} =$

3. $\frac{15}{8} =$ **4.** $\frac{17}{8} =$

5. $\frac{9}{4} =$ **6.** $\frac{23}{5} =$ **7.** $\frac{18}{7} =$ **8.** $\frac{12}{10} =$ **9.** $\frac{7}{2} =$ **10.** $\frac{23}{7} =$

11. $\frac{16}{5} =$ **12.** $\frac{26}{6} =$ **13.** $\frac{32}{5} =$ **14.** $\frac{25}{12} =$ **15.** $\frac{8}{3} =$ **16.** $\frac{17}{3} =$

17. $\frac{14}{3} =$ **18.** $\frac{7}{3} =$ **19.** $\frac{27}{5} =$ **20.** $\frac{13}{4} =$ **21.** $\frac{20}{7} =$ **22.** $\frac{37}{9} =$

23. $\frac{36}{7} =$ **24.** $\frac{19}{3} =$ **25.** $\frac{47}{8} =$ **26.** $\frac{32}{7} =$ **27.** $\frac{43}{8} =$ **28.** $\frac{13}{4} =$

29. $\frac{53}{8} =$ **30.** $\frac{29}{9} =$ **31.** $\frac{26}{4} =$ **32.** $\frac{17}{7} =$ **33.** $\frac{64}{9} =$ **34.** $\frac{25}{6} =$

35. $\frac{21}{8} =$ **36.** $\frac{26}{3} =$ **37.** $\frac{53}{9} =$ **38.** $\frac{85}{12} =$

39. $\frac{29}{5} =$ **40.** $\frac{34}{9} =$ **41.** $\frac{19}{4} =$ **42.** $\frac{65}{9} =$

Practice hard. You'll win!

Skill: Changing Mixed Numbers to Improper Fractions

Mixed Numbers

Name ______________________

Total Problems	**42**
Problems Correct	______

Change these mixed numbers to improper fractions. Show your work on another sheet. Write your answers here.

1. $3\frac{2}{5} =$ **2.** $6\frac{2}{5} =$

3. $2\frac{1}{4} =$ **4.** $7\frac{3}{8} =$

5. $4\frac{2}{7} =$ **6.** $12\frac{3}{4} =$ **7.** $8\frac{2}{3} =$ **8.** $4\frac{1}{8} =$ **9.** $3\frac{2}{4} =$ **10.** $5\frac{2}{7} =$

11. $8\frac{2}{5} =$ **12.** $4\frac{3}{7} =$ **13.** $2\frac{3}{8} =$ **14.** $9\frac{2}{3} =$ **15.** $4\frac{3}{9} =$ **16.** $8\frac{3}{5} =$

17. $15\frac{1}{3} =$ **18.** $17\frac{1}{2} =$ **19.** $32\frac{1}{3} =$ **20.** $3\frac{2}{6} =$ **21.** $8\frac{2}{5} =$ **22.** $6\frac{2}{8} =$

23. $7\frac{3}{5} =$ **24.** $4\frac{6}{7} =$ **25.** $8\frac{2}{7} =$ **26.** $9\frac{3}{4} =$ **27.** $6\frac{2}{8} =$ **28.** $8\frac{2}{6} =$

29. $5\frac{2}{8} =$ **30.** $3\frac{7}{8} =$ **31.** $9\frac{2}{5} =$ **32.** $4\frac{3}{7} =$ **33.** $8\frac{3}{6} =$ **34.** $6\frac{2}{9} =$

35. $8\frac{7}{12} =$ **36.** $5\frac{3}{9} =$ **37.** $3\frac{2}{11} =$ **38.** $9\frac{6}{12} =$

39. $7\frac{2}{8} =$ **40.** $11\frac{2}{12} =$ **41.** $15\frac{2}{3} =$ **42.** $5\frac{3}{6} =$

Practice hard. You'll win!

Skill: Changing Improper Fractions to Mixed Numbers

Fractions

Name ____________________

Change these improper fractions to mixed numbers. Show your work on another sheet. Write your answers here.

Total Problems 50

Problems Correct ______

1. $\frac{36}{6} =$ **2.** $\frac{14}{6} =$

3. $\frac{28}{9} =$ **4.** $\frac{13}{5} =$ **5.** $\frac{17}{8} =$ **6.** $\frac{51}{10} =$ **7.** $\frac{13}{6} =$

8. $\frac{43}{8} =$ **9.** $\frac{24}{5} =$ **10.** $\frac{34}{6} =$ **11.** $\frac{29}{4} =$ **12.** $\frac{91}{10} =$

13. $\frac{37}{7} =$ **14.** $\frac{21}{4} =$ **15.** $\frac{83}{9} =$ **16.** $\frac{15}{6} =$ **17.** $\frac{37}{5} =$

18. $\frac{49}{6} =$ **19.** $\frac{25}{4} =$ **20.** $\frac{48}{5} =$ **21.** $\frac{23}{7} =$ **22.** $\frac{15}{2} =$

23. $\frac{39}{6} =$ **24.** $\frac{56}{9} =$ **25.** $\frac{47}{6} =$ **26.** $\frac{23}{3} =$ **27.** $\frac{63}{8} =$

28. $\frac{75}{8} =$ **29.** $\frac{62}{7} =$ **30.** $\frac{42}{5} =$ **31.** $\frac{73}{9} =$ **32.** $\frac{47}{8} =$

33. $\frac{59}{10} =$ **34.** $\frac{78}{9} =$ **35.** $\frac{46}{5} =$ **36.** $\frac{87}{12} =$ **37.** $\frac{95}{9} =$

38. $\frac{111}{11} =$ **39.** $\frac{89}{11} =$ **40.** $\frac{123}{10} =$ **41.** $\frac{147}{12} =$ **42.** $\frac{113}{10} =$

43. $\frac{135}{12} =$ **44.** $\frac{114}{10} =$ **45.** $\frac{59}{6} =$

Anything's possible with practice!

46. $\frac{47}{4} =$ **47.** $\frac{134}{11} =$ **48.** $\frac{112}{10} =$

49. $\frac{36}{5} =$ **50.** $\frac{88}{10} =$

Fractions

Name ____________________

Total Problems 50

Problems Correct ______

Change these mixed numbers to improper fractions. Show your work on another sheet. Write your answers here.

1. $3\frac{6}{7} =$ **2.** $4\frac{2}{8} =$

3. $2\frac{1}{3} =$ **4.** $4\frac{5}{6} =$ **5.** $2\frac{2}{3} =$ **6.** $4\frac{1}{6} =$ **7.** $4\frac{3}{5} =$

8. $3\frac{4}{6} =$ **9.** $5\frac{2}{3} =$ **10.** $6\frac{3}{7} =$ **11.** $2\frac{4}{9} =$ **12.** $6\frac{2}{5} =$

13. $5\frac{2}{9} =$ **14.** $7\frac{3}{6} =$ **15.** $2\frac{3}{12} =$ **16.** $8\frac{4}{10} =$ **17.** $3\frac{4}{12} =$

18. $2\frac{6}{14} =$ **19.** $6\frac{3}{9} =$ **20.** $5\frac{1}{9} =$ **21.** $12\frac{3}{11} =$ **22.** $4\frac{5}{8} =$

23. $7\frac{6}{12} =$ **24.** $5\frac{7}{10} =$ **25.** $4\frac{6}{12} =$ **26.** $3\frac{2}{4} =$ **27.** $6\frac{1}{8} =$

28. $7\frac{2}{5} =$ **29.** $3\frac{4}{8} =$ **30.** $9\frac{2}{12} =$ **31.** $8\frac{3}{7} =$ **32.** $4\frac{6}{11} =$

33. $11\frac{3}{12} =$ **34.** $10\frac{4}{11} =$ **35.** $5\frac{6}{9} =$ **36.** $7\frac{8}{10} =$ **37.** $12\frac{4}{11} =$

38. $14\frac{2}{3} =$ **39.** $15\frac{1}{4} =$ **40.** $3\frac{2}{6} =$ **41.** $4\frac{8}{15} =$ **42.** $2\frac{1}{11} =$

43. $5\frac{1}{7} =$ **44.** $12\frac{6}{9} =$ **45.** $11\frac{3}{11} =$

46. $30\frac{2}{10} =$ **47.** $13\frac{3}{4} =$ **48.** $20\frac{2}{4} =$

49. $45\frac{1}{2} =$ **50.** $9\frac{5}{31} =$

Practice!
Practice!
Practice!

Fractions

Name ______________________

Total Problems	**40**
Problems Correct	________

Show your work on another sheet. Reduce your answers to lowest terms and write them here.

1. $\frac{2}{4} + \frac{1}{4}$ **2.** $\frac{3}{8} + \frac{4}{8}$ **3.** $\frac{3}{12} + \frac{8}{12}$

4. $\frac{1}{2} + \frac{1}{2}$ **5.** $\frac{3}{7} + \frac{2}{7}$ **6.** $\frac{2}{3} + \frac{1}{3}$ **7.** $\frac{8}{16} + \frac{3}{16}$ **8.** $\frac{1}{5} + \frac{2}{5}$ **9.** $\frac{5}{10} + \frac{2}{10}$ **10.** $\frac{2}{9} + \frac{4}{9}$ **11.** $\frac{3}{5} + \frac{1}{5}$ **12.** $\frac{2}{6} + \frac{2}{6}$ **13.** $\frac{2}{8} + \frac{1}{8}$

14. $\frac{5}{9} + \frac{1}{9}$ **15.** $\frac{6}{7} + \frac{1}{7}$ **16.** $\frac{12}{20} + \frac{4}{20}$ **17.** $\frac{5}{8} + \frac{2}{8}$ **18.** $\frac{8}{18} + \frac{5}{18}$ **19.** $\frac{4}{11} + \frac{5}{11}$ **20.** $\frac{5}{16} + \frac{9}{16}$ **21.** $\frac{8}{24} + \frac{13}{24}$ **22.** $\frac{4}{12} + \frac{2}{12}$ **23.** $\frac{5}{9} + \frac{3}{9}$

24. $\frac{9}{21} + \frac{7}{21}$ **25.** $\frac{3}{10} + \frac{6}{10}$ **26.** $\frac{4}{9} + \frac{3}{9}$ **27.** $\frac{14}{24} + \frac{7}{24}$ **28.** $\frac{2}{7} + \frac{4}{7}$ **29.** $\frac{5}{16} + \frac{7}{16}$ **30.** $\frac{2}{5} + \frac{2}{5}$ **31.** $\frac{3}{6} + \frac{2}{6}$ **32.** $\frac{7}{20} + \frac{8}{20}$ **33.** $\frac{5}{8} + \frac{3}{8}$

34. $\frac{8}{12} + \frac{3}{12}$ **35.** $\frac{11}{16} + \frac{5}{16}$ **36.** $\frac{8}{24} + \frac{9}{24}$ **37.** $\frac{15}{30} + \frac{8}{30}$ **38.** $\frac{7}{21} + \frac{10}{21}$ **39.** $\frac{3}{14} + \frac{8}{14}$ **40.** $\frac{9}{15} + \frac{4}{15}$

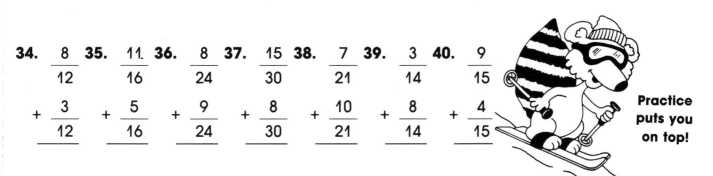

Practice puts you on top!

Skill: Addition of Like Fractions

Fractions

Name ________________________

Total Problems	**40**
Problems Correct	______

Show your work on another sheet. Reduce your answers to lowest terms and write them here.

1. $\frac{2}{3} + \frac{1}{3}$

2. $\frac{2}{6} + \frac{3}{6}$

3. $\frac{4}{12} + \frac{3}{12}$

4. $\frac{8}{16} + \frac{4}{16}$

5. $\frac{3}{25} + \frac{18}{25}$

6. $\frac{7}{15} + \frac{4}{15}$

7. $\frac{2}{5} + \frac{2}{5}$

8. $\frac{6}{30} + \frac{17}{30}$

9. $\frac{4}{9} + \frac{3}{9}$

10. $\frac{7}{11} + \frac{3}{11}$

11. $\frac{6}{8} + \frac{2}{8}$

12. $\frac{5}{16} + \frac{8}{16}$

13. $\frac{7}{10} + \frac{2}{10}$

14. $\frac{4}{8} + \frac{3}{8}$

15. $\frac{2}{17} + \frac{9}{17}$

16. $\frac{3}{9} + \frac{5}{9}$

17. $\frac{2}{7} + \frac{4}{7}$

18. $\frac{5}{12} + \frac{6}{12}$

19. $\frac{3}{48} + \frac{7}{48}$

20. $\frac{1}{6} + \frac{3}{6}$

21. $\frac{5}{28} + \frac{13}{28}$

22. $\frac{7}{30} + \frac{8}{30}$

23. $\frac{11}{22} + \frac{8}{22}$

24. $\frac{9}{14} + \frac{3}{14}$

25. $\frac{8}{64} + \frac{17}{64}$

26. $\frac{4}{7} + \frac{3}{7}$

27. $\frac{2}{8} + \frac{3}{8}$

28. $\frac{3}{6} + \frac{1}{6}$

29. $\frac{6}{28} + \frac{17}{28}$

30. $\frac{14}{50} + \frac{7}{50}$

31. $\frac{6}{10} + \frac{3}{10}$

32. $\frac{8}{16} + \frac{4}{16}$

33. $\frac{5}{35} + \frac{17}{35}$

34. $\frac{5}{11} + \frac{2}{11}$

35. $\frac{2}{9} + \frac{5}{9}$

36. $\frac{8}{90} + \frac{23}{90}$

37. $\frac{8}{12} + \frac{2}{12}$

38. $\frac{4}{8} + \frac{1}{8}$

39. $\frac{8}{14} + \frac{5}{14}$

40. $\frac{17}{28} + \frac{6}{28}$

Practice brings success!

Fractions

Name ______________________

Total Problems **40**

Problems Correct ______

Show your work on another sheet. Reduce your answers to lowest terms and write them here.

1. $\frac{1}{3} + \frac{3}{6}$ **2.** $\frac{1}{5} + \frac{3}{10}$ **3.** $\frac{1}{4} + \frac{5}{8}$

4. $\frac{1}{2} + \frac{2}{4}$ **5.** $\frac{3}{7} + \frac{2}{14}$ **6.** $\frac{5}{6} + \frac{2}{12}$ **7.** $\frac{2}{4} + \frac{5}{12}$ **8.** $\frac{2}{5} + \frac{4}{10}$ **9.** $\frac{1}{4} + \frac{2}{8}$ **10.** $\frac{1}{3} + \frac{4}{6}$ **11.** $\frac{1}{7} + \frac{5}{14}$ **12.** $\frac{3}{6} + \frac{1}{12}$ **13.** $\frac{2}{5} + \frac{7}{15}$

14. $\frac{4}{8} + \frac{3}{16}$ **15.** $\frac{2}{9} + \frac{5}{18}$ **16.** $\frac{4}{7} + \frac{5}{21}$ **17.** $\frac{2}{3} + \frac{2}{6}$ **18.** $\frac{4}{10} + \frac{5}{20}$ **19.** $\frac{1}{2} + \frac{1}{4}$ **20.** $\frac{1}{3} + \frac{2}{9}$ **21.** $\frac{3}{4} + \frac{1}{12}$ **22.** $\frac{6}{7} + \frac{2}{21}$ **23.** $\frac{6}{10} + \frac{6}{20}$

24. $\frac{4}{5} + \frac{1}{15}$ **25.** $\frac{2}{6} + \frac{7}{12}$ **26.** $\frac{2}{4} + \frac{3}{16}$ **27.** $\frac{2}{4} + \frac{3}{8}$ **28.** $\frac{4}{5} + \frac{1}{10}$ **29.** $\frac{4}{9} + \frac{3}{18}$ **30.** $\frac{1}{4} + \frac{6}{12}$ **31.** $\frac{4}{7} + \frac{3}{14}$ **32.** $\frac{2}{3} + \frac{2}{9}$ **33.** $\frac{3}{8} + \frac{7}{16}$

34. $\frac{2}{8} + \frac{5}{16}$ **35.** $\frac{1}{5} + \frac{9}{15}$ **36.** $\frac{3}{9} + \frac{7}{18}$ **37.** $\frac{5}{7} + \frac{4}{21}$ **38.** $\frac{8}{10} + \frac{1}{20}$ **39.** $\frac{1}{3} + \frac{5}{9}$ **40.** $\frac{3}{4} + \frac{2}{16}$

Practice brings success!

Fractions

Name ______________________

Total Problems	**40**
Problems Correct	______

Show your work on another sheet. Reduce your answers to lowest terms and write them here.

1. $\frac{1}{2} + \frac{3}{8}$ **2.** $\frac{1}{2} + \frac{2}{5}$ **3.** $\frac{2}{8} + \frac{2}{3}$

4. $\frac{4}{7} + \frac{1}{3}$ **5.** $\frac{2}{5} + \frac{2}{4}$ **6.** $\frac{1}{2} + \frac{2}{8}$ **7.** $\frac{2}{3} + \frac{1}{5}$ **8.** $\frac{2}{4} + \frac{7}{16}$ **9.** $\frac{3}{5} + \frac{2}{6}$ **10.** $\frac{5}{11} + \frac{1}{3}$ **11.** $\frac{3}{9} + \frac{1}{2}$ **12.** $\frac{6}{7} + \frac{2}{3}$ **13.** $\frac{2}{10} + \frac{1}{2}$

14. $\frac{1}{2} + \frac{4}{9}$ **15.** $\frac{1}{3} + \frac{6}{12}$ **16.** $\frac{1}{4} + \frac{3}{5}$ **17.** $\frac{2}{6} + \frac{1}{2}$ **18.** $\frac{1}{2} + \frac{1}{5}$ **19.** $\frac{1}{3} + \frac{3}{5}$ **20.** $\frac{4}{8} + \frac{1}{3}$ **21.** $\frac{1}{3} + \frac{5}{12}$ **22.** $\frac{1}{6} + \frac{1}{4}$ **23.** $\frac{5}{12} + \frac{1}{2}$

24. $\frac{2}{3} + \frac{5}{7}$ **25.** $\frac{3}{6} + \frac{2}{5}$ **26.** $\frac{2}{5} + \frac{1}{3}$ **27.** $\frac{2}{16} + \frac{3}{4}$ **28.** $\frac{4}{10} + \frac{1}{2}$ **29.** $\frac{2}{3} + \frac{3}{11}$ **30.** $\frac{5}{7} + \frac{1}{2}$ **31.** $\frac{1}{5} + \frac{3}{4}$ **32.** $\frac{1}{2} + \frac{1}{6}$ **33.** $\frac{1}{2} + \frac{3}{12}$

34. $\frac{1}{6} + \frac{4}{5}$ **35.** $\frac{4}{11} + \frac{1}{3}$ **36.** $\frac{3}{12} + \frac{2}{3}$ **37.** $\frac{1}{4} + \frac{9}{16}$ **38.** $\frac{5}{8} + \frac{1}{3}$ **39.** $\frac{3}{10} + \frac{1}{2}$ **40.** $\frac{3}{7} + \frac{1}{2}$

Practice and anything's possible!

Fractions

Name ____________________

Total Problems	40
Problems Correct	______

Show your work on another sheet. Reduce your answers to lowest terms and write them here.

1. $\frac{2}{3} + \frac{1}{9}$

2. $\frac{3}{4} + \frac{2}{12}$

3. $\frac{1}{5} + \frac{3}{10}$

4. $\frac{1}{6} + \frac{2}{12}$

5. $\frac{3}{4} + \frac{1}{8}$

6. $\frac{2}{8} + \frac{1}{16}$

7. $\frac{3}{5} + \frac{2}{10}$

8. $\frac{7}{12} + \frac{2}{4}$

9. $\frac{6}{7} + \frac{2}{21}$

10. $\frac{3}{5} + \frac{2}{15}$

11. $\frac{7}{14} + \frac{2}{7}$

12. $\frac{3}{6} + \frac{2}{18}$

13. $\frac{2}{14} + \frac{1}{7}$

14. $\frac{1}{8} + \frac{1}{2}$

15. $\frac{6}{8} + \frac{1}{24}$

16. $\frac{4}{12} + \frac{1}{3}$

17. $\frac{8}{14} + \frac{3}{7}$

18. $\frac{2}{3} + \frac{4}{12}$

19. $\frac{6}{14} + \frac{1}{2}$

20. $\frac{3}{6} + \frac{4}{12}$

21. $\frac{3}{8} + \frac{5}{16}$

22. $\frac{7}{21} + \frac{2}{7}$

23. $\frac{5}{15} + \frac{1}{3}$

24. $\frac{4}{16} + \frac{1}{2}$

25. $\frac{3}{9} + \frac{1}{3}$

26. $\frac{1}{5} + \frac{6}{25}$

27. $\frac{1}{4} + \frac{2}{8}$

28. $\frac{1}{2} + \frac{4}{6}$

29. $\frac{10}{20} + \frac{3}{4}$

30. $\frac{7}{30} + \frac{1}{3}$

31. $\frac{4}{8} + \frac{1}{40}$

32. $\frac{1}{4} + \frac{3}{8}$

33. $\frac{2}{5} + \frac{4}{10}$

34. $\frac{1}{5} + \frac{1}{6}$

35. $\frac{2}{9} + \frac{1}{4}$

36. $\frac{3}{7} + \frac{1}{2}$

37. $\frac{2}{5} + \frac{1}{7}$

38. $\frac{4}{8} + \frac{1}{3}$

39. $\frac{5}{9} + \frac{1}{2}$

40. $\frac{2}{7} + \frac{1}{8}$

Anything's possible with practice!

Fractions

Name ______________________

Total Problems	**40**
Problems Correct	______

Show your work on another sheet. Reduce your answers to lowest terms and write them here.

1. $\frac{2}{3} + \frac{2}{9}$ **2.** $\frac{1}{6} + \frac{2}{3}$ **3.** $\frac{1}{8} + \frac{4}{16}$

4. $\frac{4}{8} + \frac{1}{4}$ **5.** $\frac{5}{9} + \frac{3}{18}$ **6.** $\frac{5}{12} + \frac{1}{3}$ **7.** $\frac{8}{10} + \frac{1}{5}$ **8.** $\frac{4}{5} + \frac{1}{20}$ **9.** $\frac{2}{8} + \frac{1}{2}$ **10.** $\frac{1}{10} + \frac{2}{5}$ **11.** $\frac{2}{11} + \frac{1}{22}$ **12.** $\frac{3}{10} + \frac{1}{2}$ **13.** $\frac{2}{6} + \frac{1}{3}$

14. $\frac{3}{8} + \frac{1}{4}$ **15.** $\frac{2}{5} + \frac{2}{15}$ **16.** $\frac{1}{9} + \frac{1}{18}$ **17.** $\frac{3}{4} + \frac{1}{16}$ **18.** $\frac{2}{7} + \frac{3}{21}$ **19.** $\frac{4}{6} + \frac{1}{12}$ **20.** $\frac{2}{3} + \frac{2}{12}$ **21.** $\frac{2}{8} + \frac{3}{16}$ **22.** $\frac{2}{21} + \frac{2}{7}$ **23.** $\frac{1}{4} + \frac{2}{12}$

24. $\frac{3}{6} + \frac{2}{18}$ **25.** $\frac{2}{7} + \frac{6}{21}$ **26.** $\frac{1}{2} + \frac{3}{18}$ **27.** $\frac{1}{3} + \frac{2}{15}$ **28.** $\frac{1}{8} + \frac{1}{4}$ **29.** $\frac{3}{6} + \frac{3}{12}$ **30.** $\frac{2}{5} + \frac{9}{15}$ **31.** $\frac{3}{6} + \frac{5}{12}$ **32.** $\frac{1}{15} + \frac{1}{3}$ **33.** $\frac{2}{8} + \frac{1}{16}$

34. $\frac{3}{4} + \frac{1}{12}$ **35.** $\frac{1}{3} + \frac{5}{18}$ **36.** $\frac{1}{5} + \frac{4}{10}$ **37.** $\frac{2}{6} + \frac{4}{12}$ **38.** $\frac{3}{5} + \frac{2}{10}$ **39.** $\frac{1}{9} + \frac{3}{18}$ **40.** $\frac{4}{7} + \frac{2}{21}$

Anything's possible with practice!

Mixed Numbers

Name ____________________

Total Problems	**40**
Problems Correct	______

Show your work on another sheet. Reduce your answers to lowest terms and write them here.

1. $3\frac{2}{4} + 7\frac{1}{4}$
2. $8\frac{2}{7} + 5\frac{3}{7}$
3. $4\frac{6}{9} + 8\frac{2}{9}$
4. $2\frac{4}{7} + 9\frac{2}{7}$
5. $4\frac{2}{5} + 5\frac{2}{5}$
6. $7\frac{2}{4} + 9\frac{1}{4}$
7. $5\frac{2}{7} + 8\frac{3}{7}$
8. $8\frac{3}{5} + 7\frac{1}{5}$
9. $3\frac{1}{4} + 8\frac{2}{4}$
10. $5\frac{3}{9} + 6\frac{4}{9}$
11. $9\frac{2}{4} + 6\frac{1}{4}$
12. $7\frac{2}{6} + 9\frac{3}{6}$
13. $6\frac{1}{7} + 4\frac{3}{7}$
14. $4\frac{1}{6} + 7\frac{4}{6}$
15. $9\frac{3}{7} + 8\frac{2}{7}$
16. $5\frac{1}{3} + 6\frac{1}{3}$
17. $8\frac{2}{14} + 9\frac{7}{14}$
18. $4\frac{3}{9} + 6\frac{4}{9}$
19. $6\frac{1}{5} + 8\frac{3}{5}$
20. $7\frac{1}{12} + 8\frac{6}{12}$
21. $3\frac{2}{8} + 9\frac{3}{8}$
22. $9\frac{6}{9} + 4\frac{1}{9}$
23. $5\frac{2}{7} + 8\frac{3}{7}$
24. $8\frac{3}{10} + 7\frac{4}{10}$
25. $9\frac{1}{4} + 7\frac{2}{4}$
26. $2\frac{6}{8} + 9\frac{1}{8}$
27. $6\frac{3}{5} + 9\frac{1}{5}$
28. $5\frac{1}{7} + 6\frac{1}{7}$
29. $4\frac{3}{8} + 7\frac{2}{8}$
30. $7\frac{3}{6} + 8\frac{2}{6}$
31. $7\frac{2}{9} + 4\frac{3}{9}$
32. $3\frac{4}{8} + 7\frac{3}{8}$
33. $9\frac{1}{5} + 4\frac{2}{5}$
34. $7\frac{1}{3} + 9\frac{1}{3}$
35. $6\frac{2}{9} + 4\frac{3}{9}$
36. $8\frac{2}{6} + 9\frac{3}{6}$
37. $4\frac{8}{10} + 7\frac{1}{10}$
38. $5\frac{1}{7} + 7\frac{3}{7}$
39. $3\frac{2}{12} + 8\frac{3}{12}$
40. $4\frac{3}{15} + 9\frac{8}{15}$

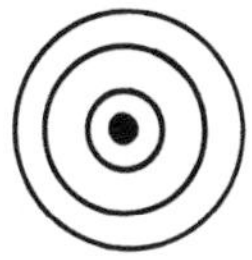

Practice hard.

You'll win.

Mixed Numbers

Name ______________________________

Show your work on another sheet. Reduce your answers to lowest terms and write them here.

Total Problems	**40**
Problems Correct	______

1. $3\frac{2}{4} + 5\frac{3}{4}$

2. $8\frac{1}{6} + 4\frac{7}{6}$

3. $4\frac{2}{5} + 9\frac{3}{5}$

4. $7\frac{2}{8} + 5\frac{7}{8}$

5. $9\frac{1}{3} + 8\frac{4}{3}$

6. $2\frac{4}{5} + 7\frac{3}{5}$

7. $4\frac{3}{8} + 7\frac{5}{8}$

8. $6\frac{3}{5} + 5\frac{6}{5}$

9. $3\frac{2}{4} + 7\frac{3}{4}$

10. $8\frac{4}{6} + 9\frac{5}{6}$

11. $5\frac{2}{5} + 8\frac{4}{5}$

12. $7\frac{3}{8} + 3\frac{7}{8}$

13. $4\frac{5}{9} + 8\frac{7}{9}$

14. $6\frac{4}{5} + 6\frac{3}{5}$

15. $8\frac{2}{7} + 9\frac{6}{7}$

16. $4\frac{2}{6} + 7\frac{5}{6}$

17. $6\frac{3}{8} + 9\frac{7}{8}$

18. $3\frac{2}{5} + 7\frac{4}{5}$

19. $7\frac{4}{6} + 5\frac{5}{6}$

20. $9\frac{2}{3} + 8\frac{2}{3}$

21. $6\frac{4}{5} + 8\frac{3}{5}$

22. $4\frac{2}{9} + 5\frac{8}{9}$

23. $8\frac{4}{7} + 8\frac{6}{7}$

24. $2\frac{2}{3} + 1\frac{2}{3}$

25. $6\frac{4}{5} + 9\frac{4}{5}$

26. $4\frac{2}{5} + 8\frac{3}{5}$

27. $8\frac{6}{10} + 3\frac{7}{10}$

28. $5\frac{2}{8} + 9\frac{7}{8}$

29. $12\frac{6}{7} + 4\frac{3}{7}$

30. $9\frac{3}{6} + 8\frac{5}{6}$

31. $14\frac{3}{5} + 7\frac{4}{5}$

32. $8\frac{2}{4} + 9\frac{3}{4}$

33. $7\frac{8}{10} + 9\frac{7}{10}$

34. $13\frac{2}{4} + 9\frac{3}{4}$

35. $5\frac{3}{7} + 8\frac{6}{7}$

36. $3\frac{2}{9} + 7\frac{8}{9}$

37. $15\frac{2}{6} + 8\frac{5}{6}$

38. $21\frac{2}{8} + 8\frac{6}{8}$

39. $4\frac{3}{5} + 7\frac{4}{5}$

40. $10\frac{2}{4} + 8\frac{3}{4}$

Practice hard. You'll win!

Skill: Addition of Mixed Numbers With Unlike Denominators

Mixed Numbers

Name ____________________

Total Problems	40
Problems Correct	______

Show your work on another sheet. Reduce your answers to lowest terms and write them here.

1. $3\frac{2}{4} + 7\frac{3}{8}$
2. $5\frac{3}{5} + 9\frac{4}{10}$
3. $8\frac{1}{6} + 4\frac{3}{12}$
4. $6\frac{2}{10} + 5\frac{3}{5}$
5. $7\frac{4}{8} + 6\frac{3}{4}$
6. $2\frac{3}{10} + 6\frac{2}{5}$
7. $9\frac{3}{4} + 3\frac{2}{12}$
8. $3\frac{2}{6} + 8\frac{1}{3}$
9. $7\frac{2}{6} + 8\frac{1}{2}$
10. $4\frac{2}{15} + 8\frac{3}{5}$
11. $5\frac{2}{7} + 9\frac{3}{21}$
12. $2\frac{6}{9} + 3\frac{1}{3}$
13. $8\frac{1}{2} + 9\frac{3}{4}$
14. $6\frac{2}{5} + 8\frac{3}{10}$
15. $4\frac{3}{8} + 6\frac{4}{16}$
16. $9\frac{2}{5} + 8\frac{3}{15}$
17. $7\frac{2}{3} + 7\frac{1}{6}$
18. $5\frac{3}{10} + 9\frac{2}{20}$
19. $2\frac{1}{8} + 8\frac{3}{24}$
20. $7\frac{3}{6} + 9\frac{1}{12}$
21. $8\frac{4}{6} + 7\frac{1}{2}$
22. $3\frac{2}{4} + 6\frac{1}{2}$
23. $9\frac{3}{9} + 7\frac{1}{3}$
24. $2\frac{3}{5} + 8\frac{1}{10}$
25. $11\frac{3}{6} + 8\frac{4}{12}$
26. $9\frac{2}{7} + 7\frac{3}{21}$
27. $6\frac{2}{5} + 8\frac{3}{15}$
28. $8\frac{1}{6} + 9\frac{2}{3}$
29. $15\frac{2}{6} + 8\frac{1}{2}$
30. $4\frac{2}{3} + 7\frac{1}{9}$
31. $13\frac{2}{8} + 8\frac{1}{2}$
32. $5\frac{3}{8} + 9\frac{6}{16}$
33. $4\frac{1}{2} + 8\frac{3}{12}$
34. $12\frac{1}{3} + 8\frac{3}{6}$
35. $8\frac{1}{5} + 9\frac{4}{10}$
36. $18\frac{1}{2} + 5\frac{3}{6}$
37. $4\frac{3}{6} + 5\frac{2}{12}$
38. $2\frac{4}{8} + 3\frac{2}{32}$
39. $5\frac{2}{12} + 8\frac{4}{36}$
40. $9\frac{2}{7} + 6\frac{3}{21}$

Practice hard.

You'll win!

Skill: Addition of Mixed Numbers With Unlike Denominators

Mixed Numbers

Name ____________________

Total Problems	40
Problems Correct	______

Show your work on another sheet. Reduce your answers to lowest terms and write them here.

1. $2\frac{1}{8} + 3\frac{2}{4}$
2. $3\frac{4}{6} + 7\frac{2}{12}$
3. $9\frac{3}{7} + 4\frac{2}{21}$
4. $5\frac{1}{20} + 3\frac{2}{4}$
5. $10\frac{1}{2} + 3\frac{2}{6}$
6. $4\frac{2}{6} + 8\frac{7}{12}$
7. $6\frac{2}{4} + 3\frac{1}{8}$
8. $7\frac{3}{4} + 2\frac{1}{2}$
9. $8\frac{4}{6} + 7\frac{7}{12}$
10. $2\frac{4}{9} + 3\frac{2}{3}$
11. $5\frac{3}{4} + 8\frac{2}{8}$
12. $3\frac{1}{4} + 2\frac{8}{12}$
13. $2\frac{4}{5} + 3\frac{5}{10}$
14. $8\frac{4}{5} + 7\frac{2}{15}$
15. $9\frac{1}{4} + 3\frac{9}{16}$
16. $8\frac{2}{8} + 8\frac{3}{4}$
17. $6\frac{2}{5} + 8\frac{1}{10}$
18. $7\frac{1}{8} + 7\frac{9}{16}$
19. $3\frac{1}{21} + 7\frac{6}{7}$
20. $5\frac{1}{15} + 6\frac{1}{3}$
21. $2\frac{3}{5} + 9\frac{2}{10}$
22. $6\frac{2}{4} + 8\frac{6}{8}$
23. $7\frac{2}{12} + 6\frac{1}{4}$
24. $2\frac{1}{4} + 6\frac{3}{12}$
25. $9\frac{2}{6} + 8\frac{2}{3}$
26. $4\frac{1}{16} + 8\frac{3}{4}$
27. $8\frac{2}{7} + 7\frac{9}{14}$
28. $6\frac{1}{4} + 3\frac{4}{16}$
29. $8\frac{2}{8} + 3\frac{1}{4}$
30. $5\frac{6}{9} + 8\frac{6}{18}$
31. $2\frac{6}{7} + 3\frac{2}{14}$
32. $9\frac{2}{16} + 6\frac{1}{4}$
33. $4\frac{2}{5} + 8\frac{1}{10}$
34. $12\frac{2}{7} + 6\frac{1}{14}$
35. $16\frac{2}{5} + 2\frac{1}{15}$
36. $3\frac{2}{12} + 4\frac{1}{24}$
37. $4\frac{1}{8} + 7\frac{2}{4}$
38. $2\frac{6}{9} + 3\frac{1}{3}$
39. $4\frac{2}{9} + 8\frac{2}{3}$
40. $7\frac{4}{21} + 2\frac{1}{3}$

Practice! Practice! Practice!

Skill: Addition of Mixed Numbers With Fractions

Mixed Numbers

Name ____________________

Total Problems	40
Problems Correct	______

Show your work on another sheet. Reduce your answers to lowest terms and write them here.

1. $5\frac{2}{6} + \frac{1}{3}$	**2.** $8\frac{3}{4} + \frac{3}{4}$	**3.** $4\frac{2}{4} + \frac{1}{8}$				
4. $12\frac{3}{6} + \frac{4}{12}$	**5.** $9\frac{2}{5} + \frac{2}{5}$	**6.** $5\frac{6}{7} + \frac{3}{14}$	**7.** $10\frac{3}{8} + \frac{2}{8}$	**8.** $4\frac{3}{6} + \frac{2}{6}$	**9.** $8\frac{2}{4} + \frac{1}{4}$	**10.** $16\frac{3}{9} + \frac{4}{18}$
11. $12\frac{3}{8} + \frac{2}{8}$	**12.** $3\frac{6}{12} + \frac{2}{12}$	**13.** $11\frac{3}{8} + \frac{4}{8}$	**14.** $3\frac{2}{7} + \frac{3}{14}$	**15.** $9\frac{3}{16} + \frac{3}{8}$	**16.** $8\frac{3}{4} + \frac{1}{2}$	**17.** $6\frac{2}{5} + \frac{3}{10}$
18. $8\frac{4}{7} + \frac{2}{7}$	**19.** $2\frac{1}{3} + \frac{7}{9}$	**20.** $8\frac{2}{3} + \frac{5}{6}$	**21.** $12\frac{2}{5} + \frac{2}{10}$	**22.** $14\frac{1}{5} + \frac{2}{5}$	**23.** $8\frac{1}{3} + \frac{2}{6}$	**24.** $9\frac{3}{5} + \frac{3}{10}$
25. $6\frac{2}{8} + \frac{1}{2}$	**26.** $8\frac{6}{9} + \frac{1}{3}$	**27.** $12\frac{1}{3} + \frac{3}{6}$	**28.** $8\frac{9}{12} + \frac{2}{3}$	**29.** $7\frac{3}{5} + \frac{2}{15}$	**30.** $3\frac{2}{5} + \frac{5}{10}$	**31.** $16\frac{2}{16} + \frac{3}{8}$
32. $8\frac{2}{10} + \frac{3}{10}$	**33.** $6\frac{3}{7} + \frac{4}{21}$	**34.** $19\frac{4}{12} + \frac{7}{12}$	**35.** $7\frac{3}{4} + \frac{2}{8}$	**36.** $14\frac{2}{9} + \frac{1}{3}$		
37. $6\frac{8}{10} + \frac{4}{5}$	**38.** $9\frac{4}{8} + \frac{2}{4}$	**39.** $3\frac{3}{16} + \frac{2}{4}$	**40.** $4\frac{8}{12} + \frac{2}{6}$			

Practice puts you on top!

Fractions

Name ____________________

Total Problems	**40**
Problems Correct	______

Show your work on another sheet. Reduce your answers to lowest terms and write them here.

1. $\frac{8}{10} - \frac{3}{10}$ **2.** $\frac{3}{6} - \frac{1}{6}$ **3.** $\frac{6}{8} - \frac{4}{8}$

4. $\frac{8}{9} - \frac{5}{9}$ **5.** $\frac{4}{5} - \frac{2}{5}$ **6.** $\frac{1}{2} - \frac{1}{2}$ **7.** $\frac{2}{3} - \frac{1}{3}$ **8.** $\frac{11}{12} - \frac{8}{12}$ **9.** $\frac{5}{7} - \frac{3}{7}$ **10.** $\frac{4}{6} - \frac{3}{6}$ **11.** $\frac{11}{14} - \frac{9}{14}$ **12.** $\frac{15}{20} - \frac{7}{20}$ **13.** $\frac{9}{16} - \frac{5}{16}$

14. $\frac{9}{12} - \frac{4}{12}$ **15.** $\frac{13}{15} - \frac{4}{15}$ **16.** $\frac{3}{4} - \frac{1}{4}$ **17.** $\frac{5}{10} - \frac{2}{10}$ **18.** $\frac{16}{24} - \frac{8}{24}$ **19.** $\frac{6}{9} - \frac{2}{9}$ **20.** $\frac{17}{20} - \frac{9}{20}$ **21.** $\frac{3}{5} - \frac{1}{5}$ **22.** $\frac{10}{12} - \frac{7}{12}$ **23.** $\frac{4}{7} - \frac{3}{7}$

24. $\frac{7}{8} - \frac{2}{8}$ **25.** $\frac{11}{20} - \frac{10}{20}$ **26.** $\frac{13}{14} - \frac{8}{14}$ **27.** $\frac{20}{24} - \frac{15}{24}$ **28.** $\frac{5}{6} - \frac{3}{6}$ **29.** $\frac{3}{4} - \frac{2}{4}$ **30.** $\frac{7}{9} - \frac{6}{9}$ **31.** $\frac{12}{16} - \frac{4}{16}$ **32.** $\frac{14}{15} - \frac{8}{15}$ **33.** $\frac{6}{8} - \frac{2}{8}$

Practice hard. You'll win!

34. $\frac{6}{7} - \frac{2}{7}$ **35.** $\frac{9}{10} - \frac{6}{10}$ **36.** $\frac{12}{14} - \frac{9}{14}$ **37.** $\frac{10}{15} - \frac{6}{15}$ **38.** $\frac{5}{8} - \frac{1}{8}$ **39.** $\frac{13}{16} - \frac{9}{16}$ **40.** $\frac{11}{22} - \frac{5}{22}$

Fractions

Name ______________________________

Total Problems	**40**
Problems Correct	______

Show your work on another sheet. Reduce your answers to lowest terms and write them here.

1. $\frac{8}{10} - \frac{3}{10}$

2. $\frac{4}{6} - \frac{3}{6}$

3. $\frac{5}{12} - \frac{3}{12}$

4. $\frac{7}{14} - \frac{5}{14}$

5. $\frac{9}{21} - \frac{6}{21}$

6. $\frac{14}{17} - \frac{8}{17}$

7. $\frac{5}{6} - \frac{3}{6}$

8. $\frac{8}{9} - \frac{5}{9}$

9. $\frac{10}{20} - \frac{7}{20}$

10. $\frac{5}{8} - \frac{2}{8}$

11. $\frac{14}{30} - \frac{7}{30}$

12. $\frac{2}{4} - \frac{1}{4}$

13. $\frac{7}{8} - \frac{3}{8}$

14. $\frac{9}{15} - \frac{3}{15}$

15. $\frac{24}{26} - \frac{15}{26}$

16. $\frac{8}{20} - \frac{3}{20}$

17. $\frac{13}{24} - \frac{7}{24}$

18. $\frac{5}{21} - \frac{2}{21}$

19. $\frac{3}{6} - \frac{1}{6}$

20. $\frac{5}{7} - \frac{4}{7}$

21. $\frac{18}{32} - \frac{7}{32}$

22. $\frac{14}{15} - \frac{8}{15}$

23. $\frac{21}{50} - \frac{15}{50}$

24. $\frac{11}{12} - \frac{4}{12}$

25. $\frac{5}{8} - \frac{4}{8}$

26. $\frac{7}{10} - \frac{3}{10}$

27. $\frac{6}{15} - \frac{3}{15}$

28. $\frac{3}{9} - \frac{1}{9}$

29. $\frac{6}{11} - \frac{2}{11}$

30. $\frac{7}{12} - \frac{5}{12}$

31. $\frac{19}{20} - \frac{12}{20}$

32. $\frac{5}{13} - \frac{2}{13}$

33. $\frac{6}{15} - \frac{2}{15}$

34. $\frac{4}{5} - \frac{2}{5}$

35. $\frac{3}{9} - \frac{2}{9}$

36. $\frac{17}{21} - \frac{8}{21}$

37. $\frac{42}{50} - \frac{13}{50}$

38. $\frac{71}{100} - \frac{40}{100}$

39. $\frac{7}{10} - \frac{1}{10}$

40. $\frac{8}{19} - \frac{3}{19}$

Success ahoy! Just practice!

Fractions

Name ____________________

Total Problems	35
Problems Correct	______

Show your work on another sheet. Reduce your answers to lowest terms and write them here.

1. $\frac{3}{8} - \frac{1}{4}$

2. $\frac{2}{5} - \frac{2}{15}$

3. $\frac{3}{4} - \frac{1}{12}$

4. $\frac{5}{6} - \frac{1}{3}$

5. $\frac{3}{5} - \frac{2}{10}$

6. $\frac{6}{7} - \frac{3}{14}$

7. $\frac{5}{8} - \frac{5}{16}$

8. $\frac{7}{10} - \frac{2}{20}$

9. $\frac{2}{4} - \frac{1}{12}$

10. $\frac{5}{15} - \frac{1}{5}$

11. $\frac{7}{16} - \frac{2}{8}$

12. $\frac{4}{9} - \frac{1}{3}$

13. $\frac{5}{7} - \frac{2}{14}$

14. $\frac{9}{10} - \frac{2}{5}$

15. $\frac{2}{3} - \frac{1}{9}$

16. $\frac{5}{8} - \frac{1}{4}$

17. $\frac{2}{4} - \frac{1}{2}$

18. $\frac{3}{6} - \frac{1}{3}$

19. $\frac{1}{2} - \frac{2}{8}$

20. $\frac{8}{9} - \frac{3}{18}$

21. $\frac{6}{8} - \frac{2}{16}$

22. $\frac{3}{4} - \frac{5}{16}$

23. $\frac{7}{16} - \frac{3}{8}$

24. $\frac{5}{6} - \frac{2}{18}$

25. $\frac{7}{21} - \frac{1}{7}$

26. $\frac{8}{24} - \frac{2}{12}$

27. $\frac{5}{8} - \frac{3}{16}$

28. $\frac{7}{10} - \frac{1}{5}$

29. $\frac{1}{2} - \frac{3}{18}$

30. $\frac{7}{9} - \frac{2}{27}$

31. $\frac{1}{2} - \frac{7}{16}$

32. $\frac{3}{4} - \frac{2}{12}$

33. $\frac{9}{10} - \frac{3}{20}$

34. $\frac{8}{10} - \frac{5}{20}$

35. $\frac{3}{15} - \frac{1}{5}$

Practice puts you on top!

Fractions

Name ____________________

Total Problems	40
Problems Correct	____

Show your work on another sheet. Reduce your answers to lowest terms and write them here.

1. $\frac{1}{2} - \frac{3}{8}$ ____ **2.** $\frac{2}{5} - \frac{3}{10}$ ____ **3.** $\frac{2}{3} - \frac{2}{9}$ ____

4. $\frac{1}{2} - \frac{1}{4}$ ____ **5.** $\frac{2}{3} - \frac{1}{6}$ ____ **6.** $\frac{7}{8} - \frac{2}{4}$ ____ **7.** $\frac{4}{5} - \frac{3}{10}$ ____ **8.** $\frac{8}{10} - \frac{1}{2}$ ____ **9.** $\frac{6}{9} - \frac{1}{3}$ ____ **10.** $\frac{3}{4} - \frac{1}{12}$ ____ **11.** $\frac{1}{4} - \frac{1}{8}$ ____ **12.** $\frac{5}{6} - \frac{2}{3}$ ____ **13.** $\frac{8}{12} - \frac{2}{6}$ ____

14. $\frac{3}{4} - \frac{2}{8}$ ____ **15.** $\frac{1}{2} - \frac{2}{4}$ ____ **16.** $\frac{5}{9} - \frac{3}{18}$ ____ **17.** $\frac{6}{8} - \frac{1}{4}$ ____ **18.** $\frac{1}{2} - \frac{2}{8}$ ____ **19.** $\frac{3}{5} - \frac{2}{10}$ ____ **20.** $\frac{12}{16} - \frac{5}{8}$ ____ **21.** $\frac{9}{14} - \frac{3}{7}$ ____ **22.** $\frac{5}{10} - \frac{1}{2}$ ____ **23.** $\frac{2}{3} - \frac{1}{6}$ ____

24. $\frac{3}{5} - \frac{6}{15}$ ____ **25.** $\frac{9}{10} - \frac{4}{5}$ ____ **26.** $\frac{13}{14} - \frac{5}{7}$ ____ **27.** $\frac{1}{2} - \frac{2}{6}$ ____ **28.** $\frac{7}{9} - \frac{2}{18}$ ____ **29.** $\frac{3}{4} - \frac{2}{8}$ ____ **30.** $\frac{7}{8} - \frac{3}{4}$ ____ **31.** $\frac{8}{9} - \frac{1}{3}$ ____ **32.** $\frac{9}{16} - \frac{2}{8}$ ____ **33.** $\frac{4}{7} - \frac{3}{14}$ ____

Practice hard. You'll win.

34. $\frac{11}{18} - \frac{4}{9}$ ____ **35.** $\frac{7}{8} - \frac{3}{16}$ ____ **36.** $\frac{7}{10} - \frac{2}{5}$ ____ **37.** $\frac{4}{5} - \frac{9}{15}$ ____ **38.** $\frac{6}{7} - \frac{5}{14}$ ____ **39.** $\frac{10}{12} - \frac{4}{6}$ ____ **40.** $\frac{6}{10} - \frac{1}{5}$ ____

Fractions

Name ____________________

Total Problems	**40**
Problems Correct	______

Show your work on another sheet. Reduce your answers to lowest terms and write them here.

1. $\frac{3}{4} - \frac{2}{5}$ **2.** $\frac{7}{9} - \frac{1}{2}$ **3.** $\frac{11}{16} - \frac{2}{4}$

4. $\frac{16}{20} - \frac{5}{10}$ **5.** $\frac{2}{3} - \frac{6}{11}$ **6.** $\frac{4}{5} - \frac{2}{4}$ **7.** $\frac{7}{8} - \frac{2}{3}$ **8.** $\frac{3}{4} - \frac{4}{16}$ **9.** $\frac{5}{6} - \frac{12}{18}$ **10.** $\frac{3}{4} - \frac{2}{6}$ **11.** $\frac{1}{3} - \frac{2}{11}$ **12.** $\frac{5}{6} - \frac{2}{4}$ **13.** $\frac{3}{4} - \frac{4}{9}$

14. $\frac{5}{6} - \frac{3}{5}$ **15.** $\frac{3}{4} - \frac{4}{6}$ **16.** $\frac{8}{10} - \frac{9}{20}$ **17.** $\frac{2}{3} - \frac{1}{6}$ **18.** $\frac{5}{9} - \frac{1}{2}$ **19.** $\frac{2}{3} - \frac{4}{8}$ **20.** $\frac{4}{5} - \frac{1}{6}$ **21.** $\frac{5}{8} - \frac{1}{3}$ **22.** $\frac{6}{7} - \frac{2}{5}$ **23.** $\frac{1}{2} - \frac{5}{14}$

24. $\frac{1}{2} - \frac{2}{9}$ **25.** $\frac{4}{5} - \frac{2}{6}$ **26.** $\frac{5}{7} - \frac{1}{2}$ **27.** $\frac{3}{5} - \frac{1}{4}$ **28.** $\frac{4}{6} - \frac{9}{18}$ **29.** $\frac{5}{7} - \frac{3}{5}$ **30.** $\frac{11}{15} - \frac{5}{30}$ **31.** $\frac{7}{16} - \frac{1}{4}$ **32.** $\frac{9}{14} - \frac{1}{2}$ **33.** $\frac{1}{2} - \frac{3}{7}$

34. $\frac{4}{6} - \frac{2}{5}$ **35.** $\frac{2}{3} - \frac{5}{8}$ **36.** $\frac{17}{18} - \frac{3}{6}$ **37.** $\frac{7}{9} - \frac{2}{4}$ **38.** $\frac{5}{9} - \frac{8}{27}$ **39.** $\frac{4}{5} - \frac{3}{7}$ **40.** $\frac{6}{12} - \frac{7}{36}$

Practice = Success!

Fractions

Name ____________________

Total Problems	40
Problems Correct	______

Show your work on another sheet. Reduce your answers to lowest terms and write them here.

1. $5 - \frac{3}{4}$ **2.** $8 - \frac{7}{8}$

3. $4 - \frac{3}{6}$ **4.** $10 - \frac{3}{8}$ **5.** $14 - \frac{2}{5}$ **6.** $11 - \frac{7}{9}$ **7.** $4 - \frac{3}{5}$ **8.** $7 - \frac{5}{8}$ **9.** $6 - \frac{2}{4}$

10. $12 - \frac{3}{6}$ **11.** $9 - \frac{5}{8}$ **12.** $3 - \frac{6}{10}$ **13.** $7 - \frac{3}{4}$ **14.** $40 - \frac{3}{7}$ **15.** $5 - \frac{2}{3}$ **16.** $8 - \frac{5}{9}$

17. $11 - \frac{6}{12}$ **18.** $4 - \frac{3}{8}$ **19.** $6 - \frac{5}{7}$ **20.** $9 - \frac{3}{4}$ **21.** $12 - \frac{3}{9}$ **22.** $4 - \frac{6}{11}$ **23.** $7 - \frac{5}{10}$

24. $32 - \frac{5}{7}$ **25.** $25 - \frac{3}{4}$ **26.** $20 - \frac{5}{8}$ **27.** $5 - \frac{3}{6}$ **28.** $8 - \frac{2}{5}$ **29.** $4 - \frac{3}{9}$ **30.** $11 - \frac{2}{4}$

31. $14 - \frac{3}{7}$ **32.** $23 - \frac{6}{8}$ **33.** $56 - \frac{3}{5}$ **34.** $12 - \frac{5}{7}$ **35.** $30 - \frac{8}{9}$ **36.** $10 - \frac{14}{20}$ **37.** $9 - \frac{5}{6}$

38. $4 - \frac{1}{4}$ **39.** $6 - \frac{7}{8}$ **40.** $9 - \frac{7}{12}$

Practice hard. You'll win.

Skill: Subtraction of Fractions From Mixed Numbers With Like and Unlike Denominators

Mixed Numbers

Name ____________________

Total Problems	**40**
Problems Correct	______

Show your work on another sheet. Reduce your answers to lowest terms and write them here.

1. $5\frac{3}{5} - \frac{1}{5}$

2. $11\frac{5}{8} - \frac{4}{8}$

3. $14\frac{6}{7} - \frac{4}{7}$

4. $10\frac{3}{6} - \frac{1}{6}$

5. $8\frac{5}{8} - \frac{3}{8}$

6. $14\frac{3}{4} - \frac{6}{8}$

7. $3\frac{6}{8} - \frac{5}{8}$

8. $7\frac{4}{5} - \frac{3}{5}$

9. $9\frac{2}{3} - \frac{2}{6}$

10. $5\frac{6}{8} - \frac{2}{8}$

11. $15\frac{4}{7} - \frac{1}{7}$

12. $8\frac{6}{9} - \frac{5}{18}$

13. $12\frac{3}{7} - \frac{1}{7}$

14. $8\frac{3}{4} - \frac{2}{8}$

15. $10\frac{5}{7} - \frac{3}{14}$

16. $4\frac{6}{8} - \frac{1}{2}$

17. $7\frac{3}{5} - \frac{4}{10}$

18. $3\frac{6}{9} - \frac{2}{3}$

19. $6\frac{7}{8} - \frac{2}{4}$

20. $9\frac{5}{6} - \frac{1}{3}$

21. $5\frac{4}{6} - \frac{1}{2}$

22. $7\frac{5}{8} - \frac{2}{4}$

23. $15\frac{7}{10} - \frac{3}{5}$

24. $10\frac{2}{5} - \frac{2}{10}$

25. $5\frac{3}{7} - \frac{4}{14}$

26. $7\frac{5}{8} - \frac{1}{2}$

27. $4\frac{6}{10} - \frac{2}{5}$

28. $8\frac{6}{7} - \frac{5}{14}$

29. $2\frac{6}{8} - \frac{3}{4}$

30. $9\frac{8}{10} - \frac{3}{5}$

31. $4\frac{5}{7} - \frac{3}{21}$

32. $10\frac{3}{5} - \frac{1}{10}$

33. $22\frac{8}{9} - \frac{2}{3}$

34. $7\frac{5}{6} - \frac{2}{3}$

35. $10\frac{5}{8} - \frac{3}{8}$

36. $8\frac{9}{10} - \frac{4}{5}$

37. $11\frac{3}{10} - \frac{1}{5}$

38. $4\frac{4}{7} - \frac{1}{7}$

39. $6\frac{5}{6} - \frac{1}{3}$

40. $12\frac{7}{8} - \frac{5}{8}$

Practice = Success!

Mixed Numbers

Name ____________________

Total Problems	**40**
Problems Correct	______

Show your work on another sheet. Reduce your answers to lowest terms and write them here.

1. $2\frac{5}{8} - 1\frac{2}{8}$

2. $6\frac{6}{10} - 2\frac{4}{10}$

3. $8\frac{3}{6} - 1\frac{1}{6}$

4. $5\frac{2}{8} - 3\frac{1}{8}$

5. $16\frac{2}{4} - 8\frac{1}{4}$

6. $12\frac{4}{6} - 3\frac{2}{6}$

7. $9\frac{6}{7} - 3\frac{4}{7}$

8. $8\frac{3}{6} - 4\frac{2}{6}$

9. $4\frac{3}{8} - 2\frac{3}{8}$

10. $15\frac{2}{7} - 8\frac{1}{7}$

11. $9\frac{6}{8} - 4\frac{2}{8}$

12. $7\frac{6}{8} - 4\frac{5}{8}$

13. $14\frac{2}{5} - 8\frac{1}{5}$

14. $3\frac{2}{6} - 1\frac{1}{6}$

15. $8\frac{11}{12} - 4\frac{8}{12}$

16. $9\frac{2}{6} - 4\frac{1}{6}$

17. $12\frac{6}{8} - 8\frac{4}{8}$

18. $4\frac{3}{6} - 3\frac{1}{6}$

19. $8\frac{2}{5} - 4\frac{1}{5}$

20. $9\frac{6}{11} - 4\frac{5}{11}$

21. $6\frac{3}{8} - 4\frac{1}{8}$

22. $12\frac{4}{6} - 9\frac{2}{6}$

23. $5\frac{2}{8} - 3\frac{1}{8}$

24. $20\frac{1}{9} - 6\frac{1}{9}$

25. $14\frac{2}{6} - 9\frac{1}{6}$

26. $7\frac{2}{9} - 5\frac{1}{9}$

27. $8\frac{6}{7} - 4\frac{2}{7}$

28. $5\frac{4}{10} - 3\frac{2}{10}$

29. $8\frac{5}{6} - 4\frac{2}{6}$

30. $2\frac{3}{6} - 1\frac{2}{6}$

31. $9\frac{4}{10} - 3\frac{3}{10}$

32. $5\frac{4}{6} - 4\frac{2}{6}$

33. $7\frac{3}{8} - 6\frac{1}{8}$

34. $4\frac{11}{20} - 2\frac{4}{20}$

35. $9\frac{6}{14} - 3\frac{2}{14}$

36. $7\frac{6}{8} - 4\frac{4}{8}$

Through practice you learn!

37. $3\frac{6}{10} - 1\frac{3}{10}$

38. $6\frac{3}{7} - 4\frac{2}{7}$

39. $10\frac{2}{5} - 5\frac{1}{5}$

40. $12\frac{4}{6} - 8\frac{2}{6}$

Skill: Subtraction of Mixed Numbers With Like Denominators-Regrouping

Mixed Numbers

Name ____________________

Total Problems	40
Problems Correct	______

Show your work on another sheet. Reduce your answers to lowest terms and write them here.

1. $8\frac{3}{5} - 2\frac{4}{5}$
2. $6\frac{1}{8} - 4\frac{5}{8}$
3. $3\frac{2}{7} - 1\frac{5}{7}$
4. $5\frac{1}{4} - 2\frac{3}{4}$
5. $7\frac{1}{5} - 4\frac{3}{5}$
6. $4\frac{2}{10} - 2\frac{3}{10}$
7. $8\frac{3}{6} - 2\frac{5}{6}$
8. $2\frac{1}{4} - 1\frac{3}{4}$
9. $12\frac{1}{6} - 8\frac{3}{6}$
10. $5\frac{1}{3} - 2\frac{2}{3}$
11. $6\frac{4}{12} - 2\frac{8}{12}$
12. $4\frac{2}{5} - 1\frac{4}{5}$
13. $8\frac{2}{7} - 2\frac{5}{7}$
14. $7\frac{2}{8} - 5\frac{4}{8}$
15. $12\frac{2}{5} - 8\frac{4}{5}$
16. $14\frac{3}{9} - 9\frac{5}{9}$
17. $3\frac{2}{5} - 1\frac{4}{5}$
18. $8\frac{4}{10} - 6\frac{8}{10}$
19. $10\frac{3}{7} - 5\frac{6}{7}$
20. $4\frac{2}{6} - 3\frac{5}{6}$
21. $2\frac{1}{4} - 1\frac{3}{4}$
22. $7\frac{3}{8} - 2\frac{4}{8}$
23. $20\frac{1}{10} - 8\frac{4}{10}$
24. $9\frac{4}{8} - 6\frac{7}{8}$
25. $2\frac{4}{7} - 1\frac{5}{7}$
26. $6\frac{3}{9} - 4\frac{8}{9}$
27. $8\frac{4}{6} - 3\frac{5}{6}$
28. $5\frac{3}{7} - 2\frac{5}{7}$
29. $12\frac{2}{11} - 8\frac{4}{11}$
30. $9\frac{3}{8} - 4\frac{7}{8}$
31. $8\frac{5}{10} - 7\frac{6}{10}$
32. $11\frac{2}{6} - 4\frac{5}{6}$
33. $4\frac{5}{7} - 1\frac{6}{7}$
34. $14\frac{2}{6} - 8\frac{4}{6}$
35. $3\frac{1}{4} - 1\frac{2}{4}$
36. $15\frac{1}{3} - 7\frac{2}{3}$
37. $8\frac{1}{6} - 4\frac{5}{6}$
38. $3\frac{2}{12} - 2\frac{6}{12}$
39. $4\frac{1}{8} - 2\frac{5}{8}$
40. $21\frac{2}{5} - 13\frac{3}{5}$

Practice! Practice!

Practice!

Mixed Numbers

Name ______________________

Total Problems **40**

Problems Correct ________

Show your work on another sheet. Reduce your answers to lowest terms and write them here.

1. $3\frac{1}{3} - 2\frac{1}{6}$

2. $8\frac{3}{4} - 3\frac{5}{8}$

3. $12\frac{3}{6} - 8\frac{1}{3}$

4. $5\frac{4}{6} - 2\frac{1}{2}$

5. $8\frac{5}{10} - 3\frac{1}{2}$

6. $12\frac{3}{4} - 5\frac{1}{2}$

7. $6\frac{5}{7} - 4\frac{2}{14}$

8. $9\frac{4}{6} - 3\frac{1}{3}$

9. $7\frac{8}{12} - 4\frac{1}{3}$

10. $4\frac{8}{10} - 2\frac{2}{5}$

11. $6\frac{3}{7} - 5\frac{1}{14}$

12. $12\frac{6}{8} - 6\frac{3}{4}$

13. $5\frac{2}{3} - 4\frac{1}{6}$

14. $12\frac{5}{8} - 8\frac{2}{4}$

15. $3\frac{2}{11} - 1\frac{1}{22}$

16. $5\frac{3}{9} - 3\frac{1}{18}$

17. $10\frac{3}{5} - 8\frac{1}{10}$

18. $14\frac{2}{3} - 8\frac{1}{6}$

19. $4\frac{3}{6} - 2\frac{1}{3}$

20. $8\frac{6}{7} - 4\frac{2}{14}$

21. $10\frac{2}{4} - 6\frac{1}{8}$

22. $12\frac{3}{5} - 8\frac{2}{10}$

23. $2\frac{6}{8} - 1\frac{1}{2}$

24. $5\frac{3}{4} - 3\frac{1}{12}$

25. $8\frac{3}{5} - 4\frac{2}{10}$

26. $3\frac{2}{4} - 1\frac{1}{8}$

27. $10\frac{2}{3} - 4\frac{2}{6}$

28. $2\frac{11}{12} - 1\frac{4}{6}$

29. $9\frac{2}{3} - 6\frac{1}{9}$

30. $2\frac{4}{8} - 1\frac{1}{4}$

31. $15\frac{2}{7} - 8\frac{1}{14}$

32. $8\frac{3}{5} - 7\frac{2}{15}$

33. $7\frac{8}{9} - 4\frac{2}{3}$

34. $7\frac{2}{3} - 4\frac{2}{9}$

35. $14\frac{8}{10} - 6\frac{4}{20}$

36. $25\frac{6}{7} - 14\frac{3}{21}$

37. $3\frac{5}{8} - 2\frac{4}{16}$

38. $9\frac{2}{4} - 6\frac{2}{12}$

39. $15\frac{3}{5} - 8\frac{2}{10}$

40. $20\frac{4}{7} - 8\frac{2}{14}$

Practice hard. You'll win.

Fractions

Name ______________________________

Total Problems	**28**
Problems Correct	________

Show your work on another sheet. Reduce your answers to lowest terms and write them here.

1. $\frac{1}{3} \times \frac{2}{4} =$

2. $\frac{1}{4} \times \frac{3}{6} =$

3. $\frac{1}{2} \times \frac{3}{4} =$

4. $\frac{1}{3} \times \frac{1}{5} =$

5. $\frac{1}{6} \times \frac{3}{7} =$

6. $\frac{2}{6} \times \frac{1}{8} =$

7. $\frac{3}{5} \times \frac{2}{4} =$

8. $\frac{2}{3} \times \frac{1}{5} =$

9. $\frac{3}{8} \times \frac{1}{6} =$

10. $\frac{1}{2} \times \frac{2}{3} =$

11. $\frac{1}{4} \times \frac{2}{5} =$

12. $\frac{4}{6} \times \frac{1}{7} =$

13. $\frac{1}{3} \times \frac{4}{5} =$

14. $\frac{1}{5} \times \frac{3}{6} =$

15. $\frac{1}{4} \times \frac{5}{6} =$

16. $\frac{2}{6} \times \frac{3}{5} =$

17. $\frac{1}{3} \times \frac{1}{4} =$

18. $\frac{3}{5} \times \frac{6}{7} =$

19. $\frac{3}{8} \times \frac{1}{9} =$

20. $\frac{1}{5} \times \frac{4}{6} =$

21. $\frac{1}{2} \times \frac{4}{7} =$

22. $\frac{1}{5} \times \frac{3}{5} =$

23. $\frac{2}{3} \times \frac{4}{5} =$

24. $\frac{1}{4} \times \frac{2}{8} =$

25. $\frac{1}{2} \times \frac{3}{7} =$

26. $\frac{2}{3} \times \frac{2}{6} =$

27. $\frac{1}{6} \times \frac{2}{3} =$

28. $\frac{1}{3} \times \frac{1}{6} =$

Practice = Success!

Skill: Multiplication of Fractions

Fractions

Name ____________________

Total Problems	**28**
Problems Correct	______

Show your work on another sheet. Reduce your answers to lowest terms and write them here.

1. $\frac{3}{4} \times \frac{5}{6} =$

2. $\frac{2}{9} \times \frac{1}{4} =$

3. $\frac{4}{5} \times \frac{1}{5} =$

4. $\frac{3}{7} \times \frac{2}{6} =$

5. $\frac{3}{4} \times \frac{1}{6} =$

6. $\frac{5}{7} \times \frac{3}{5} =$

7. $\frac{4}{6} \times \frac{2}{4} =$

8. $\frac{3}{4} \times \frac{4}{5} =$

9. $\frac{2}{7} \times \frac{4}{6} =$

10. $\frac{8}{9} \times \frac{1}{3} =$

11. $\frac{2}{4} \times \frac{5}{7} =$

12. $\frac{6}{8} \times \frac{3}{7} =$

13. $\frac{2}{3} \times \frac{4}{5} =$

14. $\frac{7}{8} \times \frac{3}{4} =$

15. $\frac{5}{8} \times \frac{2}{6} =$

16. $\frac{4}{7} \times \frac{2}{3} =$

17. $\frac{1}{12} \times \frac{4}{9} =$

18. $\frac{6}{8} \times \frac{3}{5} =$

19. $\frac{5}{8} \times \frac{1}{3} =$

20. $\frac{5}{10} \times \frac{2}{4} =$

21. $\frac{6}{7} \times \frac{2}{3} =$

22. $\frac{1}{2} \times \frac{3}{8} =$

23. $\frac{4}{7} \times \frac{3}{6} =$

24. $\frac{3}{4} \times \frac{2}{3} =$

25. $\frac{5}{11} \times \frac{2}{3} =$

26. $\frac{6}{7} \times \frac{4}{5} =$

27. $\frac{3}{8} \times \frac{2}{9} =$

28. $\frac{3}{12} \times \frac{2}{4} =$

Practice and anything's possible!

Fractions

Name ______________________________

Total Problems	**45**
Problems Correct	______

Show your work on another sheet. Reduce your answers to lowest terms and write them here.

1. $\frac{2}{3} \times \frac{4}{7} =$ **2.** $\frac{5}{6} \times \frac{2}{4} =$

3. $\frac{3}{9} \times \frac{2}{3} =$ **4.** $\frac{6}{8} \times \frac{1}{4} =$ **5.** $\frac{4}{7} \times \frac{1}{8} =$ **6.** $\frac{2}{7} \times \frac{3}{6} =$ **7.** $\frac{5}{8} \times \frac{2}{9} =$

8. $\frac{4}{10} \times \frac{3}{8} =$ **9.** $\frac{8}{11} \times \frac{3}{6} =$ **10.** $\frac{4}{5} \times \frac{2}{9} =$ **11.** $\frac{6}{10} \times \frac{5}{7} =$ **12.** $\frac{3}{6} \times \frac{2}{4} =$

13. $\frac{3}{11} \times \frac{4}{12} =$ **14.** $\frac{5}{9} \times \frac{3}{7} =$ **15.** $\frac{1}{20} \times \frac{2}{10} =$ **16.** $\frac{2}{5} \times \frac{3}{15} =$ **17.** $\frac{4}{7} \times \frac{8}{12} =$

18. $\frac{4}{13} \times \frac{2}{3} =$ **19.** $\frac{5}{6} \times \frac{3}{9} =$ **20.** $\frac{2}{13} \times \frac{4}{5} =$ **21.** $\frac{2}{3} \times \frac{1}{2} =$ **22.** $\frac{4}{5} \times \frac{2}{7} =$

23. $\frac{8}{9} \times \frac{3}{7} =$ **24.** $\frac{2}{5} \times \frac{1}{6} =$ **25.** $\frac{9}{10} \times \frac{3}{14} =$ **26.** $\frac{2}{3} \times \frac{2}{16} =$ **27.** $\frac{5}{8} \times \frac{2}{9} =$

28. $\frac{1}{5} \times \frac{2}{17} =$ **29.** $\frac{3}{4} \times \frac{2}{3} =$ **30.** $\frac{2}{7} \times \frac{5}{10} =$ **31.** $\frac{2}{3} \times \frac{6}{16} =$ **32.** $\frac{2}{8} \times \frac{4}{7} =$

33. $\frac{2}{30} \times \frac{2}{4} =$ **34.** $\frac{3}{6} \times \frac{2}{8} =$ **35.** $\frac{6}{9} \times \frac{2}{8} =$ **36.** $\frac{2}{3} \times \frac{3}{30} =$ **37.** $\frac{4}{7} \times \frac{2}{8} =$

38. $\frac{5}{6} \times \frac{2}{12} =$ **39.** $\frac{2}{10} \times \frac{3}{15} =$ **40.** $\frac{3}{8} \times \frac{4}{9} =$ **41.** $\frac{2}{6} \times \frac{5}{13} =$ **42.** $\frac{4}{6} \times \frac{8}{9} =$

43. $\frac{5}{30} \times \frac{2}{4} =$ **44.** $\frac{11}{12} \times \frac{2}{11} =$ **45.** $\frac{5}{8} \times \frac{4}{9} =$

Through practice you learn!

Fractions

Name ______________________________

Total Problems	46
Problems Correct	______

Show your work on another sheet. Reduce your answers to lowest terms and write them here.

1. $\frac{4}{7} \times \frac{3}{4} =$

2. $\frac{2}{5} \times \frac{4}{8} =$

3. $\frac{3}{12} \times \frac{4}{6} =$

4. $\frac{5}{8} \times \frac{1}{6} =$

5. $\frac{2}{9} \times \frac{3}{5} =$

6. $\frac{4}{6} \times \frac{4}{5} =$

7. $\frac{3}{6} \times \frac{4}{5} =$

8. $\frac{2}{7} \times \frac{3}{8} =$

9. $\frac{2}{7} \times \frac{4}{14} =$

10. $\frac{5}{12} \times \frac{2}{4} =$

11. $\frac{3}{7} \times \frac{4}{5} =$

12. $\frac{3}{7} \times \frac{5}{8} =$

13. $\frac{5}{7} \times \frac{2}{5} =$

14. $\frac{3}{8} \times \frac{2}{5} =$

15. $\frac{4}{5} \times \frac{1}{4} =$

16. $\frac{2}{3} \times \frac{5}{6} =$

17. $\frac{1}{4} \times \frac{6}{12} =$

18. $\frac{3}{8} \times \frac{5}{9} =$

19. $\frac{2}{8} \times \frac{1}{12} =$

20. $\frac{2}{8} \times \frac{4}{5} =$

21. $\frac{5}{8} \times \frac{6}{7} =$

22. $\frac{4}{5} \times \frac{3}{7} =$

23. $\frac{6}{18} \times \frac{2}{3} =$

24. $\frac{5}{7} \times \frac{4}{8} =$

25. $\frac{3}{6} \times \frac{1}{2} =$

26. $\frac{4}{8} \times \frac{3}{7} =$

27. $\frac{8}{9} \times \frac{2}{5} =$

28. $\frac{4}{6} \times \frac{3}{4} =$

29. $\frac{3}{6} \times \frac{1}{2} =$

30. $\frac{8}{12} \times \frac{5}{8} =$

31. $\frac{10}{11} \times \frac{1}{10} =$

32. $\frac{11}{12} \times \frac{2}{3} =$

33. $\frac{7}{8} \times \frac{2}{3} =$

34. $\frac{2}{7} \times \frac{1}{10} =$

35. $\frac{3}{5} \times \frac{6}{9} =$

36. $\frac{3}{6} \times \frac{2}{4} =$

37. $\frac{5}{6} \times \frac{2}{4} =$

38. $\frac{8}{10} \times \frac{2}{20} =$

39. $\frac{4}{8} \times \frac{5}{12} =$

40. $\frac{3}{6} \times \frac{8}{9} =$

41. $\frac{7}{11} \times \frac{4}{5} =$

42. $\frac{7}{8} \times \frac{2}{14} =$

43. $\frac{3}{8} \times \frac{11}{12} =$

44. $\frac{11}{12} \times \frac{4}{8} =$

45. $\frac{2}{7} \times \frac{4}{8} =$

46. $\frac{3}{6} \times \frac{5}{10} =$

Practice!
Practice!
Practice!

Fractions

Name ____________________

Total Problems	**28**
Problems Correct	______

Show your work on another sheet. Reduce your answers to lowest terms and write them here.

1. $3 \times \frac{4}{6} =$

2. $8 \times \frac{2}{4} =$

3. $\frac{2}{8} \times 2 =$

4. $3 \times \frac{1}{7} =$

5. $6 \times \frac{3}{6} =$

6. $9 \times \frac{2}{9} =$

7. $\frac{2}{5} \times 2 =$

8. $\frac{2}{3} \times 9 =$

9. $\frac{2}{10} \times 3 =$

10. $\frac{3}{6} \times 4 =$

11. $\frac{3}{8} \times 3 =$

12. $5 \times \frac{1}{11} =$

13. $10 \times \frac{2}{4} =$

14. $8 \times \frac{1}{12} =$

15. $\frac{3}{12} \times 3 =$

16. $8 \times \frac{1}{2} =$

17. $\frac{4}{12} \times 6 =$

18. $14 \times \frac{2}{30} =$

19. $\frac{6}{10} \times 5 =$

20. $6 \times \frac{2}{14} =$

21. $\frac{3}{12} \times 2 =$

22. $16 \times \frac{2}{40} =$

23. $\frac{1}{3} \times 1 =$

24. $3 \times \frac{3}{6} =$

25. $\frac{2}{4} \times 12 =$

26. $15 \times \frac{1}{18} =$

27. $4 \times \frac{2}{11} =$

28. $\frac{1}{3} \times 2 =$

Practice hard. You'll win!

Mixed Numbers

Name ______________________

Total Problems **50**

Problems Correct ________

Show your work on another sheet. Reduce your answers to lowest terms and write them here.

1. $3 \times 2\frac{1}{3} =$ **2.** $2\frac{1}{4} \times 8 =$

3. $5 \times 1\frac{1}{9} =$ **4.** $3\frac{1}{2} \times 6 =$ **5.** $2 \times 3\frac{2}{4} =$ **6.** $14 \times 2\frac{1}{2} =$

7. $5 \times 3\frac{1}{4} =$ **8.** $7 \times 2\frac{2}{4} =$ **9.** $3 \times 2\frac{4}{5} =$ **10.** $2 \times 2\frac{4}{6} =$

11. $2\frac{1}{4} \times 9 =$ **12.** $5 \times 3\frac{1}{4} =$ **13.** $6\frac{2}{4} \times 5 =$ **14.** $3\frac{1}{5} \times 6 =$

15. $12 \times 1\frac{1}{4} =$ **16.** $7\frac{1}{2} \times 4 =$ **17.** $3\frac{2}{6} \times 2 =$ **18.** $4\frac{2}{3} \times 2 =$

19. $2 \times 1\frac{1}{3} =$ **20.** $3\frac{1}{6} \times 10 =$ **21.** $3 \times 1\frac{1}{8} =$ **22.** $2\frac{4}{5} \times 4 =$

23. $4\frac{1}{4} \times 3 =$ **24.** $5 \times 6\frac{2}{3} =$ **25.** $3 \times 1\frac{1}{2} =$ **26.** $4 \times 2\frac{1}{2} =$

27. $1\frac{1}{4} \times 3 =$ **28.** $2\frac{1}{3} \times 5 =$ **29.** $3 \times 1\frac{1}{8} =$ **30.** $1\frac{1}{5} \times 4 =$

31. $14 \times 1\frac{1}{2} =$ **32.** $6\frac{1}{2} \times 2 =$ **33.** $4\frac{1}{6} \times 2 =$ **34.** $5\frac{2}{4} \times 6 =$

35. $2\frac{1}{2} \times 4 =$ **36.** $1\frac{1}{3} \times 4 =$ **37.** $7 \times 1\frac{1}{5} =$ **38.** $15 \times 1\frac{1}{3} =$

39. $2\frac{1}{4} \times 4 =$ **40.** $5\frac{1}{3} \times 3 =$ **41.** $6\frac{1}{3} \times 6 =$ **42.** $5\frac{1}{2} \times 8 =$

43. $2 \times 3\frac{1}{8} =$ **44.** $4 \times 2\frac{1}{5} =$ **45.** $9 \times 1\frac{1}{4} =$ **46.** $1\frac{1}{5} \times 3 =$

47. $6\frac{1}{8} \times 4 =$ **48.** $3 \times 2\frac{1}{5} =$

49. $7\frac{1}{4} \times 2 =$ **50.** $20 \times 1\frac{1}{2} =$

With practice, you can do it!

Mixed Numbers

Name ______________________________

Total Problems	**50**
Problems Correct	______

Show your work on another sheet. Reduce your answers to lowest terms and write them here.

1. $1\frac{1}{3} \times 2\frac{1}{2} =$

2. $1\frac{1}{8} \times 2\frac{1}{3} =$

3. $2\frac{1}{4} \times \frac{3}{4} =$

4. $1\frac{1}{3} \times 1\frac{1}{5} =$

5. $2\frac{2}{3} \times 1\frac{1}{6} =$

6. $4\frac{1}{2} \times 2\frac{1}{3} =$

7. $1\frac{1}{9} \times 1\frac{1}{3} =$

8. $2\frac{1}{4} \times 3\frac{1}{3} =$

9. $3\frac{1}{6} \times 1\frac{1}{2} =$

10. $4\frac{1}{2} \times \frac{2}{4} =$

11. $\frac{1}{6} \times 1\frac{1}{3} =$

12. $3\frac{2}{4} \times \frac{3}{8} =$

13. $2\frac{1}{12} \times 1\frac{1}{3} =$

14. $\frac{6}{8} \times 3\frac{1}{2} =$

15. $\frac{3}{5} \times 1\frac{1}{5} =$

16. $\frac{4}{8} \times 2\frac{1}{4} =$

17. $1\frac{1}{10} \times \frac{3}{4} =$

18. $3\frac{2}{4} \times 1\frac{1}{5} =$

19. $1\frac{1}{8} \times 1\frac{3}{7} =$

20. $1\frac{2}{5} \times \frac{6}{8} =$

21. $4\frac{2}{4} \times \frac{3}{5} =$

22. $1\frac{3}{4} \times 3\frac{1}{5} =$

23. $1\frac{1}{6} \times 3\frac{2}{4} =$

24. $1\frac{4}{5} \times 2\frac{1}{6} =$

25. $2\frac{1}{6} \times 1\frac{4}{8} =$

26. $3\frac{2}{5} \times 2\frac{1}{6} =$

27. $5\frac{1}{4} \times \frac{2}{3} =$

28. $2\frac{1}{4} \times \frac{4}{6} =$

29. $\frac{2}{7} \times 3\frac{1}{6} =$

30. $4\frac{1}{3} \times \frac{6}{7} =$

31. $3\frac{1}{4} \times 2\frac{3}{5} =$

32. $1\frac{1}{8} \times 3\frac{2}{6} =$

33. $2\frac{1}{6} \times \frac{4}{5} =$

34. $1\frac{1}{4} \times \frac{6}{8} =$

35. $3\frac{1}{2} \times \frac{2}{5} =$

36. $1\frac{1}{6} \times 2\frac{1}{3} =$

37. $4\frac{1}{3} \times \frac{2}{3} =$

38. $\frac{4}{5} \times 2\frac{1}{4} =$

39. $1\frac{5}{7} \times \frac{2}{3} =$

40. $1\frac{1}{2} \times \frac{4}{5} =$

41. $2\frac{3}{10} \times \frac{4}{5} =$

42. $5\frac{4}{6} \times 1\frac{1}{3} =$

43. $3\frac{1}{4} \times 2\frac{1}{3} =$

44. $\frac{3}{7} \times 4\frac{3}{5} =$

45. $1\frac{2}{4} \times \frac{3}{5} =$

46. $2\frac{4}{5} \times 3\frac{1}{6} =$

47. $1\frac{2}{4} \times \frac{2}{3} =$

48. $3\frac{2}{5} \times \frac{4}{8} =$

49. $\frac{6}{7} \times 2\frac{1}{3} =$

50. $8\frac{2}{3} \times \frac{1}{6} =$

Practice!
Practice!
Practice!

Fractions

Name ______________________

Total Problems	**28**
Problems Correct	______

Show your work on another sheet. Reduce your answers to lowest terms and write them here.

1. $6 \div \frac{1}{2} =$

2. $5 \div \frac{1}{3} =$

3. $7 \div \frac{1}{6} =$

4. $3 \div \frac{1}{9} =$

5. $7 \div \frac{1}{8} =$

6. $4 \div \frac{1}{6} =$

7. $8 \div \frac{1}{10} =$

8. $5 \div \frac{1}{6} =$

9. $12 \div \frac{1}{6} =$

10. $5 \div \frac{2}{4} =$

11. $15 \div \frac{1}{2} =$

12. $3 \div \frac{2}{6} =$

13. $5 \div \frac{1}{8} =$

14. $12 \div \frac{1}{3} =$

15. $10 \div \frac{1}{9} =$

16. $7 \div \frac{2}{4} =$

17. $6 \div \frac{2}{5} =$

18. $12 \div \frac{3}{4} =$

19. $6 \div \frac{1}{8} =$

20. $7 \div \frac{3}{6} =$

21. $12 \div \frac{1}{4} =$

22. $7 \div \frac{2}{6} =$

23. $4 \div \frac{2}{7} =$

24. $8 \div \frac{3}{6} =$

25. $10 \div \frac{2}{5} =$

Practice = Success!

26. $15 \div \frac{1}{3} =$

27. $8 \div \frac{1}{2} =$

28. $14 \div \frac{2}{4} =$

Fractions

Name ______________________

Total Problems	**28**
Problems Correct	______

Show your work on another sheet. Reduce your answers to lowest terms and write them here.

1. $\frac{2}{5} \div \frac{3}{6} =$

2. $\frac{3}{8} \div \frac{2}{5} =$

3. $\frac{2}{8} \div \frac{3}{6} =$

4. $\frac{1}{5} \div \frac{2}{7} =$

5. $\frac{3}{7} \div \frac{4}{5} =$

6. $\frac{2}{8} \div \frac{3}{9} =$

7. $\frac{4}{6} \div \frac{3}{7} =$

8. $\frac{6}{8} \div \frac{7}{8} =$

9. $\frac{7}{9} \div \frac{7}{8} =$

10. $\frac{4}{8} \div \frac{3}{7} =$

11. $\frac{4}{5} \div \frac{6}{7} =$

12. $\frac{8}{9} \div \frac{3}{4} =$

13. $\frac{6}{8} \div \frac{5}{12} =$

14. $\frac{3}{5} \div \frac{4}{8} =$

15. $\frac{11}{12} \div \frac{5}{6} =$

16. $\frac{4}{6} \div \frac{3}{9} =$

17. $\frac{7}{9} \div \frac{4}{5} =$

18. $\frac{6}{8} \div \frac{4}{11} =$

19. $\frac{4}{5} \div \frac{2}{7} =$

20. $\frac{8}{9} \div \frac{5}{6} =$

21. $\frac{4}{5} \div \frac{10}{12} =$

22. $\frac{7}{9} \div \frac{3}{4} =$

23. $\frac{8}{9} \div \frac{3}{7} =$

24. $\frac{8}{9} \div \frac{2}{4} =$

25. $\frac{4}{6} \div \frac{2}{9} =$

26. $\frac{3}{4} \div \frac{1}{7} =$

27. $\frac{6}{8} \div \frac{3}{9} =$

28. $\frac{3}{7} \div \frac{5}{12} =$

Practice! Practice! Practice!

Fractions

Name ____________________

Total Problems	**50**
Problems Correct	______

Show your work on another sheet. Reduce your answers to lowest terms and write them here.

1. $\frac{2}{8} \div \frac{3}{4} =$

2. $\frac{4}{7} \div \frac{1}{2} =$

3. $\frac{2}{6} \div \frac{8}{9} =$

4. $\frac{3}{9} \div \frac{3}{5} =$

5. $\frac{7}{8} \div \frac{2}{4} =$

6. $\frac{3}{9} \div \frac{2}{6} =$

7. $\frac{4}{8} \div \frac{1}{7} =$

8. $\frac{2}{3} \div \frac{5}{8} =$

9. $\frac{2}{10} \div \frac{3}{4} =$

10. $\frac{2}{6} \div \frac{5}{8} =$

11. $\frac{3}{6} \div \frac{2}{8} =$

12. $\frac{7}{8} \div \frac{2}{5} =$

13. $\frac{11}{12} \div \frac{2}{3} =$

14. $\frac{1}{8} \div \frac{9}{12} =$

15. $\frac{1}{6} \div \frac{5}{7} =$

16. $\frac{3}{10} \div \frac{2}{6} =$

17. $\frac{2}{7} \div \frac{8}{12} =$

18. $\frac{2}{9} \div \frac{3}{8} =$

19. $\frac{3}{4} \div \frac{6}{9} =$

20. $\frac{1}{11} \div \frac{7}{9} =$

21. $\frac{4}{5} \div \frac{3}{4} =$

22. $\frac{6}{8} \div \frac{7}{10} =$

23. $\frac{10}{12} \div \frac{3}{4} =$

24. $\frac{1}{2} \div \frac{4}{5} =$

25. $\frac{6}{7} \div \frac{4}{5} =$

26. $\frac{3}{8} \div \frac{4}{7} =$

27. $\frac{3}{5} \div \frac{4}{6} =$

28. $\frac{7}{8} \div \frac{5}{6} =$

29. $\frac{2}{4} \div \frac{3}{5} =$

30. $\frac{6}{10} \div \frac{3}{5} =$

31. $\frac{7}{9} \div \frac{2}{6} =$

32. $\frac{11}{12} \div \frac{3}{6} =$

33. $\frac{11}{15} \div \frac{4}{8} =$

34. $\frac{9}{12} \div \frac{8}{10} =$

35. $\frac{4}{6} \div \frac{5}{8} =$

36. $\frac{7}{9} \div \frac{4}{6} =$

37. $\frac{8}{9} \div \frac{3}{5} =$

38. $\frac{6}{7} \div \frac{8}{12} =$

39. $\frac{6}{12} \div \frac{7}{10} =$

40. $\frac{8}{12} \div \frac{3}{4} =$

41. $\frac{7}{10} \div \frac{8}{12} =$

42. $\frac{4}{15} \div \frac{6}{7} =$

43. $\frac{16}{20} \div \frac{3}{4} =$

44. $\frac{10}{12} \div \frac{5}{8} =$

45. $\frac{7}{8} \div \frac{10}{11} =$

46. $\frac{3}{12} \div \frac{4}{11} =$

47. $\frac{6}{10} \div \frac{8}{13} =$

48. $\frac{5}{6} \div \frac{6}{7} =$

49. $\frac{4}{5} \div \frac{11}{12} =$

50. $\frac{7}{8} \div \frac{12}{14} =$

Through practice you learn!

Mixed Numbers

Name ____________________

Total Problems 50

Problems Correct ______

Show your work on another sheet. Reduce your answers to lowest terms and write them here.

1. $3 \div 2\frac{1}{4} =$ **2.** $3\frac{1}{4} \div 6 =$

3. $2 \div 4\frac{1}{3} =$ **4.** $5\frac{2}{3} \div 6 =$ **5.** $4 \div 2\frac{1}{5} =$ **6.** $3\frac{1}{4} \div 8 =$

7. $2\frac{3}{6} \div 5 =$ **8.** $4\frac{1}{2} \div 8 =$ **9.** $6\frac{1}{4} \div 7 =$ **10.** $3\frac{2}{3} \div 9 =$

11. $2\frac{1}{3} \div 4 =$ **12.** $4\frac{2}{6} \div 2 =$ **13.** $5\frac{2}{3} \div 2 =$ **14.** $4 \div 6\frac{1}{3} =$

15. $2\frac{1}{5} \div 6 =$ **16.** $10 \div 1\frac{1}{8} =$ **17.** $5\frac{2}{6} \div 4 =$ **18.** $3 \div 1\frac{4}{7} =$

19. $5 \div 1\frac{1}{3} =$ **20.** $9 \div 3\frac{2}{4} =$ **21.** $4 \div 1\frac{3}{6} =$ **22.** $2 \div 5\frac{1}{3} =$

23. $5 \div 2\frac{3}{5} =$ **24.** $4\frac{1}{2} \div 7 =$ **25.** $6\frac{2}{3} \div 3 =$ **26.** $8 \div 2\frac{4}{5} =$

27. $9 \div 2\frac{2}{4} =$ **28.** $4\frac{2}{3} \div 8 =$ **29.** $6\frac{2}{4} \div 4 =$ **30.** $2\frac{1}{3} \div 6 =$

31. $8\frac{1}{3} \div 3 =$ **32.** $7\frac{2}{4} \div 9 =$ **33.** $1\frac{3}{7} \div 4 =$ **34.** $7\frac{1}{2} \div 3 =$

35. $1\frac{2}{4} \div 7 =$ **36.** $9 \div 2\frac{1}{5} =$ **37.** $2\frac{4}{6} \div 8 =$ **38.** $1\frac{8}{9} \div 4 =$

39. $3\frac{2}{4} \div 6 =$ **40.** $8 \div 1\frac{1}{4} =$ **41.** $3\frac{2}{6} \div 5 =$ **42.** $2 \div 3\frac{1}{2} =$

43. $8\frac{1}{2} \div 7 =$ **44.** $15 \div 2\frac{1}{4} =$ **45.** $4 \div 2\frac{1}{6} =$ **46.** $10 \div 2\frac{4}{8} =$

47. $7 \div 2\frac{2}{3} =$ **48.** $3\frac{2}{4} \div 8 =$

49. $4\frac{1}{6} \div 2 =$ **50.** $3 \div 1\frac{1}{4} =$

Practice = Success!

Skill: Changing Proper Fractions and Mixed Numbers to Decimals

Fractions

Name ______________________________

Total Problems __48__

Problems Correct ________

Change these proper fractions and mixed numbers to decimals. Round to the nearest hundredth. Show your work on another sheet. Write your answers here.

1. $\frac{3}{4}$ = **2.** $\frac{2}{5}$ =

3. $\frac{8}{9}$ = **4.** $\frac{3}{5}$ = **5.** $2\frac{1}{4}$ = **6.** $7\frac{2}{3}$ = **7.** $\frac{14}{15}$ =

8. $\frac{3}{50}$ = **9.** $\frac{5}{6}$ = **10.** $\frac{7}{8}$ = **11.** $\frac{2}{9}$ = **12.** $32\frac{1}{8}$ =

13. $4\frac{4}{5}$ = **14.** $\frac{1}{8}$ = **15.** $\frac{7}{12}$ = **16.** $\frac{2}{15}$ = **17.** $42\frac{1}{3}$ =

18. $\frac{21}{30}$ = **19.** $15\frac{2}{3}$ = **20.** $4\frac{2}{9}$ = **21.** $\frac{1}{4}$ = **22.** $\frac{21}{25}$ =

23. $\frac{1}{2}$ = **24.** $3\frac{2}{6}$ = **25.** $\frac{1}{5}$ = **26.** $16\frac{1}{4}$ = **27.** $3\frac{3}{8}$ =

28. $\frac{4}{5}$ = **29.** $\frac{7}{40}$ = **30.** $\frac{23}{25}$ = **31.** $\frac{9}{25}$ = **32.** $8\frac{1}{5}$ =

33. $6\frac{3}{5}$ = **34.** $\frac{39}{40}$ = **35.** $6\frac{1}{3}$ = **36.** $17\frac{4}{5}$ = **37.** $\frac{5}{8}$ =

38. $\frac{4}{25}$ = **39.** $84\frac{3}{8}$ = **40.** $\frac{7}{20}$ = **41.** $\frac{7}{16}$ = **42.** $\frac{6}{25}$ =

43. $\frac{13}{20}$ = **44.** $\frac{16}{33}$ = **45.** $1\frac{3}{5}$ =

46. $8\frac{2}{3}$ = **47.** $6\frac{3}{5}$ = **48.** $\frac{4}{9}$ =

Practice! Practice! Practice!

Fractions

Name ____________________

Total Problems	**50**
Problems Correct	______

Change these decimals to proper fractions or mixed numbers in lowest terms. Show your work on another sheet. Write your answers here.

1. 0.75 =	**2.** 3.4 =			
3. 0.5 =	**4.** 3.25 =	**5.** 0.875 =	**6.** 5.05 =	**7.** 6.10 =
8. 0.315 =	**9.** 0.45 =	**10.** 0.6 =	**11.** 0.2 =	**12.** 9.125 =
13. 7.4 =	**14.** 6.875 =	**15.** 0.84 =	**16.** 0.319 =	**17.** 8.09 =
18. 0.405 =	**19.** 0.73 =	**20.** 0.17 =	**21.** 16.8 =	**22.** 32.05 =
23. 4.3 =	**24.** 10.84 =	**25.** 3.6 =	**26.** 0.56 =	**27.** 9.02 =
28. 8.25 =	**29.** 6.4 =	**30.** 7.5 =	**31.** 24.03 =	**32.** 0.93 =
33. 0.36 =	**34.** 0.24 =	**35.** 2.875 =	**36.** 8.2 =	**37.** 5.1 =
38. 14.05 =	**39.** 7.25 =	**40.** 0.029 =	**41.** 0.749 =	**42.** 0.237 =
43. 1.07 =	**44.** 4.375 =	**45.** 2.23 =	**46.** 5.125 =	
47. 16.9 =	**48.** 3.05 =	**49.** 0.006 =	**50.** 4.25 =	

Practice makes perfect!

Fractions

Name ____________________

Total Problems 48

Problems Correct ______

Show your work on another sheet. Write your answers here.

1. $\frac{2}{3}$ of 9 =
2. $\frac{7}{8}$ of 16 =
3. $\frac{4}{5}$ of 20 =
4. $\frac{5}{7}$ of 49 =
5. $\frac{3}{7}$ of 21 =
6. $\frac{4}{6}$ of 18 =
7. $\frac{3}{8}$ of 24 =
8. $\frac{5}{9}$ of 18 =
9. $\frac{4}{7}$ of 28 =
10. $\frac{5}{10}$ of 20 =
11. $\frac{6}{8}$ of 24 =
12. $\frac{5}{6}$ of 18 =
13. $\frac{7}{9}$ of 36 =
14. $\frac{5}{8}$ of 24 =
15. $\frac{2}{9}$ of 27 =
16. $\frac{10}{12}$ of 24 =
17. $\frac{5}{8}$ of 48 =
18. $\frac{2}{3}$ of 24 =
19. $\frac{2}{5}$ of 10 =
20. $\frac{4}{6}$ of 36 =
21. $\frac{3}{9}$ of 36 =
22. $\frac{7}{8}$ of 72 =
23. $\frac{6}{9}$ of 63 =
24. $\frac{8}{10}$ of 90 =
25. $\frac{4}{11}$ of 121 =
26. $\frac{5}{9}$ of 90 =
27. $\frac{3}{12}$ of 60 =
28. $\frac{6}{12}$ of 72 =
29. $\frac{1}{2}$ of 18 =
30. $\frac{2}{3}$ of 21 =
31. $\frac{4}{7}$ of 56 =
32. $\frac{3}{9}$ of 63 =
33. $\frac{1}{4}$ of 24 =
34. $\frac{3}{8}$ of 72 =
35. $\frac{5}{9}$ of 108 =
36. $\frac{4}{7}$ of 84 =
37. $\frac{2}{8}$ of 88 =
38. $\frac{8}{10}$ of 100 =
39. $\frac{9}{10}$ of 120 =
40. $\frac{4}{12}$ of 144 =
41. $\frac{8}{10}$ of 30 =
42. $\frac{4}{11}$ of 132 =
43. $\frac{3}{11}$ of 132 =
44. $\frac{8}{9}$ of 108 =
45. $\frac{4}{7}$ of 35 =
46. $\frac{8}{11}$ of 121 =
47. $\frac{9}{10}$ of 110 =
48. $\frac{6}{9}$ of 81 =

Practice = Success!

Percents

Name ______________________________

Change these decimals to percents. Show your work on another sheet. Write your answers here.

Total Problems	50
Problems Correct	______

1. 0.07 =	**2.** 0.82 =			
3. 0.01 =	**4.** 0.74 =	**5.** 0.85 =	**6.** 0.32 =	**7.** 0.02 =
8. 0.18 =	**9.** 0.7 =	**10.** 0.9 =	**11.** 0.37 =	**12.** 0.69 =
13. 0.08 =	**14.** 0.72 =	**15.** 0.48 =	**16.** 0.3 =	**17.** 0.6 =
18. 0.05 =	**19.** 7.36 =	**20.** 0.83 =	**21.** 0.4 =	**22.** 0.21 =
23. 0.1 =	**24.** 0.24 =	**25.** 0.91 =	**26.** 0.79 =	**27.** 0.81 =
28. 8.92 =	**29.** 0.38 =	**30.** 3.24 =	**31.** 0.83 =	**32.** 0.42 =
33. 0.45 =	**34.** 9.27 =	**35.** 0.5 =	**36.** 0.47 =	**37.** 0.78 =
38. 0.03 =	**39.** 0.76 =	**40.** 0.12 =	**41.** 0.88 =	**42.** 0.03 =
43. 0.8 =	**44.** 0.87 =	**45.** 0.04 =	**46.** 0.94 =	**47.** 0.27 =
48. 0.93 =	**49.** 0.27 =	**50.** 0.71 =		

With practice, you can do it!

Skill: Changing Percents to Proper Fractions or Mixed Numbers

Percents

Name ______________________

Total Problems 50

Problems Correct ________

Change these percents to proper fractions or mixed numbers. Show your work on another sheet. Reduce your answers to lowest terms and write them here.

1. 7% =	**2.** 48% =			
3. 120% =	**4.** 12% =	**5.** 1% =	**6.** 160% =	**7.** 2% =
8. 21% =	**9.** 750% =	**10.** 59% =	**11.** 43% =	**12.** 250% =
13. 3% =	**14.** 140% =	**15.** 4% =	**16.** 260% =	**17.** 9% =
18. 675% =	**19.** 850% =	**20.** 36% =	**21.** 75% =	**22.** 85% =
23. 27% =	**24.** 73% =	**25.** 230% =	**26.** 5% =	**27.** 180% =
28. 37% =	**29.** 6% =	**30.** 12% =	**31.** 290% =	**32.** 15% =
33. 87% =	**34.** 53% =	**35.** 95% =	**36.** 125% =	**37.** 420% =
38. 19% =	**39.** 79% =	**40.** 23% =	**41.** 825% =	**42.** 77% =
43. 61% =	**44.** 29% =	**45.** 80% =	**46.** 28% =	**47.** 25% =
48. 93% =	**49.** 83% =	**50.** 39% =		

Through practice you learn!

Percents

Name ______________________

Change these percents to decimals. Show your work on another sheet. Write your answers here.

Total Problems 50

Problems Correct ______

1. 50% =	**2.** 42% =			
3. 8% =	**4.** 43% =	**5.** 12% =	**6.** 32% =	**7.** 79% =
8. 49% =	**9.** 31% =	**10.** 68% =	**11.** 3% =	**12.** 41% =
13. 40% =	**14.** 23% =	**15.** 75% =	**16.** 24% =	**17.** 89% =
18. 98% =	**19.** 8% =	**20.** 2% =	**21.** 17% =	**22.** 18% =
23. 6% =	**24.** 49% =	**25.** 73% =	**26.** 64% =	**27.** 1% =
28. 58% =	**29.** 96% =	**30.** 16% =	**31.** 25% =	**32.** 82% =
33. 14% =	**34.** 22% =	**35.** 71% =	**36.** 4% =	**37.** 27% =
38. 61% =	**39.** 83% =	**40.** 7% =	**41.** 28% =	**42.** 13% =
43. 81% =	**44.** 99% =	**45.** 91% =	**46.** 5% =	**47.** 39% =
48. 28% =	**49.** 94% =	**50.** 88% =		

Practice = Success!

Percents

Name ____________________

Change these proper fractions and mixed numbers to percents. Show your work on another sheet. Write your answers here.

Total Problems 50

Problems Correct ______

1. $\frac{37}{100} =$

2. $\frac{3}{100} =$

3. $\frac{65}{100} =$

4. $\frac{49}{100} =$

5. $\frac{1}{4} =$

6. $\frac{12}{100} =$

7. $\frac{11}{50} =$

8. $\frac{71}{100} =$

9. $4\frac{1}{2} =$

10. $3\frac{1}{4} =$

11. $1\frac{3}{4} =$

12. $\frac{2}{5} =$

13. $\frac{3}{10} =$

14. $\frac{63}{100} =$

15. $\frac{1}{20} =$

16. $\frac{1}{5} =$

17. $\frac{17}{20} =$

18. $\frac{57}{100} =$

19. $\frac{3}{5} =$

20. $\frac{1}{25} =$

21. $\frac{7}{10} =$

22. $5\frac{1}{4} =$

23. $\frac{37}{50} =$

24. $\frac{23}{100} =$

25. $\frac{1}{2} =$

26. $\frac{9}{10} =$

27. $\frac{81}{100} =$

28. $\frac{39}{100} =$

29. $3\frac{3}{4} =$

30. $\frac{73}{100} =$

31. $\frac{7}{20} =$

32. $9\frac{1}{2} =$

33. $\frac{4}{5} =$

34. $\frac{1}{10} =$

35. $\frac{13}{20} =$

36. $\frac{91}{100} =$

37. $\frac{51}{100} =$

38. $5\frac{1}{4} =$

39. $\frac{11}{100} =$

40. $\frac{3}{20} =$

41. $8\frac{1}{2} =$

42. $\frac{47}{50} =$

43. $2\frac{1}{5} =$

44. $1\frac{4}{5} =$

45. $\frac{7}{100} =$

46. $6\frac{1}{2} =$

47. $\frac{21}{50} =$

48. $\frac{21}{100} =$

49. $\frac{53}{100} =$

50. $\frac{67}{100} =$

Practice! Practice! Practice!

Percents

Name ______________________

Show your work on another sheet. Write your answers here.

Total Problems 50

Problems Correct ______

1. 10% of 80 = **2.** 35% of 60 =

3. 50% of 20 = **4.** 15% of 20 = **5.** 10% of 60 = **6.** 20% of 50 =

7. 30% of 60 = **8.** 5% of 100 = **9.** 25% of 100 = **10.** 5% of 25 =

11. 15% of 40 = **12.** 20% of 45 = **13.** 24% of 60 = **14.** 20% of 10 =

15. 50% of 32 = **16.** 28% of 35 = **17.** 18% of 25 = **18.** 50% of 36 =

19. 18% of 32 = **20.** 30% of 70 = **21.** 30% of 40 = **22.** 44% of 34 =

23. 25% of 20 = **24.** 5% of 60 = **25.** 10% of 70 = **26.** 25% of 64 =

27. 8% of 21 = **28.** 50% of 48 = **29.** 4% of 20 = **30.** 75% of 200 =

31. 28% of 40 = **32.** 35% of 80 = **33.** 26% of 50 = **34.** 32% of 18 =

35. 19% of 25 = **36.** 10% of 90 = **37.** 80% of 30 = **38.** 66% of 40 =

39. 45% of 60 = **40.** 95% of 30 = **41.** 46% of 80 = **42.** 10% of 50 =

43. 95% of 20 = **44.** 31% of 40 = **45.** 36% of 22 =

46. 40% of 30 = **47.** 20% of 80 = **48.** 10% of 76 =

49. 86% of 40 = **50.** 56% of 20 =

Practice puts you on top!

Percents

Name ____________________

Show your work on another sheet. Write your answers here.

Total Problems ___50___

Problems Correct ________

1. 5 is ____% of 20

2. 6 is ____% of 40

3. 8 is ____% of 40

4. 10 is ____% of 50

5. 2 is ____% of 4

6. 5 is ____% of 25

7. 14 is ____% of 20

8. 6 is ____% of 30

9. 18 is ____% of 36

10. 7 is ____% of 10

11. 24 is ____% of 30

12. 22 is ____% of 100

13. 36 is ____% of 40

14. 12 is ____% of 40

15. 2 is ____% of 8

16. 5 is ____% of 50

17. 38 is ____% of 50

18. 6 is ____% of 15

19. 6 is ____% of 24

20. 26 is ____% of 40

21. 9 is ____% of 20

22. 26 is ____% of 50

23. 48 is ____% of 100

24. 27 is ____% of 30

25. 68 is ____% of 200

26. 7 is ____% of 70

27. 12 is ____% of 60

28. 16 is ____% of 40

29. 36 is ____% of 80

30. 14 is ____% of 50

31. 74 is ____% of 100

32. 39 is ____% of 50

33. 38 is ____% of 76

34. 36 is ____% of 200

35. 48 is ____% of 200

36. 72 is ____% of 80

37. 43 is ____% of 50

38. 89 is ____% of 100

39. 28 is ____% of 80

40. 24 is ____% of 96

41. 8 is ____% of 160

42. 16 is ____% of 32

43. 10 is ____% of 100

44. 8 is ____% of 80

45. 15 is ____% of 60

46. 9 is ____% of 36

47. 36 is ____% of 72

48. 6 is ____% of 50

49. 4 is ____% of 80

50. 9 is ____% of 180

Practice brings success!

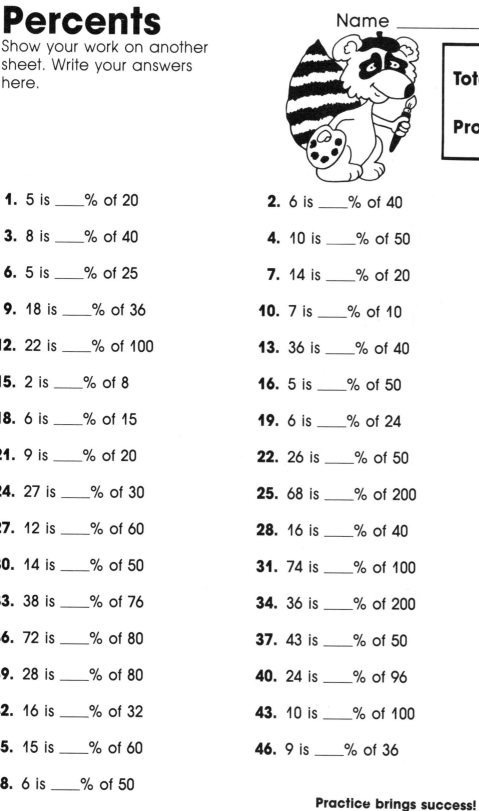

Proportions

Show your work on another sheet. Write your answers here.

Name ____________________

Total Problems	50
Problems Correct	______

1. $\frac{2}{4} = \frac{n}{8}$ n =

2. $\frac{3}{x} = \frac{9}{15}$ x =

3. $\frac{n}{20} = \frac{5}{4}$ n =

4. $\frac{5}{6} = \frac{30}{n}$ n =

5. $\frac{27}{n} = \frac{9}{10}$ n =

6. $\frac{3}{14} = \frac{n}{42}$ n =

7. $\frac{2}{n} = \frac{24}{72}$ n =

8. $\frac{3}{9} = \frac{x}{54}$ x =

9. $\frac{3}{7} = \frac{x}{42}$ x =

10. $\frac{6}{12} = \frac{12}{n}$ n =

11. $\frac{7}{8} = \frac{42}{x}$ x =

12. $\frac{3}{8} = \frac{n}{48}$ n =

13. $\frac{12}{13} = \frac{24}{x}$ x =

14. $\frac{7}{9} = \frac{21}{n}$ n =

15. $\frac{7}{4} = \frac{x}{28}$ x =

16. $\frac{n}{30} = \frac{5}{3}$ n =

17. $\frac{5}{40} = \frac{2}{m}$ m =

18. $\frac{6}{2} = \frac{t}{20}$ t =

19. $\frac{3}{9} = \frac{x}{15}$ x =

20. $\frac{6}{n} = \frac{4}{8}$ n =

21. $\frac{7}{4} = \frac{49}{y}$ y =

22. $\frac{6}{8} = \frac{n}{48}$ n =

23. $\frac{y}{15} = \frac{1}{3}$ y =

24. $\frac{40}{120} = \frac{4}{n}$ n =

25. $\frac{9}{3} = \frac{27}{y}$ y =

26. $\frac{14}{6} = \frac{n}{3}$ n =

27. $\frac{12}{3} = \frac{12}{n}$ n =

28. $\frac{1}{8} = \frac{24}{m}$ m =

29. $\frac{25}{6} = \frac{75}{n}$ n =

30. $\frac{3}{12} = \frac{x}{48}$ x =

31. $\frac{2}{30} = \frac{y}{60}$ y =

32. $\frac{6}{t} = \frac{4}{6}$ t =

33. $\frac{n}{44} = \frac{2}{4}$ n =

34. $\frac{7}{21} = \frac{m}{9}$ m =

35. $\frac{42}{4} = \frac{t}{22}$ t =

36. $\frac{18}{3} = \frac{x}{2}$ x =

37. $\frac{y}{10} = \frac{4}{5}$ y =

38. $\frac{n}{24} = \frac{4}{12}$ n =

39. $\frac{5}{2} = \frac{20}{x}$ x =

40. $\frac{6}{24} = \frac{3}{n}$ n =

41. $\frac{13}{2} = \frac{39}{x}$ x =

42. $\frac{2}{8} = \frac{14}{m}$ m =

43. $\frac{6}{t} = \frac{24}{12}$ t =

44. $\frac{9}{2} = \frac{y}{4}$ y =

45. $\frac{n}{55} = \frac{2}{11}$ n =

46. $\frac{5}{7} = \frac{10}{m}$ m =

47. $\frac{8}{10} = \frac{64}{y}$ y =

48. $\frac{3}{4} = \frac{12}{n}$ n =

49. $\frac{5}{25} = \frac{t}{20}$ t =

50. $\frac{16}{2} = \frac{32}{x}$ x =

Practice = Success!

Skill: Addition of Integers

Integers

Name __________________________

Show your work on another sheet. Write your answers here.

Total Problems 50

Problems Correct ________

1. $4 + {}^{-}5 =$

2. $6 + {}^{-}8 =$

3. ${}^{-}3 + {}^{-}4 =$

4. $8 + 9 =$

5. ${}^{-}4 + 8 =$

6. $3 + {}^{-}9 =$

7. $13 + {}^{-}14 =$

8. ${}^{-}8 + 0 =$

9. ${}^{-}5 + {}^{-}5 =$

10. ${}^{-}6 + 8 =$

11. ${}^{-}12 + 1 =$

12. ${}^{-}7 + 9 =$

13. ${}^{-}2 + 10 =$

14. ${}^{-}5 + 6 =$

15. ${}^{-}14 + 7 =$

16. ${}^{-}12 + 12 =$

17. ${}^{-}14 + 3 =$

18. ${}^{-}10 + {}^{-}10 =$

19. ${}^{-}5 + 0 =$

20. $12 + {}^{-}11 =$

21. ${}^{-}6 + 9 =$

22. ${}^{-}8 + 14 =$

23. ${}^{-}6 + 5 =$

24. ${}^{-}5 + 3 =$

25. ${}^{-}1 + 12 =$

26. $15 + {}^{-}10 =$

27. ${}^{-}2 + 8 =$

28. ${}^{-}30 + 2 =$

29. ${}^{-}4 + 5 =$

30. $7 + 8 =$

31. $14 + {}^{-}12 =$

32. ${}^{-}14 + 8 =$

33. ${}^{-}12 + 6 =$

34. ${}^{-}4 + 12 =$

35. ${}^{-}24 + 14 =$

36. ${}^{-}3 + 15 =$

37. ${}^{-}5 + 10 =$

38. ${}^{-}15 + 5 =$

39. ${}^{-}18 + 25 =$

40. ${}^{-}15 + 16 =$

41. ${}^{-}16 + 16 =$

42. ${}^{-}7 + 14 =$

43. ${}^{-}14 + 30 =$

44. ${}^{-}30 + 15 =$

45. ${}^{-}10 + {}^{-}7 =$

46. ${}^{-}2 + 12 =$

47. ${}^{-}3 + 10 =$

48. $20 + {}^{-}10 =$

49. ${}^{-}5 + 21 =$

50. ${}^{-}13 + 2 =$

Practice makes perfect!

Integers

Name ______________________

Total Problems **50**

Problems Correct ______

Show your work on another sheet. Write your answers here.

1. $10 - {}^{-}2 =$	**2.** $7 - {}^{-}4 =$		
3. ${}^{-}6 - 8 =$	**4.** $8 - {}^{-}9 =$	**5.** ${}^{-}4 - 2 =$	**6.** ${}^{-}6 - 9 =$
7. ${}^{-}18 - 9 =$	**8.** ${}^{-}5 - {}^{-}8 =$	**9.** $15 - 20 =$	**10.** ${}^{-}32 - {}^{-}10 =$
11. ${}^{-}7 - 10 =$	**12.** $10 - {}^{-}14 =$	**13.** $14 - {}^{-}7 =$	**14.** $10 - {}^{-}3 =$
15. ${}^{-}10 - 6 =$	**16.** ${}^{-}5 - {}^{-}5 =$	**17.** ${}^{-}8 - {}^{-}9 =$	**18.** $20 - {}^{-}6 =$
19. ${}^{-}6 - 3 =$	**20.** ${}^{-}8 - 3 =$	**21.** $30 - {}^{-}8 =$	**22.** ${}^{-}14 - 9 =$
23. $16 - {}^{-}4 =$	**24.** $20 - 30 =$	**25.** ${}^{-}10 - 4 =$	**26.** $15 - {}^{-}8 =$
27. ${}^{-}15 - 7 =$	**28.** ${}^{-}21 - {}^{-}1 =$	**29.** $20 - {}^{-}5 =$	**30.** ${}^{-}3 - {}^{-}8 =$
31. ${}^{-}9 - 3 =$	**32.** $14 - {}^{-}3 =$	**33.** ${}^{-}8 - {}^{-}8 =$	**34.** $15 - {}^{-}5 =$
35. ${}^{-}3 - {}^{-}3 =$	**36.** ${}^{-}5 - {}^{-}6 =$	**37.** $25 - {}^{-}5 =$	**38.** $18 - {}^{-}4 =$
39. $60 - {}^{-}5 =$	**40.** $12 - 15 =$	**41.** $18 - {}^{-}3 =$	**42.** $21 - 40 =$
43. $83 - {}^{-}21 =$	**44.** $35 - {}^{-}5 =$	**45.** ${}^{-}10 - {}^{-}7 =$	**46.** $39 - {}^{-}18 =$
47. $12 - {}^{-}42 =$	**48.** $25 - {}^{-}10 =$		
49. ${}^{-}20 - 5 =$	**50.** ${}^{-}28 - 30 =$		

Practice hard. You'll win.

Equations

Name ____________________

Show your work on another sheet. Write your answers here.

Total Problems	**50**
Problems Correct	______

1. $2 + 7 - 3 =$

2. $16 \div 4 + 3 =$

3. $4 + 6 - 7 =$

4. $2 \times 6 \div 3 =$

5. $6 \times 4 \div 12 =$

6. $10 - 7 + 6 =$

7. $36 \div 6 + 4 =$

8. $7 \times 4 + 2 =$

9. $5 \times 5 - 5 =$

10. $12 \div 4 + 7 =$

11. $6 + 9 - 3 =$

12. $13 + 6 - 7 =$

13. $14 \div 2 \times 3 =$

14. $4 + 8 - 7 =$

15. $(16 + 9) \div 5 =$

16. $9 \times 4 \div 6 =$

17. $3 \times 9 - 17 =$

18. $5 + 5 \times 3 =$

19. $6 \times 6 \div 12 =$

20. $12 + 7 - 9 =$

21. $6 + 12 \div 2 =$

22. $9 \times 3 + 4 =$

23. $9 + 6 - 8 =$

24. $64 \div 8 + 9 =$

25. $16 \div 2 + 9 =$

26. $18 \div 2 \times 3 =$

27. $16 + 18 - 8 =$

28. $14 - 7 + 3 =$

29. $6 \times 7 - 6 =$

30. $24 \div 6 \times 7 =$

31. $32 \div 8 \times 5 =$

32. $16 + 4 \div 2 =$

33. $9 \times 9 + 6 =$

34. $13 + 5 - 7 =$

35. $15 \div 3 \times 2 =$

36. $7 + (3 \times 9) =$

37. $6 + (2 \times 4) =$

38. $(4 + 8) \div 2 =$

39. $9 + 9 \times 2 =$

40. $6 \times 3 + 4 =$

41. $(9 + 16) \div 5 =$

42. $16 + 18 - 7 =$

43. $(60 \div 5) \div 4 =$

44. $36 + (4 \times 8) =$

45. $9 \times 9 + 12 =$

46. $32 \div 4 - 3 =$

47. $12 \div 3 \times 9 =$

48. $6 + 9 - 7 =$

49. $8 \times 9 + 7 =$

50. $8 + 3 \times 8 =$

Success ahoy! Just practice!

Equations

Name ____________________

Show your work on another sheet. Write your answers here.

Total Problems	50
Problems Correct	______

1. $5 + 6 - 4 =$
2. $3 \times 4 \div 3 =$
3. $32 \div 8 + 3 =$
4. $40 \div 8 - 2 =$
5. $6 + 8 \times 3 =$
6. $14 + 12 - 6 =$
7. $2 \times 9 + 4 =$
8. $8 \times 8 + 6 =$
9. $5 + 8 \div 2 =$
10. $6 + 6 \div 6 =$
11. $45 \div 5 \times 3 =$
12. $9 + 7 - 10 =$
13. $15 \times 2 \div 3 =$
14. $3 \times 7 - 1 =$
15. $18 \div 9 \times 8 =$
16. $36 \div 9 + 8 =$
17. $21 \div 7 + 6 =$
18. $7 + 8 - 8 =$
19. $9 + 6 - 12 =$
20. $12 + 7 - 8 =$
21. $56 \div 8 + 4 =$
22. $64 \div 8 + 5 =$
23. $14 + (2 \times 8) =$
24. $(7 + 9) \div 2 =$
25. $15 \div 3 \times 2 =$
26. $(5 + 3) \times 3 =$
27. $15 - 7 + 3 =$
28. $(3 + 7) \times 2 \div 10 =$
29. $6 + 8 \div 2 =$
30. $3 \times (5 + 6) =$
31. $12 \times 2 + 2 =$
32. $15 + 3 \times 2 =$
33. $14 - (8 - 2) - 1 =$
34. $16 - (10 - 4) =$
35. $(14 + 6) \div 5 =$
36. $(3 + 2) \times (4 + 6) =$
37. $12 \times (3 + 2) =$
38. $9 \times (15 - 7) =$
39. $6 \times (4 + 5) =$
40. $3 + 6 \times 2 + 5 =$
41. $8 + 4 \times 5 =$
42. $6 \times 8 + 2 =$
43. $30 + 16 \times 2 =$
44. $3 \times (9 + 2) =$
45. $52 - (5 + 3) =$
46. $64 \div 8 \times 3 =$
47. $25 - (3 + 8) =$
48. $21 \div (3 + 4) =$
49. $12 + 32 \div 4 =$
50. $16 + (4 \times 3) =$

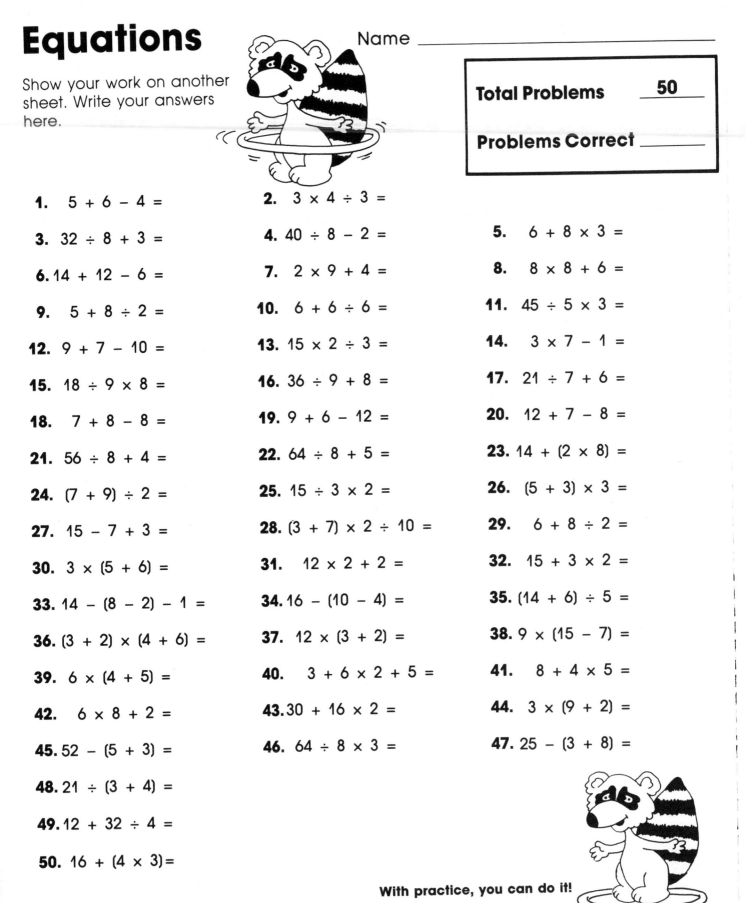

With practice, you can do it!

Equations

Name ____________________

Solve these equations using this information: **a** = 2, **b** = 3, **c** = 4. Show your work on another sheet. Write your answers here.

Total Problems	48
Problems Correct	______

1. $a + 7 =$	**2.** $23 + c =$		
3. $12 \div b =$	**4.** $ab =$	**5.** $2a - b =$	**6.** $48 \div c =$
7. $15b =$	**8.** $5a + 10 =$	**9.** $b + 13 =$	**10.** $6a + c =$
11. $bc =$	**12.** $7a - c =$	**13.** $3c + -8 =$	**14.** $ac + 6 =$
15. $14 \div a =$	**16.** $b + 24 =$	**17.** $ac =$	**18.** $10a + b =$
19. $6b + 7c =$	**20.** $15 - ab =$	**21.** $13 + ac =$	**22.** $5b + c =$
23. $a + c =$	**24.** $36 \div b =$	**25.** $20 - 4c =$	**26.** $62 + a =$
27. $2a + -6 =$	**28.** $21 \div (b + c) =$	**29.** $9a + 2b =$	**30.** $5b + -12 =$
31. $ac + 24 =$	**32.** $4a - 5 =$	**33.** $8a + 2b =$	**34.** $bc + a =$
35. $36 \div c =$	**36.** $7b + 3c =$	**37.** $ac + 9 =$	**38.** $ab + -14 =$
39. $ac + b =$	**40.** $4b + -5 =$	**41.** $6c - b =$	**42.** $14 + ac =$
43. $20a - b =$	**44.** $12c - 17 =$	**45.** $ab + c =$	
46. $a + 27 =$	**47.** $3b - c =$	**48.** $b + -6 =$	

Practice brings success!

Equations

Name ______________________________

Solve these equations using this information: $a = 2$, $b = 3$, $x = 4$, $y = 5$. Show your work on another sheet. Write your answers here.

Total Problems	50
Problems Correct	______

1. $a + 14 =$

2. $x + 23 =$

3. $3x - 7 =$

4. $14 - y =$

5. $62 + x =$

6. $ab + 3 =$

7. $48 \div x =$

8. $y + ab =$

9. $6a - 7 =$

10. $5a + y =$

11. $7y - 10 =$

12. $6b \div 3 =$

13. $8x + {}^{-}9 =$

14. $a^2 + y =$

15. $17 + b =$

16. $x + 12 =$

17. $y + {}^{-}16 =$

18. $3b - 7 =$

19. $6x \div 12 =$

20. $12 + xy =$

21. $ax + 3 =$

22. $bx - 6 =$

23. $y + {}^{-}18 =$

24. $ab + xy =$

25. $y + 32 =$

26. $12a - 14 =$

27. $3y + {}^{-}12 =$

28. $6x - y =$

29. $b^2 + 14 =$

30. $25 - xy =$

31. $6x + {}^{-}2y =$

32. $16a - xy =$

33. $10b \div y =$

34. $20 \div x =$

35. $10 + 3x =$

36. $29 - 3b =$

37. $60 - ab =$

38. $16 + b =$

39. $27 + y =$

40. $3a + 6x =$

41. $42 \div b =$

42. $39 + y =$

43. $32a \div 8 =$

44. $ab \div 2 =$

45. $12a - 2b =$

46. $2a + 18 =$

47. $81 \div b^2 =$

48. $xy + {}^{-}18 =$

49. $12 + ax =$

50. $6b - 7 =$

Practice! Practice! Practice!

Equations

Name ____________________

Show your work on another sheet. Write your answers here.

Total Problems	39
Problems Correct	______

1. $d + 7 = 12$
$d =$

2. $a + 8 = 26$
$a =$

3. $17 + a = 34$
$a =$

4. $18 + n = 0$
$n =$

5. $24 + q = 34$
$q =$

6. $a + 3 = 24$
$a =$

7. $15 + m = 31$
$m =$

8. $d + 14 = 37$
$d =$

9. $m + 8 = 21$
$m =$

10. $36 = n + 9$
$n =$

11. $q + 4 = 36$
$q =$

12. $t + 8 = 15$
$t =$

13. $47 + c = 58$
$c =$

14. $43 = m + 17$
$m =$

15. $56 = n + 14$
$n =$

16. $m + 15 = 34$
$m =$

17. $13 + d = 28$
$d =$

18. $28 + n = 47$
$n =$

19. $t + 30 = 43$
$t =$

20. $32 + d = 49$
$d =$

21. $16 + n = 40$
$n =$

22. $2 + m = 14$
$m =$

23. $e + 12 = 43$
$e =$

24. $14 + q = 62$
$q =$

25. $93 = 32 + m$
$m =$

26. $m + 82 = 94$
$m =$

27. $n + 3 = 49$
$n =$

28. $49 = 27 + f$
$f =$

29. $d + 45 = 80$
$d =$

30. $18 = n + 10$
$n =$

31. $60 = n + 29$
$n =$

32. $a + 13 = 17$
$a =$

33. $t + 23 = 40$
$t =$

34. $x + 30 = 54$
$x =$

35. $58 + n = 106$
$n =$

36. $42 + d = 68$
$d =$

37. $15 = y + 15$
$y =$

38. $y + 14 = 36$
$y =$

39. $60 + n = 86$
$n =$

Practice = Success!

Equations

Name ______________________

Total Problems 40

Problems Correct ______

Show your work on another sheet. Write your answers here.

1. $\frac{m}{12} = 3$ m =
2. $\frac{n}{6} = 5$ n =
3. $\frac{r}{3} = 4$ r =
4. $16 = \frac{n}{2}$ n =
5. $9 = \frac{n}{9}$ n =
6. $9 = \frac{r}{2}$ r =
7. $12 = \frac{r}{3}$ r =
8. $14 = \frac{n}{3}$ n =
9. $\frac{n}{6} = 12$ n =
10. $\frac{t}{8} = 4$ t =
11. $\frac{x}{5} = 4$ x =
12. $\frac{n}{5} = 20$ n =
13. $\frac{d}{3} = 8$ d =
14. $\frac{d}{5} = 12$ d =
15. $\frac{m}{8} = 14$ m =
16. $\frac{r}{6} = 7$ r =
17. $\frac{r}{12} = 12$ r =
18. $\frac{n}{10} = 11$ n =
19. $15 = \frac{n}{6}$ n =
20. $8 = \frac{r}{11}$ r =
21. $12 = \frac{n}{13}$ n =
22. $20 = \frac{n}{5}$ n =
23. $13 = \frac{r}{7}$ r =
24. $\frac{n}{12} = 9$ n =
25. $\frac{r}{16} = 3$ r =
26. $18 = \frac{d}{4}$ d =
27. $\frac{r}{9} = 36$ r =
28. $\frac{r}{13} = 3$ r =
29. $\frac{n}{6} = 8$ n =
30. $\frac{m}{15} = 3$ m =
31. $\frac{n}{10} = 18$ n =
32. $\frac{m}{15} = 5$ m =
33. $\frac{m}{5} = 8$ m =
34. $\frac{n}{9} = 27$ n =
35. $\frac{m}{6} = 13$ m =
36. $\frac{n}{11} = 14$ n =
37. $\frac{x}{4} = 9$ x =
38. $\frac{d}{5} = 25$ d =
39. $\frac{y}{4} = 12$ y =
40. $\frac{d}{12} = 6$ d =

Through practice you learn!

Answer Key

Addition

Name ______________

Total Problems 40

Problems Correct ______

1. 6,429 + 5,857 = 12,286
2. 9,247 + 6,938 = 16,185
3. 4,862 + 2,379 = 7,241
4. 8,563 + 4,784 = 13,347
5. 7,437 + 6,829 = 14,266
6. 5,649 + 9,857 = 15,506
7. 7,368 + 8,249 = 15,617
8. 36,483 + 8,279 = 44,762
9. 76,475 + 71,948 = 148,423
10. 95,468 + 32,785 = 128,253
11. 48,263 + 61,178 = 109,441
12. 72,674 + 19,239 = 91,913
13. 74,865 + 94,573 = 169,438
14. 91,768 + 27,347 = 119,115
15. 45,276 + 32,949 = 78,225
16. 39,265 + 94,381 = 133,646
17. 28,394 + 9,158 = 37,552
18. 85,237 + 73,296 = 158,533
19. 64,879 + 82,387 = 147,266
20. 79,365 + 12,847 = 92,212
21. 54,783 + 69,814 = 124,597
22. 88,603 + 43,529 = 132,132
23. 506,486 + 48,237 = 554,723
24. 756,983 + 181,249 = 938,232
25. 926,548 + 297,619 = 1,224,167
26. 470,869 + 81,473 = 552,342
27. 672,457 + 759,264 = 1,431,721
28. 946,309 + 717,846 = 1,664,155
29. 642,038 + 85,297 = 727,335
30. 248,365 + 923,982 = 1,172,347
31. 743,654 + 7,196 = 750,850
32. 458,964 + 824,395 = 1,283,359
33. 532,486 + 925,747 = 1,458,233
34. 810,156 + 364,512 = 1,174,668
35. 289,547 + 408,968 = 698,515
36. 568,495 + 287,147 = 855,642
37. 723,108 + 298,349 = 1,021,457
38. 764,258 + 429,169 = 1,193,427
39. 462,197 + 389,245 = 851,442
40. 265,478 + 396,584 = 662,062

Practice! Practice! Practice!

Page 1

Skill: Addition of Four- to Eight-Digit Numbers

Addition

Name ______________

Total Problems 41

Problems Correct ______

1. 3,708 + 2,949 = 6657
2. 7,365 + 7,482 = 14,847
3. 4,984 + 4,363 = 9347
4. 6,507 + 5,824 = 12,331
5. 9,234 + 4,928 = 14,162
6. 5,240 + 8,929 = 14,169
7. 2,895 + 4,927 = 7822
8. 4,627 + 5,248 = 9875
9. 37,241 + 8,469 = 45,710
10. 53,209 + 4,648 = 57,857
11. 77,241 + 8,679 = 85,920
12. 94,216 + 9,867 = 104,083
13. 81,476 + 8,925 = 90,401
14. 62,418 + 5,526 = 67,944
15. 62,147 + 24,928 = 87,075
16. 97,612 + 26,748 = 124,360
17. 45,036 + 47,948 = 92,984
18. 27,528 + 68,487 = 96,015
19. 85,436 + 62,795 = 148,231
20. 55,326 + 27,493 = 82,819
21. 93,218 + 82,925 = 176,143
22. 74,621 + 72,943 = 147,564
23. 46,247 + 81,964 = 128,211
24. 36,219 + 48,143 = 84,362
25. 50,819 + 68,627 = 119,446
26. 64,217 + 86,946 = 151,163
27. 717,402 + 816,784 = 1,534,186
28. 649,217 + 432,964 = 1,082,181
29. 824,913 + 712,847 = 1,537,760
30. 254,726 + 941,645 = 1,196,371
31. 524,613 + 452,814 = 977,427
32. 968,213 + 84,928 = 1,053,141
33. 734,216 + 29,832 = 764,048
34. 462,519 + 589,423 = 1,051,942
35. 643,817 + 267,423 = 911,240
36. 542,611 + 627,498 = 1,170,109
37. 812,436 + 419,845 = 1,232,281
38. 7,240,452 + 2,991,829 = 10,232,281
39. 64,615,215 + 8,416,548 = 73,031,763
40. 75,602,527 + 6,519,728 = 82,122,255
41. 45,825,187 + 18,742,649 = 64,567,836

Practice hard. You'll win!

Page 2

Skill: Addition of Four-, Five- and Six-Digit Numbers

Addition

Name ______________

Total Problems 25

Problems Correct ______

1. 764,120 + 215,328 + 342,509 + 56,282 + 9,164 = 1,387,403
2. 46,812 + 527,193 + 615,739 + 3,265 + 434,347 = 1,627,356
3. 62,102 + 423,216 + 4,823 + 1,169 + 532,342 = 1023,652
4. 47,264 + 721,436 + 85,249 + 2,111 + 9,327 = 865,387
5. 303,215 + 24,148 + 912,325 + 2,298 + 56,413 = 1,298,399
6. 49,325 + 321,264 + 723,127 + 3,836 + 94,243 = 1,191,795
7. 624,125 + 86,257 + 9,582 + 323,123 + 4,448 = 1,047,535
8. 5,426 + 625,132 + 5,588 + 47,245 + 123,136 = 806,527
9. 7,778 + 524,432 + 7,845 + 52,136 + 6,629 = 598,820
10. 706,147 + 621,542 + 92,285 + 346,127 + 9,325 = 1,775,426
11. 925,292 + 32,145 + 626,327 + 5,893 + 8,476 = 1,598,133
12. 721,625 + 39,237 + 61,343 + 132,183 + 242,152 = 1,196,540
13. 3,216 + 321,423 + 416,342 + 8,124 + 52,306 = 801,411
14. 981,624 + 724,157 + 8,216 + 43,564 + 132,438 = 1,889,999
15. 623,415 + 364,127 + 251,362 + 142,125 + 131,236 = 1,512,265
16. 743,212 + 62,193 + 4,324 + 8,659 + 9,924 = 828,312
17. 521,243 + 162,135 + 8,262 + 10,418 + 63,124 = 765,182
18. 600,030 + 49,243 + 123,136 + 9,419 + 62,132 = 843,930
19. 2,284 + 325,721 + 82,413 + 56,296 + 124,132 = 590,846
20. 316,423 + 47,215 + 923,134 + 1,927 + 6,421 = 1,295,120
21. 42,146 + 137,247 + 8,312 + 231,436 + 283,142 = 702,283
22. 132,326 + 49,123 + 261,242 + 96,134 + 2,808 = 541,633
23. 2,233 + 85,216 + 429,463 + 912,322 + 83,147 = 1,512,381
24. 261,342 + 83,148 + 9,233 + 3,892 + 56,125 = 413,740
25. 4,449 + 8,426 + 729,137 + 4,728 + 5,213 = 751,953

Practice = Success!

Page 3

Skill: Addition of Four-, Five- and Six-Digit Numbers

Addition

Name ______________

Total Problems 20

Problems Correct ______

1. 45,624 + 305,231 + 723,715 + 51,256 + 2,425 = 1,128,251
2. 5,201 + 672,316 + 1,841 + 3,462 + 756,295 = 1,439,115
3. 840,316 + 3,723 + 56,104 + 92,457 + 295,262 = 1,287,862
4. 35,206 + 742,527 + 1,282 + 74,653 + 5,474 = 859,142
5. 642,563 + 51,284 + 549,326 + 74,419 + 638,247 = 1,955,839
6. 364,218 + 3,423 + 542,852 + 84,336 + 92,574 = 1,087,403
7. 46,359 + 862,432 + 8,274 + 434,648 + 2,423 = 1,354,136
8. 4,682 + 56,243 + 81,425 + 563,839 + 845,158 = 1,551,347
9. 546,523 + 852,196 + 2,465 + 65,287 + 473,324 = 1,939,795
10. 642,394 + 1,237 + 36,248 + 3,855 + 3,464 = 687,198
11. 365,496 + 246,278 + 121,362 + 384,629 + 937,845 = 2,055,610
12. 6,514 + 362,825 + 58,263 + 823,647 + 634,739 = 1,886,008
13. 350,002 + 86,247 + 932,351 + 8,963 + 4,688 = 1,382,251
14. 816,243 + 42,686 + 924,312 + 8,197 + 539,438 = 2,330,876
15. 56,421 + 962,536 + 8,923 + 84,368 + 547,827 = 1,660,075
16. 6,764 + 826,283 + 9,436 + 58,149 + 932,527 = 1,833,159
17. 463,192 + 6,824 + 732,648 + 37,352 + 546,475 = 1,786,491
18. 843,619 + 65,243 + 924,306 + 1,896 + 347,247 = 2,182,311
19. 362,485 + 925,247 + 36,523 + 922,587 + 364,254 = 2,611,096
20. 625,143 + 463,258 + 142,324 + 368,432 + 724,897 = 2,324,054

Practice takes you to the top!

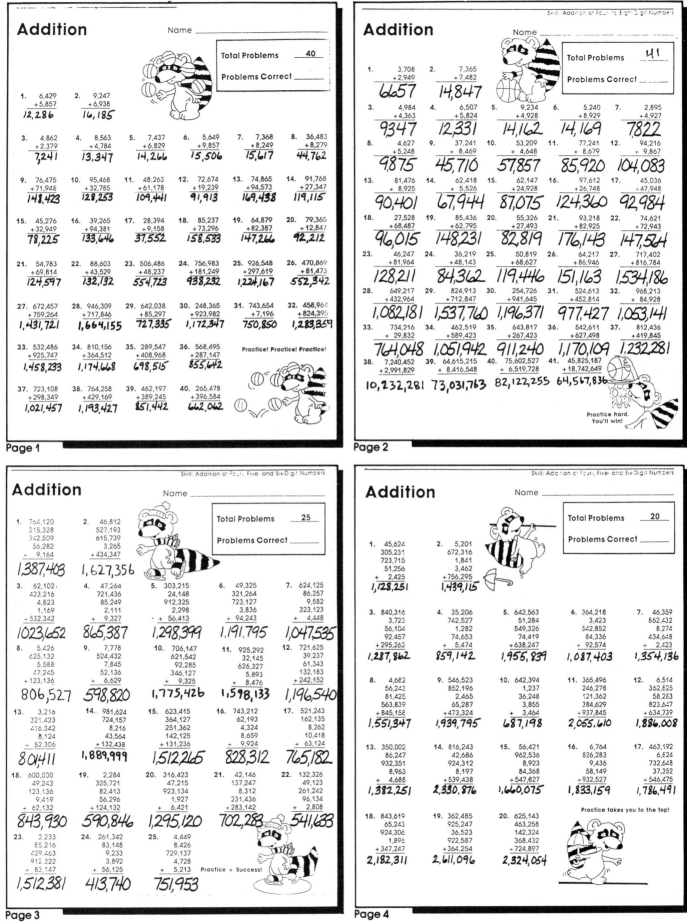

Page 4

Answer Key

Subtraction

Skill: Subtraction of Four- and Five-Digit Numbers

Name ______________________

Total Problems	40
Problems Correct	______

No.	Problem	Answer
1.	8,913 − 6,346	2,567
2.	5,137 − 2,986	2,151
3.	4,876 − 1,989	2,887
4.	7,348 − 2,479	4,869
5.	9,600 − 3,834	5,766
6.	6,524 − 4,259	2,265
7.	3,726 − 1,958	1,768
8.	8,432 − 5,649	2,783
9.	2,986 − 1,498	1,488
10.	7,543 − 2,798	4,745
11.	5,849 − 4,967	882
12.	8,643 − 4,857	3,786
13.	48,362 − 9.625	38,737
14.	84,758 − 61,269	23,489
15.	57,648 − 8,729	48,919
16.	74,682 − 52,797	21,885
17.	96,200 − 57,456	38,744
18.	74,649 − 15,783	58,866
19.	65,428 − 8,279	57,149
20.	88,427 − 49,383	39,044
21.	57,436 − 13,683	43,753
22.	96,425 − 67,248	29,177
23.	48,615 − 29,784	18,831
24.	72,106 − 41,728	30,378
25.	25,423 − 19,146	6,277
26.	63,289 − 46,195	17,094
27.	58,314 − 9,426	48,888
28.	76,249 − 27,413	48,836
29.	43,628 − 28,349	15,279
30.	94,562 − 5,728	88,834
31.	87,658 − 52,879	34,779
32.	53,628 − 38,249	15,379
33.	62,495 − 35,718	26,777
34.	79,645 − 63,257	16,388
35.	43,625 − 16,476	27,149
36.	89,235 − 32,487	56,748
37.	46,387 − 31,824	14,563
38.	29,357 − 14,189	15,168
39.	58,437 − 29,148	29,289
40.	35,428 − 26,139	9,289

Practice brings success!

Page 5

Subtraction

Skill: Subtraction of Four- to Eight-Digit Numbers

Name ______________________

Total Problems	42
Problems Correct	______

No.	Problem	Answer
1.	76,004 − 9,212	66,792
2.	7,421 − 1,546	5,875
3.	8,914 − 2,389	6,525
4.	73,125 − 24,314	48,811
5.	6,143 − 2,684	3,459
6.	42,156 − 8,219	33,937
7.	476,214 − 28,156	448,058
8.	62,146 − 8,527	53,619
9.	74,216 − 29,348	44,868
10.	9,215 − 2,647	6,568
11.	264,319 − 125,123	139,196
12.	4,000 − 2,184	1,816
13.	70,547 − 9,262	61,285
14.	524,615 − 241,328	283,287
15.	5,016 − 2,428	2,588
16.	41,646 − 8,293	33,353
17.	842,196 − 8,049	834,147
18.	92,004 − 27,123	64,881
19.	4,215,302 − 804,921	3,410,381
20.	7,006 − 2,439	4,567
21.	65,214 − 27,183	38,031
22.	47,215 − 28,306	18,909
23.	82,147 − 27,328	54,819
24.	726,154 − 8,239	717,915
25.	42,156,142 − 21,327,027	20,829,115
26.	8,147 − 2,473	5,674
27.	31,426 − 28,248	3,178
28.	91,346 − 28,127	63,219
29.	502,142 − 84,261	417,881
30.	4,312,006 − 916,124	3,395,882
31.	28,416 − 14,249	14,167
32.	27,416,545 − 8,312,287	19,104,258
33.	43,216 − 28,409	14,807
34.	71,000 − 25,242	45,758
35.	347,214 − 152,148	195,066
36.	5,614 − 2,852	2,762
37.	9,214,685 − 826,248	8,388,437
38.	5,214,599 − 2,843,288	2,371,311
39.	3,008 − 1,764	1,244
40.	4,020 − 2,452	1,568
41.	56,413,219 − 24,246,143	32,167,076
42.	76,423 − 4,247	72,176

Practice = Success!

Page 6

Subtraction

Skill: Subtraction of Five- to Eight-Digit Numbers

Name ______________________

Total Problems	41
Problems Correct	______

No.	Problem	Answer
1.	621,435 − 340,829	280,606
2.	924,365 − 742,826	181,539
3.	7,645,124 − 824,539	6,820,585
4.	4,620,000 − 341,362	4,278,638
5.	9,245,156 − 316,249	8,928,907
6.	807,421 − 324,618	482,803
7.	436,124 − 89,365	346,759
8.	29,006 − 22,438	6,568
9.	743,615 − 361,784	381,831
10.	9,432,106 − 521,817	8,910,289
11.	56,418 − 27,243	29,175
12.	762,415 − 215,423	546,992
13.	924,065 − 18,472	905,593
14.	5,000,462 − 326,248	4,674,214
15.	425,147 − 216,083	209,064
16.	7,624,508 − 815,142	6,809,366
17.	3,201,426 − 614,819	2,586,607
18.	5,421,879 − 210,342	5,211,537
19.	8,641,526 − 88,249	8,553,277
20.	46,517 − 29,284	17,233
21.	9,246,132 − 652,824	8,593,308
22.	812,456 − 19,582	792,874
23.	38,614 − 22,927	15,687
24.	462,517 − 324,618	137,899
25.	3,214,684 − 815,742	2,398,942
26.	6,421,007 − 614,143	5,806,864
27.	5,142,542 − 3,164,231	1,978,311
28.	8,401,624 − 3,216,418	5,185,206
29.	7,642,145 − 86,589	7,555,556
30.	89,654 − 77,497	12,157
31.	9,614,506 − 718,247	8,896,259
32.	5,432,187 − 4,286,324	1,145,863
33.	52,146,513 − 27,423,241	24,723,272
34.	32,146,892 − 4,382,971	27,763,921
35.	8,324,695 − 683,742	7,640,953
36.	92,436,149 − 825,426	91,610,723
37.	57,243,615 − 9,621,242	47,622,373
38.	25,408 − 12,629	12,779
39.	66,421,547 − 8,342,125	58,079,422
40.	7,615,243 − 3,246,318	4,368,925
41.	3,892,146 − 1,941,183	1,950,963

Practice! Practice! Practice!

Page 7

Subtraction

Skill: Subtraction of Six-, Seven- and Eight-Digit Numbers

Name ______________________

Total Problems	34
Problems Correct	______

No.	Problem	Answer
1.	305,628 − 187,849	117,779
2.	743,629 − 281,783	461,846
3.	640,321 − 192,846	447,475
4.	843,216 − 372,642	470,574
5.	462,317 − 281,548	180,769
6.	964,374 − 172,846	791,528
7.	465,389 − 127,694	337,695
8.	864,397 − 671,648	192,749
9.	843,108 − 381,423	461,685
10.	462,009 − 185,236	276,773
11.	565,432 − 279,247	286,185
12.	646,374 − 493,189	153,185
13.	762,348 − 531,459	230,889
14.	926,348 − 345,653	580,695
15.	463,899 − 285,946	177,953
16.	964,302 − 481,428	482,874
17.	762,498 − 478,824	283,674
18.	784,537 − 396,846	387,691
19.	463,402 − 234,761	228,641
20.	648,514 − 529,348	119,166
21.	385,387 − 191,298	194,089
22.	524,318 − 341,846	182,472
23.	829,416 − 435,824	393,592
24.	475,234 − 387,613	87,621
25.	629,432 − 436,829	192,603
26.	928,316 − 731,264	197,052
27.	8,462,103 − 741,316	7,720,787
28.	5,432,148 − 3,651,829	1,780,319
29.	7,431,645 − 2,640,859	4,790,786
30.	3,218,643 − 809,751	2,408,892
31.	6,257,431 − 4,319,614	1,937,817
32.	5,642,918 − 1,853,486	3,789,432
33.	78,430,615 − 9,511,283	68,919,332
34.	96,431,265 − 48,514,391	47,916,874

Practice takes you to the top!

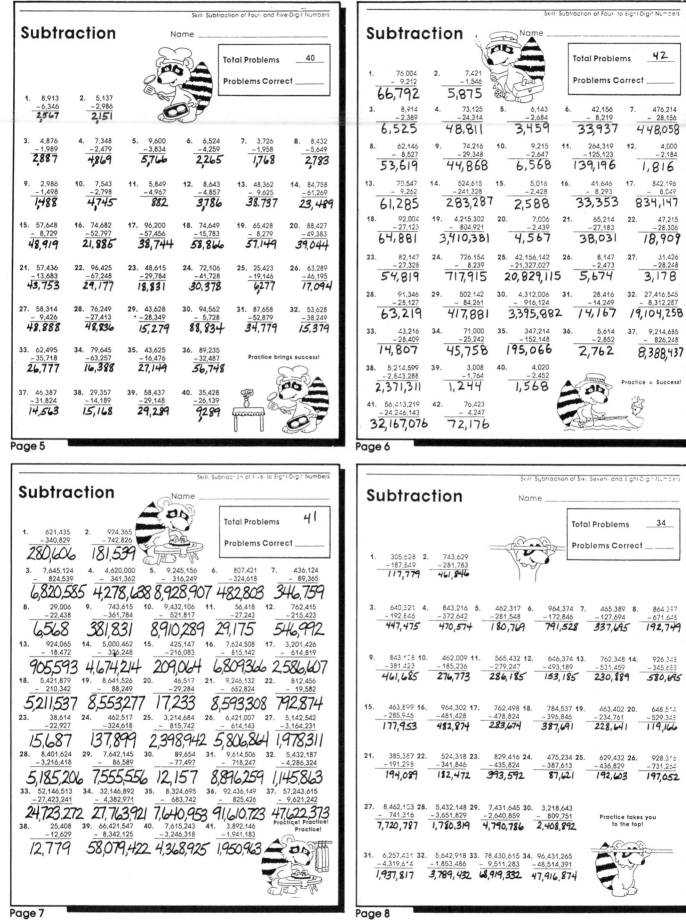

Page 8

Answer Key

Multiplication

Skill: Multiplying by One-Digit Numbers

Name ____________

Total Problems 40

Problems Correct ______

No.	Number	Multiplier	Answer
1.	649	×8	5,192
2.	858	×7	6,006
3.	7,642	×5	38,210
4.	8,219	×3	24,657
5.	5,238	×6	31,428
6.	4,623	×9	41,607
7.	8,249	×4	32,996
8.	6,518	×7	45,626
9.	8,943	×9	80,487
10.	3,268	×5	16,340
11.	4,637	×8	37,096
12.	8,924	×6	53,544
13.	5,387	×4	21,548
14.	8,264	×9	74,376
15.	4,875	×7	34,125
16.	5,689	×8	45,512
17.	9,243	×4	36,972
18.	7,643	×9	68,787
19.	8,540	×6	51,240
20.	3,726	×5	18,630
21.	83,243	×6	499,458
22.	74,254	×7	519,778
23.	62,435	×9	561,915
24.	95,201	×5	476,005
25.	73,643	×8	589,144
26.	51,476	×4	205,904
27.	73,629	×5	368,145
28.	87,642	×7	613,494
29.	25,624	×4	102,496
30.	63,928	×8	511,424
31.	98,215	×6	589,290
32.	41,826	×9	376,434
33.	53,214	×8	425,712
34.	83,265	×4	333,060
35.	65,429	×5	327,145
36.	79,267	×3	237,801
37.	46,254	×7	323,778
38.	91,242	×8	729,936
39.	73,263	×6	439,578
40.	35,584	×2	71,168

Anything's possible with practice!

Page 9

Multiplication

Skill: Multiplying by Two-Digit Numbers

Name ____________

Show your work on another sheet. Write your answers here.

Total Problems 40

Problems Correct ______

No.	Number	Multiplier	Answer
1.	467	×35	16,345
2.	538	×47	25,286
3.	393	×82	32,226
4.	724	×56	40,544
5.	821	×75	61,575
6.	463	×43	19,909
7.	522	×68	35,496
8.	326	×92	29,992
9.	735	×45	33,075
10.	268	×39	10,452
11.	534	×76	40,584
12.	232	×98	22,736
13.	845	×63	53,235
14.	928	×81	75,168
15.	625	×33	20,625
16.	856	×42	35,952
17.	932	×58	54,056
18.	734	×54	39,636
19.	487	×72	35,064
20.	289	×79	22,831
21.	824	×75	61,800
22.	936	×47	43,992
23.	365	×28	10,220
24.	573	×65	37,245
25.	792	×34	26,928
26.	476	×83	39,508
27.	468	×57	26,676
28.	323	×92	29,716
29.	645	×73	47,085
30.	765	×48	36,720
31.	859	×63	54,117
32.	368	×87	32,016
33.	428	×61	26,108
34.	537	×44	23,628
35.	804	×87	69,948
36.	348	×29	10,092
37.	437	×73	31,901
38.	725	×52	37,700
39.	639	×38	24,282
40.	457	×86	39,302

Practice makes perfect!

Page 10

Multiplication

Skill: Multiplying by One- and Two-Digit Numbers

Name ____________

Show your work on another sheet. Write your answers here.

Total Problems 48

Problems Correct ______

No.	Number	Multiplier	Answer
1.	6,142	×3	18,426
2.	4,921	×5	24,605
3.	3,168	×8	25,344
4.	2,482	×9	22,338
5.	8,142	×3	24,426
6.	4,628	×7	32,396
7.	9,874	×2	19,748
8.	7,425	×6	44,550
9.	5,487	×4	21,948
10.	6,849	×7	47,943
11.	9,240	×8	73,920
12.	7,645	×4	30,580
13.	4,208	×9	37,872
14.	8,004	×2	16,008
15.	43,619	×6	261,714
16.	54,613	×4	218,452
17.	86,423	×9	777,807
18.	56,984	×7	398,888
19.	82,412	×3	247,236
20.	46,304	×8	370,432
21.	82,425	×5	412,125
22.	51,403	×9	462,627
23.	413,642	×3	1,240,926
24.	549,627	×8	4,397,016
25.	840,205	×7	5,881,435
26.	1,364	×42	57,288
27.	2,423	×57	138,111
28.	3,920	×84	329,280
29.	5,549	×30	166,470
30.	6,847	×27	184,869
31.	2,925	×56	163,800
32.	2,427	×93	225,711
33.	3,240	×64	207,360
34.	5,149	×80	411,920
35.	6,847	×92	629,924
36.	5,148	×24	123,552
37.	5,492	×76	417,392
38.	6,284	×33	207,372
39.	62,003	×34	2,108,102
40.	82,413	×47	3,873,411
41.	81,404	×76	6,186,704
42.	38,243	×91	3,480,113
43.	54,128	×24	1,299,072
44.	24,136	×58	1,399,888
45.	76,132	×49	3,730,468
46.	59,149	×26	1,537,874
47.	62,427	×78	4,869,306
48.	51,264	×32	1,640,448

Practice hard. You'll win.

Page 11

Multiplication

Skill: Multiplying by Three-Digit Numbers

Name ____________

Show your work on another sheet. Write your answers here.

Total Problems 40

Problems Correct ______

No.	Number	Multiplier	Answer
1.	325	×614	199,550
2.	463	×527	244,001
3.	265	×921	244,065
4.	429	×304	130,416
5.	724	×630	456,120
6.	512	×825	422,400
7.	189	×432	81,648
8.	382	×265	101,230
9.	361	×543	196,023
10.	465	×734	341,310
11.	412	×398	163,976
12.	252	×726	182,952
13.	736	×413	303,968
14.	425	×817	347,225
15.	832	×625	520,000
16.	923	×542	500,266
17.	234	×489	114,426
18.	564	×820	462,480
19.	713	×256	182,528
20.	468	×375	175,500
21.	568	×943	535,624
22.	726	×245	177,870
23.	364	×545	198,380
24.	463	×982	454,666
25.	523	×764	399,572
26.	624	×846	527,904
27.	821	×265	217,565
28.	486	×631	306,666
29.	824	×532	438,368
30.	842	×701	590,242
31.	523	×438	229,074
32.	265	×835	221,275
33.	547	×325	177,775
34.	406	×982	398,692
35.	397	×768	304,896
36.	725	×424	307,400
37.	481	×632	303,992
38.	254	×825	209,550
39.	932	×364	339,248
40.	589	×746	439,394

With practice, you can do it!

Page 12

Answer Key

Page 13

Skill: Multiplying by Three-Digit Numbers

Multiplication

Name

Show your work on another sheet. Write your answers here.

Total Problems 48

Problems Correct

No.	Problem	Answer
1.	628 × 403	253,084
2.	531 × 724	384,444
3.	248 × 265	65,720
4.	304 × 529	160,816
5.	246 × 824	202,704
6.	146 × 532	77,672
7.	308 × 236	72,688
8.	813 × 432	351,216
9.	385 × 274	105,490
10.	284 × 621	176,364
11.	486 × 513	249,318
12.	314 × 249	78,186
13.	485 × 613	297,305
14.	461 × 920	424,120
15.	212 × 685	145,220
16.	329 × 400	131,600
17.	215 × 548	117,820
18.	243 × 824	200,232
19.	149 × 632	94,168
20.	475 × 362	171,950
21.	140 × 523	73,220
22.	147 × 250	36,750
23.	827 × 342	282,834
24.	389 × 921	358,269
25.	142 × 265	37,630
26.	527 × 462	243,474
27.	3,615 × 204	737,460
28.	4,014 × 325	1,304,550
29.	3,614 × 827	2,988,778
30.	1,464 × 532	778,848
31.	5,621 × 764	4,294,444
32.	2,619 × 483	1,264,977
33.	5,762 × 728	4,194,736
34.	3,147 × 482	1,516,854
35.	2,418 × 625	1,511,250
36.	8,145 × 327	2,663,415
37.	5,134 × 842	4,322,828
38.	8,040 × 532	4,277,280
39.	3,015 × 604	1,821,060
40.	3,802 × 824	3,132,848
41.	5,124 × 324	1,660,176
42.	7,241 × 530	3,837,730
43.	6,030 × 724	4,365,720
44.	2,043 × 821	1,677,303
45.	5,341 × 231	1,233,771
46.	7,624 × 342	2,607,408
47.	3,146 × 620	1,950,520
48.	4,252 × 482	2,049,464

Success ahoy! Just practice!

Page 14

Skill: Multiplying by Four-Digit Numbers

Multiplication

Name

Show your work on another sheet. Write your answers here.

Total Problems 48

Problems Correct

No.	Problem	Answer
1.	5,406 × 2,142	11,579,652
2.	2,482 × 4,321	10,724,722
3.	2,042 × 9,123	18,629,166
4.	2,489 × 4,300	10,702,700
5.	4,364 × 5,127	22,374,228
6.	1,481 × 6,824	10,106,344
7.	1,348 × 3,421	4,611,508
8.	3,901 × 4,612	17,991,412
9.	3,842 × 3,615	13,888,830
10.	3,246 × 1,482	4,810,572
11.	1,498 × 8,003	11,988,494
12.	2,514 × 3,486	8,763,804
13.	3,628 × 2,749	9,973,372
14.	4,215 × 1,321	5,568,015
15.	1,347 × 5,621	7,571,487
16.	1,541 × 2,824	4,351,784
17.	3,045 × 9,120	27,770,400
18.	1,423 × 6,215	8,843,945
19.	2,653 × 5,214	13,832,742
20.	1,434 × 8,172	11,718,648
21.	1,545 × 8,432	13,027,440
22.	9,242 × 6,132	56,671,944
23.	1,356 × 3,642	4,938,552
24.	2,405 × 9,163	22,037,015
25.	2,348 × 1,405	3,298,940
26.	1,450 × 3,642	5,280,900
27.	1,456 × 7,214	10,503,584
28.	3,014 × 6,215	18,732,010
29.	8,042 × 3,217	25,871,114
30.	3,289 × 5,116	16,826,524
31.	8,649 × 5,472	47,327,328
32.	5,892 × 3,246	19,125,432
33.	3,264 × 7,132	23,278,848
34.	1,327 × 4,263	5,657,001
35.	1,283 × 6,245	8,012,335
36.	3,415 × 1,200	4,098,000
37.	1,523 × 3,649	5,557,427
38.	1,629 × 4,725	7,697,025
39.	5,412 × 2,743	14,845,116
40.	2,341 × 8,649	20,247,309
41.	1,006 × 3,215	3,234,290
42.	3,012 × 1,264	3,807,168
43.	1,262 × 5,215	6,581,330
44.	1,423 × 4,201	5,978,023
45.	2,512 × 2,642	6,636,704
46.	8,132 × 3,614	29,389,048
47.	1,482 × 9,125	13,523,250
48.	8,541 × 3,264	27,877,824

Anything's possible with practice!

Page 15

Skill: Multiplication Patterns

Multiplication

Name

Show your work on another sheet. Write your answers here.

Total Problems 50

Problems Correct

1. 3 × (2 × 2) = 12
2. 4 × (1 × 6) = 24
3. 7 × (3 × 2) = 42
4. (2 × 2) × 6 = 24
5. (6 × 2) × 4 = 48
6. (4 × 2) × 3 = 24
7. 5 × (2 × 3) = 30
8. 9 × (2 × 3) = 54
9. 7 × (2 × 4) = 56
10. (3 × 2) × 4 = 24
11. 3 × (3 × 2) = 18
12. 2 × (4 × 3) = 24
13. 5 × (4 + 2) = 30
14. (8 × 1) × 5 = 40
15. 3 × (4 + 4) = 24
16. 9 × (6 × 2) = 108
17. (3 × 2) + (4 × 2) = 14
18. 8 × (3 + 1) = 32
19. (4 × 2) + (6 × 3) = 26
20. (7 × 1) × 6 = 42
21. (5 + 5) × 3 = 30
22. 6 × (3 × 3) = 54
23. (5 × 5) + 8 = 33
24. (2 × 3) × 8 = 48
25. (4 × 2) + (3 × 4) = 20
26. (3 × 3) × 6 = 54
27. (3 + 4) × (2 + 5) = 49
28. (6 × 2) × 5 = 60
29. (6 × 1) × (2 × 3) = 36
30. (9 × 1) × 7 = 63
31. (3 × 2) × 8 = 48
32. (5 + 3) × 8 = 64
33. (4 × 3) × 4 = 48
34. (3 × 2) × 5 = 30
35. (3 × 4) + 9 = 21
36. 3 × (5 × 2) = 30
37. 5 × (3 × 3) = 45
38. (3 × 3) + (4 × 2) = 17
39. 6 × (3 × 4) = 72
40. 7 × (3 + 5) = 56
41. (6 + 2) × (2 + 2) = 32
42. (7 × 3) + 6 = 27
43. 8 + (9 × 12) = 116
44. 6 × (6 × 2) = 72
45. (3 × 8) + (4 × 9) = 60
46. 9 × (3 × 4) = 108
47. 5 × (2 × 5) = 50
48. (6 × 3) + 8 = 26
49. (4 + 5) × (2 × 4) = 72
50. (7 × 6) + (5 × 12) = 102

With practice, you can do it!

Page 16

Skill: One-Digit Divisors

Division

Name

Show your work on another sheet. Write your answers here.

Total Problems 40

Problems Correct

No.	Problem	Answer
1.	8) 3,216	402
2.	4) 1,272	318
3.	7) 1,502	214 R4
4.	3) 296	98 R2
5.	6) 4,811	801 R5
6.	9) 788	87 R5
7.	5) 554	110 R4
8.	8) 1,143	142 R7
9.	4) 362	90 R2
10.	3) 1,553	517 R2
11.	6) 5,554	925 R4
12.	7) 487	69 R4
13.	2) 1,694	847
14.	4) 1,550	387 R2
15.	9) 7,155	795
16.	5) 2,093	418 R3
17.	7) 4,778	682 R4
18.	3) 316	105 R1
19.	6) 483	80 R3
20.	4) 515	128 R3
21.	5) 2,013	402 R3
22.	8) 1,886	235 R6
23.	9) 2,591	287 R8
24.	7) 3,330	475 R5
25.	2) 219	109 R1
26.	3) 632	210 R2
27.	5) 1,835	367
28.	8) 567	70 R7
29.	6) 6,150	1025
30.	4) 1,278	319 R2
31.	5) 4,250	850
32.	2) 819	409 R1
33.	9) 11,232	1,248
34.	7) 22,734	3,247 R5
35.	8) 11,269	1,408 R5
36.	3) 8,693	2,897 R2
37.	4) 20,868	5,217
38.	6) 24,645	4,107 R3
39.	9) 10,889	1,209 R8
40.	8) 9,198	1,149 R6

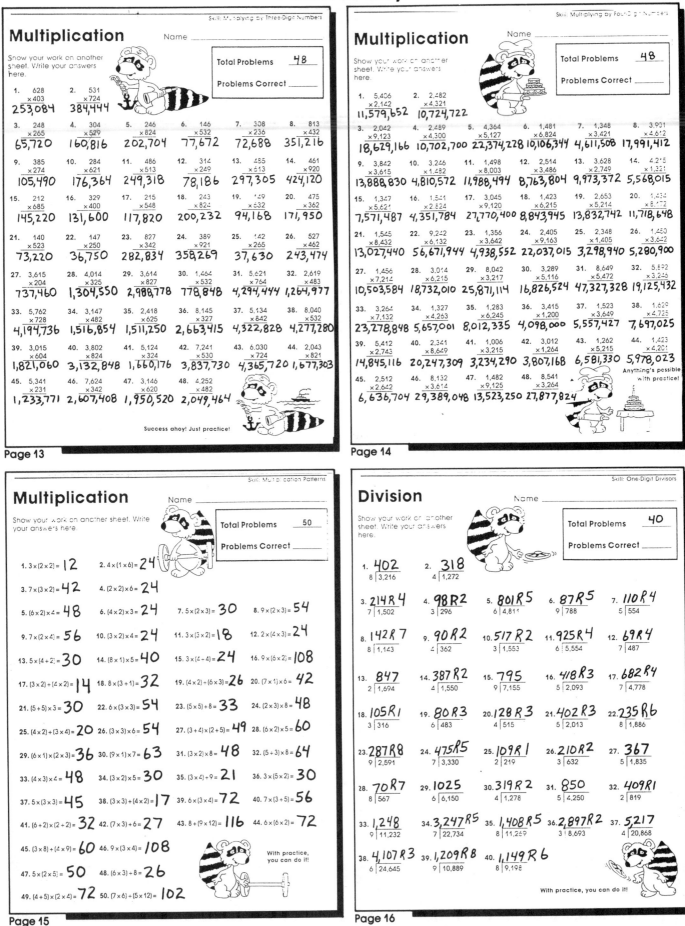

With practice, you can do it!

Answer Key

Division

Skill: Division With Two-Digit Divisors and One-Digit Quotients

Name ____________________

Show your work on another sheet. Write your answers here.

Total Problems 43

Problems Correct ______

No.	Problem	Answer
1.	27)216	8
2.	48)432	9
3.	35)245	7
4.	81)729	9
5.	32)192	6
6.	21)168	8
7.	84)588	7
8.	74)444	6
9.	65)520	8
10.	25)225	9
11.	92)644	7
12.	75)450	6
13.	24)192	8
14.	58)464	8
15.	42)252	6
16.	65)455	7
17.	86)278	3R20
18.	29)128	4R12
19.	36)302	8R14
20.	43)265	6R7
21.	82)427	5R17
22.	95)596	6R26
23.	61)594	9R45
24.	49)126	2R28
25.	82)753	9R15
26.	91)366	4R2
27.	56)420	7R28
28.	43)270	6R12
29.	68)662	9R50
30.	51)323	6R17
31.	37)310	8R14
32.	88)547	6R19
33.	48)359	7R23
34.	37)228	6R6
35.	67)362	5R27
36.	92)742	8R6
37.	73)687	9R30
38.	89)541	6R7
39.	25)188	7R13
40.	46)239	5R9
41.	73)646	8R62
42.	38)292	7R26
43.	63)552	8R48

Practice makes perfect!

Page 17

Division

Skill: Division With Two-Digit Quotients

Name ____________________

Show your work on another sheet. Write your answers here.

Total Problems 45

Problems Correct ______

No.	Problem	Answer
1.	14)326	23R4
2.	34)888	26R4
3.	21)298	14R4
4.	46)690	15
5.	31)843	27R6
6.	17)578	34
7.	54)918	17
8.	62)1,143	18R27
9.	20)706	35R6
10.	42)675	16R3
11.	23)653	28R9
12.	81)2,195	27R8
13.	71)3,550	50
14.	24)872	36R8
15.	19)825	43R8
16.	32)1,997	62R13
17.	44)1,678	38R6
18.	38)2,482	65R12
19.	15)398	26R8
20.	82)2,952	36
21.	11)996	90R6
22.	27)432	16
23.	64)1,988	31R4
24.	45)1,292	28R32
25.	33)462	14
26.	22)933	42R9
27.	30)2,467	82R7
28.	43)989	23
29.	37)976	26R14
30.	28)1,576	56R8
31.	84)2,304	27R36
32.	16)304	19
33.	92)4,356	47R32
34.	40)1,573	39R13
35.	75)3,756	50R6
36.	13)1,101	84R9
37.	41)2,583	63
38.	61)1,731	28R23
39.	73)1,799	24R47
40.	80)1,360	17
41.	32)1,946	60R26
42.	20)1,047	52R7
43.	18)1,248	69R6
44.	26)1,932	74R8
45.	35)634	18R4

Page 18

Division

Skill: Division With Two-Digit Quotients

Name ____________________

Show your work on another sheet. Write your answers here.

Total Problems 43

Problems Correct ______

No.	Problem	Answer
1.	35)2,170	62
2.	42)4,032	96
3.	64)5,443	85R3
4.	81)5,200	64R16
5.	73)1,254	17R13
6.	94)2,553	27R15
7.	62)4,426	71R24
8.	96)4,044	42R12
9.	46)3,889	84R25
10.	31)1,705	55
11.	75)3,635	48R35
12.	48)3,861	80R21
13.	86)2,336	27R14
14.	37)3,451	93R10
15.	28)1,834	65R14
16.	97)7,979	82R25
17.	63)2,990	47R29
18.	74)4,993	67R35
19.	68)3,234	47R38
20.	96)7,358	76R62
21.	45)3,702	82R12
22.	26)2,494	95R24
23.	38)2,636	69R14
24.	49)3,514	71R35
25.	74)4,476	60R36
26.	96)5,585	58R17
27.	82)6,074	74R6
28.	43)3,637	84R25
29.	87)5,509	63R28
30.	56)4,402	78R34
31.	27)2,307	85R12
32.	47)3,543	75R18
33.	95)7,921	83R36
34.	28)2,645	94R13
35.	78)3,886	49R64
36.	46)3,246	70R26
37.	83)3,908	47R7
38.	92)6,288	68R32
39.	27)1,875	69R12
40.	48)3,673	76R25
41.	37)3,581	96R29
42.	62)5,371	86R39
43.	88)5,045	57R29

With practice, you can do it!

Page 19

Division

Skill: Division With Two-Digit Quotients

Name ____________________

Show your work on another sheet. Write your answers here.

Total Problems 43

Problems Correct ______

No.	Problem	Answer
1.	14)1,170	83R8
2.	82)5,539	67R45
3.	43)3,905	90R35
4.	65)1,899	29R14
5.	27)1,450	53R19
6.	32)3,018	94R10
7.	54)3,846	71R12
8.	75)3,699	49R24
9.	48)3,972	82R36
10.	21)1,611	76R15
11.	25)1,521	60R21
12.	48)4,015	83R31
13.	39)3,574	91R25
14.	86)6,169	71R63
15.	94)2,174	23R12
16.	75)5,876	78R26
17.	55)4,909	89R14
18.	71)3,592	50R42
19.	48)3,243	67R27
20.	62)5,236	84R28
21.	39)2,390	61R11
22.	21)1,966	93R13
23.	59)4,523	76R39
24.	28)1,926	68R22
25.	47)2,796	59R23
26.	87)8,147	93R56
27.	65)4,506	69R21
28.	43)3,644	84R32
29.	72)6,523	90R43
30.	51)3,236	63R23
31.	96)4,597	47R85
32.	58)4,085	70R25
33.	63)5,178	82R12
34.	49)4,583	93R26
35.	83)3,962	47R61
36.	74)5,142	69R36
37.	29)2,334	80R14
38.	59)4,456	75R31
39.	23)1,830	79R13
40.	95)8,197	86R27
41.	72)6,023	83R47
42.	46)3,287	71R21
43.	28)2,646	94R14

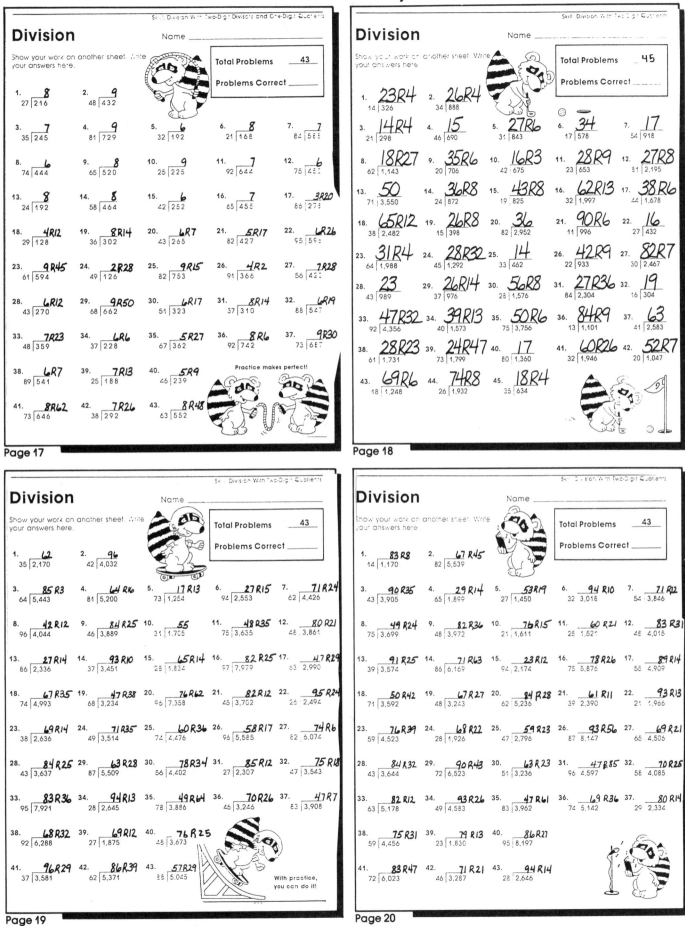

Page 20

Answer Key

Division

Name ____________________

Show your work on another sheet. Write your answers here.

Total Problems 40

Problems Correct ______

No.	Divisor	Dividend	Answer
1.	12	7,620	635
2.	23	9,476	412
3.	14	5,166	369
4.	18	8,802	489
5.	16	8,000	500
6.	19	7,885	415
7.	21	4,914	234
8.	25	7,875	315
9.	32	7,520	235
10.	15	9,375	625
11.	11	8,679	789
12.	22	6,732	306
13.	35	9,275	265
14.	17	7,854	462
15.	23	6,647	289
16.	42	6,216	148
17.	65	6,630	102
18.	24	7,800	325
19.	18	7,164	398
20.	13	8,554	658
21.	16	7,648	478
22.	25	8,525	341
23.	13	7,657	589
24.	40	9,400	235
25.	31	8,494	274
26.	17	6,273	369
27.	20	9,360	468
28.	52	7,407	142 R23
29.	86	8,900	103 R42
30.	14	7,371	526 R7
31.	33	8,889	269 R12
32.	24	8,366	348 R14
33.	15	7,298	486 R8
34.	17	8,030	472 R6
35.	89	9,282	104 R26
36.	94	9,494	101
37.	27	6,954	257 R15
38.	74	8,324	112 R36
39.	32	9,628	300 R28
40.	22	7,916	359 R18

Page 21

Division

Name ____________________

Show your work on another sheet. Write your answers here.

Total Problems 43

Problems Correct ______

No.	Divisor	Dividend	Answer
1.	14	7,415	529 R9
2.	22	6,750	306 R18
3.	16	7,672	479 R8
4.	19	5,640	296 R16
5.	51	7,749	151 R48
6.	32	8,558	267 R14
7.	12	7,543	628 R7
8.	15	5,856	390 R6
9.	24	8,757	364 R21
10.	31	7,991	257 R24
11.	23	8,314	361 R11
12.	13	4,536	348 R12
13.	17	4,872	286 R10
14.	25	9,240	369 R15
15.	33	7,085	214 R23
16.	20	9,657	482 R17
17.	14	7,244	517 R6
18.	48	6,960	145
19.	27	8,617	319 R4
20.	13	8,133	625 R8
21.	29	8,340	287 R17
22.	32	8,275	258 R19
23.	16	7,577	473 R9
24.	21	8,316	396
25.	18	5,400	300
26.	34	4,279	125 R29
27.	52	5,559	106 R47
28.	13	3,529	271 R6
29.	27	7,227	267 R18
30.	36	5,391	149 R27
31.	40	5,112	127 R32
32.	16	7,655	478 R7
33.	82	8,276	100 R76
34.	50	7,628	152 R28
35.	63	8,568	136
36.	91	9,305	102 R23
37.	24	6,225	258 R13
38.	16	7,719	482 R7
39.	12	9,471	789 R3
40.	86	8,930	103 R72
41.	53	5,972	112 R36
42.	47	8,249	175 R24
43.	28	4,282	152 R26

With practice, you can do it!

Page 22

Division

Name ____________________

Show your work on another sheet. Write your answers here.

Total Problems 44

Problems Correct ______

No.	Divisor	Dividend	Answer
1.	14	3,010	215
2.	25	8,130	325 R5
3.	32	5,696	178
4.	41	15,100	368 R12
5.	20	2,900	145
6.	53	5,565	105
7.	27	6,943	257 R4
8.	71	9,111	128 R23
9.	82	11,361	138 R45
10.	43	13,510	314 R8
11.	23	9,568	416
12.	62	14,942	241
13.	19	6,620	348 R8
14.	36	11,346	315 R6
15.	52	11,336	218
16.	21	7,763	369 R14
17.	73	7,379	101 R6
18.	40	10,333	258 R13
19.	84	12,542	149 R26
20.	15	9,384	625 R9
21.	34	15,389	452 R21
22.	45	8,433	187 R18
23.	72	7,812	108 R36
24.	22	16,031	728 R15
25.	42	10,812	257 R18
26.	64	15,552	243
27.	54	7,304	135 R14
28.	47	24,839	528 R23
29.	33	20,394	618
30.	86	12,687	147 R45
31.	50	15,700	314
32.	17	11,875	698 R9
33.	30	3,614	120 R14
34.	16	14,743	921 R7
35.	24	5,160	215
36.	74	11,715	158 R23
37.	46	7,291	158 R23
38.	91	9,671	106 R25
39.	78	24,851	318 R47
40.	92	12,052	131
41.	35	9,954	284 R14
42.	84	35,148	418 R36
43.	44	10,220	232 R12
44.	26	6,370	245

Practice makes perfect!

Page 23

Division

Name ____________________

Show your work on another sheet. Write your answers here.

Total Problems 33

Problems Correct ______

No.	Divisor	Dividend	Answer
1.	24	16,440	685
2.	52	50,128	964
3.	36	31,536	876
4.	48	44,496	927
5.	72	53,856	748
6.	58	39,672	684
7.	64	58,112	908
8.	92	72,354	786 R42
9.	43	38,478	894 R36
10.	21	15,724	748 R16
11.	86	82,599	960 R39
12.	76	63,051	829 R47
13.	48	45,495	947 R39
14.	97	84,380	869 R87
15.	54	31,698	587
16.	31	28,978	934 R24
17.	27	24,314	900 R14
18.	42	35,602	847 R28
19.	39	24,960	640
20.	84	81,051	964 R75
21.	57	49,275	864 R27
22.	95	73,093	769 R38
23.	17	15,436	908
24.	70	58,425	834 R45
25.	53	36,882	695 R47
26.	23	21,798	947 R17
27.	59	38,291	649
28.	37	22,484	607 R25
29.	81	54,729	675 R54
30.	93	69,313	745 R28
31.	73	69,934	958
32.	29	11,223	387
33.	50	33,999	679 R49

Practice and anything's possible!

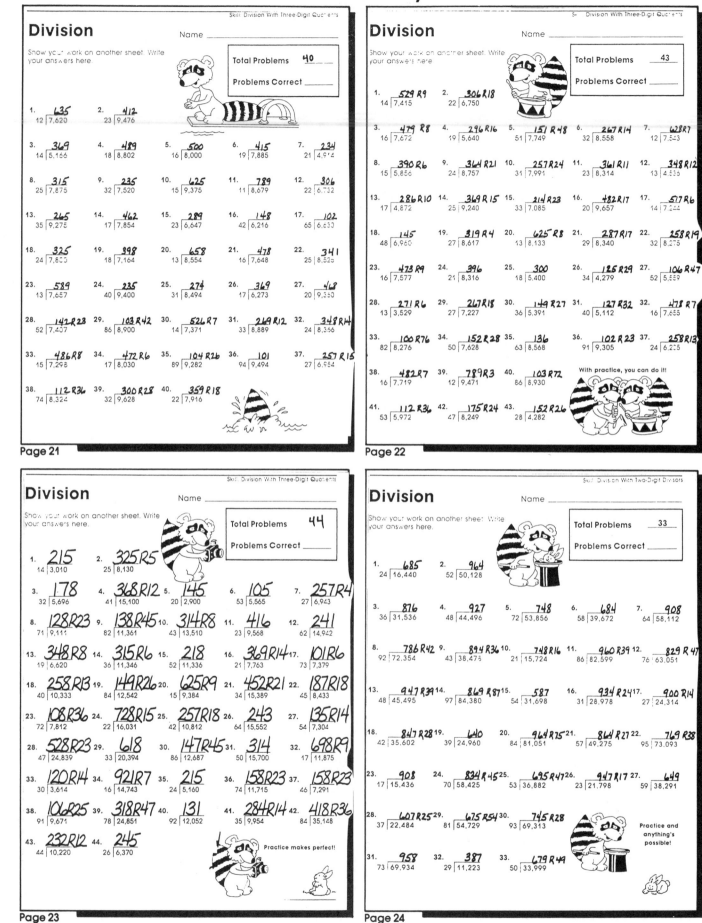

Page 24

Answer Key

Skill: Two-Digit Divisors

Division

Name ____________

Show your work on another sheet. Write your answers here.

Total Problems 45

Problems Correct ______

No.	Problem	Answer
1.	21 ⟌ 852	40R12
2.	14 ⟌ 784	56
3.	12 ⟌ 1,016	84R8
4.	31 ⟌ 730	23R17
5.	40 ⟌ 386	9R26
6.	74 ⟌ 2,085	28R13
7.	25 ⟌ 1,950	78
8.	16 ⟌ 569	35R9
9.	26 ⟌ 1,222	47
10.	78 ⟌ 1,652	21R14
11.	51 ⟌ 1,339	26R13
12.	32 ⟌ 1,616	50R16
13.	93 ⟌ 2,567	27R56
14.	18 ⟌ 291	16R3
15.	22 ⟌ 897	40R17
16.	43 ⟌ 669	15R24
17.	53 ⟌ 1,500	28R16
18.	50 ⟌ 462	9R12
19.	41 ⟌ 1,163	28R15
20.	36 ⟌ 658	18R10
21.	20 ⟌ 1,054	52R14
22.	97 ⟌ 4,658	48R2
23.	66 ⟌ 663	10R3
24.	62 ⟌ 3,732	60R12
25.	42 ⟌ 466	11R4
26.	54 ⟌ 3,888	72
27.	35 ⟌ 551	15R26
28.	95 ⟌ 783	8R23
29.	23 ⟌ 328	14R6
30.	77 ⟌ 6,935	90R5
31.	44 ⟌ 1,240	28R8
32.	68 ⟌ 2,085	30R45
33.	81 ⟌ 8,505	105
34.	61 ⟌ 13,063	214R9
35.	39 ⟌ 4,615	118R13
36.	52 ⟌ 16,640	320
37.	47 ⟌ 8,402	178R36
38.	10 ⟌ 8,428	842R8
39.	45 ⟌ 9,872	219R17
40.	27 ⟌ 4,039	149R16
41.	82 ⟌ 8,739	106R47
42.	33 ⟌ 6,849	207R18
43.	13 ⟌ 6,851	527
44.	24 ⟌ 19,812	825R12
45.	34 ⟌ 21,243	624R27

Practice! Practice! Practice!

Page 25

Skill: Three-Digit Divisors

Division

Name ____________

Show your work on another sheet. Write your answers here.

Total Problems 45

Problems Correct ______

No.	Problem	Answer
1.	143 ⟌ 1,287	9
2.	623 ⟌ 12,460	20
3.	431 ⟌ 3,448	8
4.	264 ⟌ 2,376	9
5.	172 ⟌ 2,064	12
6.	532 ⟌ 3,747	7R23
7.	803 ⟌ 12,090	15R45
8.	515 ⟌ 3,138	6R48
9.	634 ⟌ 17,443	27R325
10.	572 ⟌ 8,033	14R25
11.	145 ⟌ 5,539	38R29
12.	924 ⟌ 7,448	8R56
13.	232 ⟌ 4,908	21R36
14.	297 ⟌ 3,888	13R27
15.	128 ⟌ 2,304	18
16.	400 ⟌ 9,249	23R49
17.	103 ⟌ 2,101	20R41
18.	745 ⟌ 12,693	17R28
19.	312 ⟌ 3,149	10R29
20.	692 ⟌ 5,578	8R42
21.	154 ⟌ 2,950	19R24
22.	265 ⟌ 3,236	12R56
23.	857 ⟌ 12,027	14R29
24.	657 ⟌ 15,111	23
25.	746 ⟌ 21,013	28R125
26.	114 ⟌ 4,123	36R19
27.	256 ⟌ 13,824	54
28.	789 ⟌ 32,388	41R39
29.	364 ⟌ 17,472	48
30.	205 ⟌ 12,963	63R48
31.	108 ⟌ 4,052	37R56
32.	693 ⟌ 29,106	42
33.	624 ⟌ 5,361	8R369
34.	126 ⟌ 7,850	62R38
35.	642 ⟌ 17,976	28
36.	283 ⟌ 7,766	27R125
37.	456 ⟌ 10,488	23
38.	982 ⟌ 34,102	34R714
39.	537 ⟌ 26,886	50R36
40.	134 ⟌ 8,308	62
41.	224 ⟌ 8,551	38R39
42.	238 ⟌ 19,540	82R24
43.	842 ⟌ 62,308	74
44.	427 ⟌ 38,430	90
45.	216 ⟌ 67,824	314

Page 26

Skill: Addition of Decimals

Decimals

Name ____________

Total Problems 40

Problems Correct ______

No.	Problem	Answer
1.	3.85 + 2.46	6.31
2.	6.08 + 9.23	15.31
3.	39.8 + 56.7	96.5
4.	4.32 + 0.89	5.21
5.	98.6 + 43.5	142.1
6.	0.68 + 3.47	4.15
7.	78.6 + 83.9	162.5
8.	43.7 + 98.2	141.9
9.	42.37 + 34.85	77.22
10.	92.65 + 82.83	175.48
11.	27.36 + 90.24	117.6
12.	47.32 + 71.83	119.15
13.	56.34 + 92.43	148.77
14.	9.326 + 3.417	12.743
15.	643.2 + 481.9	1125.1
16.	37.48 + 42.32	79.8
17.	964.3 + 382.4	1346.7
18.	426.3 + 442.3	868.6
19.	87.43 + 42.74	130.17
20.	7.306 + 4.037	11.343
21.	9.234 + 2.641	11.875
21.	49.83 + 52.57	102.4
23.	56.27 + 83.53	139.8
24.	362.5 + 243.9	606.4
25.	76.38 + 35.24	111.62
26.	62.85 + 43.46	106.31
27.	482.51 + 801.03	1283.54
28.	36.059 + 42.482	78.541
29.	924.38 + 643.92	1568.3
30.	623.42 + 85.36	708.78
31.	83.04 + 9.28	92.32
32.	0.38 + 9.43	9.81
33.	564.32 + 9.08	573.4
34.	68.42 + 924.39	992.81
35.	836.40 + 93.84	930.24
36.	4.65 + 859.23	863.88
37.	364.94 + 725.38	1090.32
38.	629.38 + 842.45	1471.83
39.	89.006 + 92.848	181.854
40.	4.6258 + 5.2923	9.9181

Practice hard. You'll win.

Page 27

Skill: Addition of Decimals

Decimals

Name ____________

Total Problems 42

Problems Correct ______

No.	Problem	Answer
1.	26.9 + 427.22	454.12
2.	324.05 + 48.94	372.99
3.	82.495 + 49.28	131.775
4.	3,245.6 + 89.5	3,335.1
5.	4.804 + 3.29	8.094
6.	9.62 + 39.407	49.027
7.	84.005 + 746.92	830.925
8.	76.09 + 384.87	460.96
9.	5.72 + 87.479	93.199
10.	89.8 + 786.92	876.72
11.	346.08 + 79.96	426.04
12.	2.02 + 49.869	51.889
13.	94.568 + 487.8	582.368
14.	700.08 + 98.89	798.97
15.	4.8469 + 0.7889	5.6358
16.	8.92 + 768.724	777.644
17.	4.06 + 765.976	770.036
18.	604.72 + 87.99	692.71
19.	8,462.9 + 97.09	8,559.99
20.	76.46 + 497.9	574.36
21.	86.479 + 9.36	95.839
22.	7.04 + 86.798	93.838
23.	4.897 + 8.24	13.137
24.	80.46 + 9.87	90.33
25.	8.496 + 0.897	9.393
26.	9.71 + 87.642	97.352
27.	4.06 + 87.8	91.86
28.	8.465 + 7.008	15.473
29.	645.176 + 787.846	1,433.022
30.	46.07 + 878.787	924.857
31.	8.76 + 79.878	88.638
32.	8.91 + 78.489	87.399
33.	897.4 + 43.62 + 0.97	941.99
34.	9.7 + 62.46 + 423.09	495.25
35.	0.406 + 7.009 + 6.89	14.305
36.	84.076 + 2.89 + 25.8	112.766
37.	764.25 + 42.146 + 9.352	815.748
38.	6.2 + 847.09 + 24.76	878.05
39.	7.9 + 82.46 + 9.476	99.836
40.	0.476 + 46.219 + 7.4821	54.1771
41.	23.462 + 6.248 + 2.689	32.399
42.	0.215 + 236.89 + 4.234	241.339

Practice puts you on top!

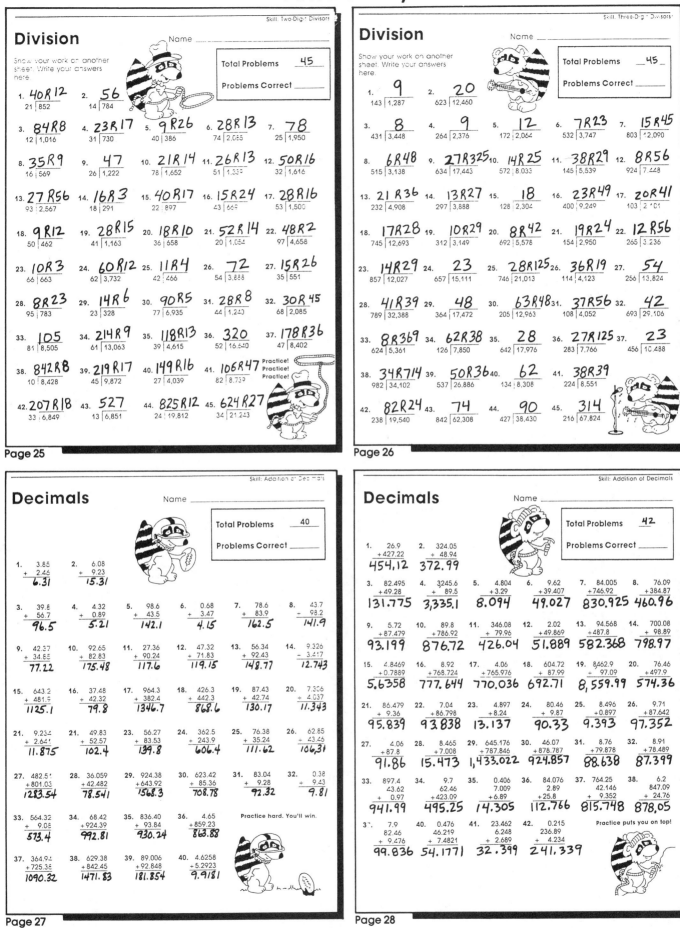

Page 28

Answer Key

Decimals

Skill: Addition of Decimals

Name ______________

Total Problems 40

Problems Correct ______

1. 32.50, 0.89, + 46.27 = 79.66
2. 842.9, 56.32, + 912.8 = 1812.02
3. 362.54, 3.85, + 46.39 = 412.78
4. 200.69, 463.2, + 8.56 = 672.45
5. 0.87, 6.42, + 8.965 = 16.255
6. 642.36, 58.29, + 0.37 = 701.02
7. 845.236, 32.873, + 0.46 = 878.569
8. 27.5, 34.62, + 5.38 = 67.5
9. 37.46, - 29.583 = 67.043
10. 526.9, 38.62, + 300.18 = 865.7
11. 9642.31, 821.24, + 9.56 = 10473.11
12. 47.312, 314.25, + 82.74 = 444.302
13. 602.45, 86.37, + 2.48 = 691.3
14. 68.75, 214.23, + 9.462 = 292.442
15. 312.46, 46.231, + 0.59 = 359.281
16. 84.06, 246.23, + 38.4 = 368.69
17. 918.06, 54.08, + 312.04 = 1284.18
18. 0.75, 28.14, + 7.32 = 36.21
19. 4.72, 32.25, + 6.9 = 43.87
20. 602.43, 35.26, + 432.52 = 1070.21
21. 426.08, 62.32, + 513.23 = 1001.63
22. 22.31, 624.15, + 8.04 = 654.5
23. 856.24, 0.89, + 46.03 = 903.16
24. 0.96, 123.14, + 84.03 = 208.13
25. 4.15, 36.124, + 82.354 = 122.628
26. 362.45, 121.32, + 143.65 = 627.42
27. 42.395, 6.25, + 4.8 = 53.445
28. 62.46, 3.821, + 543.4 = 609.681
29. 365.1, 2.326, + 28.45 = 395.876
30. 430.65, 84.32, + 312.46 = 827.43
31. 842.34, 26.15, + 8.56 = 877.05
32. 64.59, 302.152, + 8.71 = 375.452
33. 546.09, 52.43, + 3.43 = 601.95
34. 782.08, 96.23, + 214.41 = 1092.72
35. 20.415, 4.28, + 321.14 = 345.835
36. 643.38, 51.412, + 0.32 = 695.112
37. 364.25, 8.46, - 45.25 = 417.96
38. 920.04, 36.4, + 24.25 = 980.69
39. 0.64, 321.02, + 8.5 = 330.16
40. 462.98, 0.55, + 48.21 = 511.74

Success ahoy! Just practice!

Page 29

Decimals

Skill: Addition of Decimals

Name ______________

Total Problems 36

Problems Correct ______

1. 6.042, 8.253, + 4.628 = 18.923
2. 6.54, 58.47, + 9.384 = 74.394
3. 94.025, 3.684, + 9.74 = 107.449
4. 654.207, 6.87, + 92.5 = 753.577
5. 76.8, 842.78, + 8.43 = 928.01
6. 562.43, 94.2, + 3.57 = 660.2
7. 29.43, 37.52, + 48.25 = 115.2
8. 64.57, 2.76, + 85.218 = 152.548
9. 6.51, 82.43, + 9.25 = 98.19
10. 3.26, 46.38, + 8.79 = 58.43
11. 5.214, 0.36, + 2.582 = 8.156
12. 76.002, 321.4, + 8.65 = 406.052
13. 0.572, 82.41, - 5.743 = 88.725
14. 643.5, 26.43, + 52.86 = 722.79
15. 64.316, 2.465, 31.21, + 5.562 = 103.553
16. 748.21, 36.48, 7.24, + 2.53 = 794.46
17. 76.21, 8.36, 4.01, + 52.14 = 140.72
18. 852.15, 4215.3, 82.7, + 3.64 = 5,153.79
19. 464.06, 35.12, 6.94, + 57.23 = 563.35
20. 312.24, 63.45, 92.37, + 654.52 = 1,122.58
21. 24.32, 65.27, 48.51, + 23.49 = 161.59
22. 5.163, 2.413, 3.242, + 5.161 = 15.979
23. 36.215, 8.46, 21.15, + 3.271 = 69.096
24. 851.2, 46.35, 912.5, + 9.21 = 1819.26
25. 342.3, 26.5, 68.42, + 521.35 = 958.57
26. 62.4, 572.52, 24.08, + 345.21 = 1004.21
27. 501.26, 46.87, 24.35, + 59.23 = 631.71
28. 43.215, 1.486, 5.143, + 68.472 = 118.316
29. 92.54, 324.21, 65.148, + 28.352 = 510.25
30. 542.6, 28.45, 3.215, + 34.52 = 608.785
31. 3521.3, 264.56, 486.1, + 5124.3 = 9396.26
32. 69.24, 524.03, 51.36, + 48.13 = 692.76
33. 2.15, 4.82, 16.51, + 9.72 = 33.2
34. 36.22, 41.52, 8.21, + 3.46 = 89.41
35. 38.472, 3.21, 5.481, + 2.124 = 49.287
36. 5.2105, 0.465, 2.724, + 0.8131 = 9.2126

Practice takes you to the top!

Page 30

Decimals

Skill: Subtraction of Decimals

Name ______________

Total Problems 40

Problems Correct ______

1. 62.42, - 24.23 = 38.19
2. 93.56, - 42.38 = 51.18
3. 47.32, - 14.28 = 33.04
4. 3.25, - 2.67 = 0.58
5. 40.05, - 23.28 = 16.77
6. 8.621, - 3.248 = 5.373
7. 90.5, - 62.9 = 27.6
8. 583.7, - 392.4 = 191.3
9. 7.642, - 5.269 = 2.373
10. 36.49, - 29.82 = 6.67
11. 500.6, - 341.2 = 159.4
12. 80.94, - 28.23 = 52.71
13. 69.48, - 42.93 = 26.55
14. 9.302, - 7.281 = 2.021
15. 6.94, - 4.83 = 2.11
16. 76.4, - 52.8 = 23.6
17. 94.53, - 42.82 = 51.71
18. 64.07, - 52.82 = 11.25
19. 300.2, - 225.4 = 74.8
20. 500.5, - 432.2 = 68.3
21. 85.245, - 43.462 = 41.783
22. 300.24, - 142.48 = 157.76
23. 38.325, - 13.146 = 25.179
24. 564.02, - 325.24 = 238.78
25. 306.95, - 212.28 = 94.67
26. 762.14, - 341.25 = 420.89
27. 52.432, - 26.514 = 25.918
28. 746.34, - 482.16 = 264.18
29. 241.36, - 118.18 = 123.18
30. 462.5, - 293.8 = 168.7
31. 5.206, - 3.642 = 1.564
32. 842.36, - 381.64 = 460.72
33. 745.32, - 382.64 = 362.68
34. 546.07, - 327.18 = 218.89
35. 8.4162, - 5.5216 = 2.8946
36. 7.6241, - 6.8413 = 0.7828
37. 632.45, - 424.27 = 208.18
38. 82.611, - 41.802 = 40.809
39. 3642.5, - 1861.9 = 1780.6
40. 700.45, - 346.26 = 354.19

Success ahoy! Just practice!

Page 31

Decimals

Skill: Subtraction of Decimals

Name ______________

Total Problems 40

Problems Correct ______

1. 324.6, - 52.41 = 272.19
2. 26.39, - 8.246 = 18.144
3. 642.51, - 58.3 = 584.21
4. 742.8, - 6.35 = 736.45
5. 89.625, - 3.84 = 85.785
6. 4.006, - 2.85 = 1.156
7. 524.06, - 62.952 = 461.108
8. 62.05, - 8.226 = 53.824
9. 58.214, - 9.64 = 48.574
10. 8.11, - 2.325 = 5.785
11. 64.04, - 9.8 = 54.24
12. 462.51, - 38.823 = 423.687
13. 84.006, - 2.439 = 81.567
14. 4.625, - 0.259 = 4.366
15. 584.0, - 32.45 = 551.55
16. 364.25, - 8.364 = 355.886
17. 18.01, - 4.743 = 13.267
18. 392.1, - 246.81 = 145.29
19. 762.4, - 5.264 = 757.136
20. 564.7, - 58.65 = 506.05
21. 30.615, - 8.28 = 22.335
22. 716.8, - 47.28 = 669.52
23. 46.02, - 2.307 = 43.713
24. 6354.2, - 87.19 = 6267.01
25. 532.4, - 8.245 = 524.155
26. 574.04, - 0.321 = 573.719
27. 47.321, - 3.845 = 43.476
28. 26.001, - 3.245 = 22.756
29. 8.4182, - 0.2328 = 8.1854
30. 376.06, - 8.239 = 367.821
31. 6.32, - 0.489 = 5.831
32. 764.2, - 8.465 = 755.735
33. 57.018, - 6.14 = 50.878
34. 84.03, - 0.645 = 83.385
35. 916.2, - 82.9 = 833.3
36. 3642.9, - 3.625 = 3639.275
37. 478.1, - 7.25 = 470.85
38. 600.14, - 84.36 = 515.78
39. 723.8, - 64.35 = 659.45
40. 21.3, - 8.4365 = 12.8635

Anything's possible with practice!

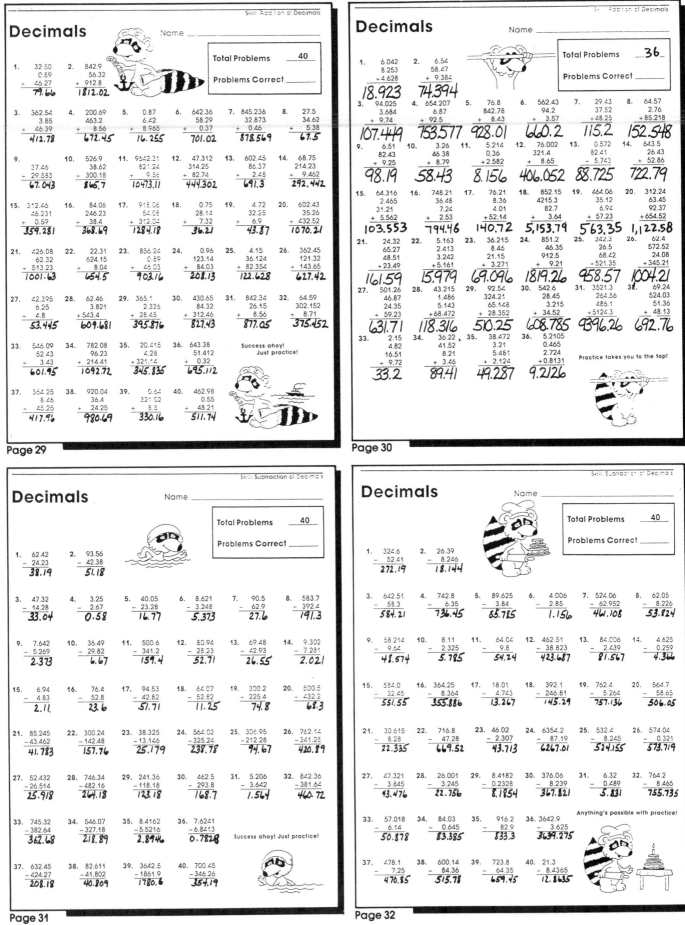

Page 32

Answer Key

Decimals

Skill: Subtraction of Decimals

Name ______________________

Total Problems 46

Problems Correct ______

1. 4.51 − 3.247 = 1.263
2. 36.2 − 18.416 = 17.784
3. 754.21 − 8.462 = 745.748
4. 17.1 − 2.145 = 14.955
5. 36.1 − 0.362 = 35.738
6. 6421.15 − 36.438 = 6384.712
7. 85.413 − 2.245 = 83.168
8. 92.5 − 3.462 = 89.038
9. 27.348 − 0.419 = 26.929
10. 32.147 − 8.56 = 23.587
11. 0.416 − 0.145 = 0.271
12. 54.007 − 3.12 = 50.887
13. 584.215 − 8.324 = 575.891
14. 852.4 − 0.146 = 852.254
15. 74.2 − 5.165 = 69.035
16. 9.22 − 1.248 = 7.972
17. 47.215 − 8.64 = 38.575
18. 946.01 − 57.16 = 888.85
19. 83.012 − 4.16 = 78.852
20. 3.14625 − 1.463 = 1.68325
21. 764.08 − 246.26 = 517.82
22. 59.16 − 8.425 = 50.735
23. 762.15 − 248.9 = 513.25
24. 46.21 − 28.5 = 17.71
25. 5421.7 − 0.3472 = 5421.3528
26. 10.5 − 0.465 = 10.035
27. 572.6 − 0.464 = 572.136
28. 854.216 − 81.9 = 772.316
29. 50.41 − 8.562 = 41.848
30. 900.001 − 46.14 = 853.861
31. 842.15 − 56.47 = 785.68
32. 542.16 − 58.72 = 483.44
33. 856.19 − 4.247 = 851.943
34. 345.1 − 6.527 = 338.573
35. 564.21 − 86.541 = 477.669
36. 6724.2 − 2.149 = 6722.051
37. 48.12 − 4.564 = 43.556
38. 89.142 − 3.86 = 85.282
39. 52.73 − 0.4234 = 52.3066
40. 9.45 − 0.24 = 9.21
41. 623.46 − 248.1 = 375.36
42. 5424.16 − 365.24 = 5058.92
43. 847.145 − 8.95 = 838.195
44. 3745.2 − 8.84 = 3736.36
45. 6241.6 − 5.3215 = 6236.2785
46. 584.1 − 2.51642 = 581.58358

Practice brings success!

Page 33

Decimals

Skill: Subtraction of Decimals

Name ______________________

Total Problems 48

Problems Correct ______

1. 8.98 − 4.73 = 4.25
2. 7.88 − 0.465 = 7.415
3. 600.42 − 49.81 = 550.61
4. 72.465 − 8.79 = 63.675
5. 80.004 − 7.492 = 72.512
6. 5.245 − 0.869 = 4.376
7. 72.462 − 8.294 = 64.168
8. 602.47 − 47.09 = 555.38
9. 4,674.98 − 8.321 = 4,666.659
10. 764.217 − 89.148 = 675.069
11. 4.009 − 0.872 = 3.137
12. 82.476 − 4.088 = 78.388
13. 27.8 − 2.432 = 25.368
14. 800.08 − 32.42 = 767.66
15. 0.369 − 0.281 = 0.088
16. 874.9 − 288.3 = 586.6
17. 3.4169 − 0.8423 = 2.5746
18. 7.03 − 2.89 = 4.14
19. 43.4107 − 8.2619 = 35.1488
20. 6.98 − 2.4694 = 4.5106
21. 34.007 − 2.43 = 31.577
22. 600.08 − 23.12 = 576.96
23. 3,214.8 − 2,187.3 = 1,027.5
24. 84.329 − 8.46 = 75.869
25. 7.87 − 0.3294 = 7.5406
26. 47.463 − 6.872 = 40.591
27. 20.006 − 8.43 = 11.576
28. 6,489.3 − 2.468 = 6,486.832
29. 46.24 − 8.265 = 37.975
30. 7.69 − 2.96 = 4.73
31. 36.423 − 2.894 = 33.529
32. 6.047 − 2.89 = 3.157
33. 642.98 − 0.432 = 642.548
34. 8.99 − 0.4657 = 8.5243
35. 72.09 − 8.462 = 63.628
36. 16.19 − 4.764 = 11.426
37. 40.07 − 8.325 = 31.745
38. 67.46 − 2.897 = 64.563
39. 0.399 − 0.276 = 0.123
40. 92.463 − 8.272 = 84.191
41. 8.39 − 2.598 = 5.792
42. 6,742.8 − 86.42 = 6,656.38
43. 27.6 − 4.6321 = 22.9679
44. 76.45 − 8.3264 = 68.1236
45. 9.96 − 2.145 = 7.815
46. 464.25 − 85.472 = 378.778
47. 76.59 − 8.432 = 68.158
48. 464.98 − 0.3264 = 464.6536

Practice hard.

Page 34

Decimals

Skill: Multiplication of Decimals by Whole Numbers

Name ______________________

Total Problems 40

Problems Correct ______

1. 3.64 × 4 = 14.56
2. 7.8 × 6 = 46.8
3. 26.5 × 9 = 238.5
4. 3.89 × 7 = 27.23
5. 0.24 × 5 = 1.2
6. 7.9 × 8 = 63.2
7. 0.65 × 9 = 5.85
8. 3.97 × 5 = 19.85
9. 12.63 × 6 = 75.78
10. 143.8 × 8 = 1150.4
11. 158.4 × 5 = 792.0
12. 98.62 × 8 = 788.96
13. 4.613 × 7 = 32.291
14. 0.146 × 4 = 0.584
15. 0.516 × 9 = 4.644
16. 0.849 × 7 = 5.943
17. 0.326 × 5 = 1.63
18. 12.89 × 6 = 77.34
19. 0.54 × 9 = 4.86
20. 421.5 × 7 = 2950.5
21. 0.8 × 6 = 4.8
22. 3.87 × 9 = 34.83
23. 3.338 × 2 = 6.676
24. 4.31 × 8 = 34.48
25. 0.895 × 6 = 5.370
26. 7.362 × 9 = 66.258
27. 3.3156 × 8 = 26.5248
28. 32.416 × 7 = 226.912
29. 642.17 × 9 = 5779.53
30. 78.148 × 3 = 234.444
31. 9465.3 × 5 = 47326.5
32. 46.418 × 3 = 139.254
33. 0.15426 × 8 = 1.23408
34. 62.517 × 4 = 250.068
35. 56.58 × 9 = 590.22
36. 3.618 × 7 = 25.326
37. 8.7154 × 4 = 34.8616
38. 0.1578 × 7 = 1.1046
39. 476.24 × 8 = 3809.92
40. 74.389 × 2 = 148.778

With practice, you can do it!

Page 35

Decimals

Skill: Multiplication of Tenths and Hundredths

Name ______________________

Show your work on another sheet. Write your answers here.

Total Problems 40

Problems Correct ______

1. 0.9 × 0.7 = 0.63
2. 0.7 × 0.4 = 0.28
3. 0.8 × 0.3 = 0.24
4. 1.9 × 0.6 = 1.14
5. 1.45 × 0.7 = 1.02
6. 4.8 × 1.6 = 7.68
7. 4.3 × 3.6 = 15.48
8. 5.87 × 3.6 = 21.13
9. 7.9 × 0.86 = 6.79
10. 12.3 × 0.45 = 5.54
11. 3.14 × 2.7 = 8.48
12. 7.46 × 3.8 = 28.35
13. 84.6 × 0.27 = 22.84
14. 24.5 × 8.2 = 200.9
15. 23.6 × 0.49 = 11.56
16. 0.8 × 0.4 = 0.32
17. 0.6 × 0.5 = 0.30
18. 21.4 × 0.94 = 20.12
19. 31.2 × 0.64 = 19.97
20. 46.9 × 0.85 = 39.87
21. 1.59 × 0.4 = 0.64
22. 12.8 × 3.7 = 47.36
23. 14.5 × 0.57 = 8.27
24. 94.6 × 0.24 = 22.70
25. 51.2 × 5.6 = 286.72
26. 14.9 × 0.76 = 11.32
27. 46.2 × 0.23 = 10.63
28. 7.25 × 3.9 = 28.28
29. 33.2 × 6.8 = 225.76
30. 61.6 × 0.73 = 44.97
31. 31.5 × 0.34 = 10.71
32. 14.5 × 0.56 = 8.12
33. 41.5 × 0.89 = 36.94
34. 13.2 × 0.34 = 4.49
35. 14.6 × 0.86 = 12.56
36. 1.6 × 0.54 = 0.86
37. 21.4 × 0.36 = 7.70
38. 14.6 × 3.7 = 54.02
39. 9.25 × 7.6 = 70.30
40. 8.16 × 5.6 = 45.70

Practice! Practice! Practice!

Page 36

Answer Key

Page 37

Skill: Multiplication of Decimals With Zeroes in the Products

Decimals

Name ______________________

Show your work on another sheet. Write your answers here.

Total Problems 40

Problems Correct ______

1. 0.2 × 0.2 = 0.04
2. 0.9 × 0.1 = 0.09
3. 1.7 × 0.03 = 0.051
4. 1.6 × 0.04 = 0.064
5. 0.39 × 0.2 = 0.078
6. 1.6 × 0.02 = 0.032
7. 2.3 × 0.04 = 0.092
8. 0.33 × 0.3 = 0.099
9. 0.08 × 0.8 = 0.064
10. 0.03 × 0.7 = 0.021
11. 0.15 × 0.04 = 0.006
12. 0.13 × 0.7 = 0.091
13. 4.3 × 0.02 = 0.086
14. 0.07 × 0.6 = 0.042
15. 0.35 × 0.2 = 0.07
16. 0.17 × 0.3 = 0.051
17. 0.09 × 0.4 = 0.036
18. 0.36 × 0.2 = 0.072
19. 0.07 × 0.2 = 0.014
20. 0.006 × 3 = 0.018
21. 0.01 × 5 = 0.05
22. .03 × 2 = 0.06
23. 0.03 × 0.4 = 0.012
24. 0.028 × 3 = 0.084
25. 0.02 × 4 = 0.08
26. 0.049 × 2 = 0.098
27. 0.4 × 0.1 = 0.04
28. 0.01 × 9 = 0.09
29. 0.08 × 1 = 0.08
30. 0.002 × 7 = 0.014
31. 0.09 × 0.3 = 0.027
32. 0.03 × 0.5 = 0.015
33. 0.1 × 0.8 = 0.08
34. 0.3 × 0.3 = 0.09
35. 0.05 × 0.6 = 0.03
36. 0.51 × 0.01 = 0.0051
37. 0.024 × 3 = 0.072
38. 0.01 × 6 = 0.06
39. 0.005 × 5 = 0.025
40. 0.3 × 0.2 = 0.06

Practice brings success!

Page 37

Page 38

Skill: Multiplication of Decimals

Decimals

Name ______________________

Show your work on another sheet. Write your answers here.

Total Problems 42

Problems Correct ______

1. 36.5 × 8.4 = 306.6
2. 516.24 × 0.3 = 154.872
3. 3.614 × 0.57 = 2.05998
4. 516.4 × 0.04 = 20.656
5. 462.3 × 7.1 = 3282.33
6. 742.01 × 3.4 = 2522.834
7. 0.316 × 1.7 = 0.5372
8. 486.1 × 5.6 = 2722.16
9. 56.01 × 0.8 = 44.808
10. 20.147 × 3.8 = 76.5586
11. 43.4 × 0.67 = 29.078
12. 64.8 × 3.2 = 207.36
13. 1.015 × 0.3 = 0.3045
14. 61.3 × 5.4 = 331.02
15. 4621.4 × 0.42 = 1940.988
16. 874.7 × 4.3 = 3761.21
17. 0.148 × 0.7 = 0.1036
18. 23.52 × 7.8 = 183.456
19. 51.6 × 4.9 = 252.84
20. 8.64 × 3.4 = 29.376
21. 6.454 × 5.6 = 36.1424
22. 1.462 × 0.83 = 1.21346
23. 21.362 × 5.7 = 121.7634
24. 7.218 × 0.68 = 4.90824
25. 6.145 × 7.4 = 45.473
26. 92.32 × 0.94 = 86.7808
27. 314.6 × 0.7 = 220.22
28. 864.25 × 8.5 = 7346.125
29. 57.328 × 0.64 = 36.68992
30. 74.25 × 0.8 = 59.4
31. 3.145 × 9.6 = 30.192
32. 2.145 × 0.4 = 0.858
33. 624.9 × 8.5 = 5311.65
34. 326.1 × 9.2 = 3000.12
35. 43.15 × 0.08 = 3.452
36. 59.46 × 8.2 = 487.572
37. 926.8 × 3.7 = 3429.16
38. 8.41 × 0.7 = 5.887
39. 4.361 × 0.7 = 3.0527
40. 5.004 × 0.65 = 3.2526
41. 37.48 × 0.21 = 7.8708
42. 214.61 × .08 = 17.1688

Practice hard. You'll win!

Page 38

Page 39

Skill: Multiplication of Decimals

Decimals

Name ______________________

Show your work on another sheet. Write your answers here.

Total Problems 50

Problems Correct ______

1. 48.8 × 7.4 = 361.12
2. 5.184 × 2.7 = 13.9968
3. 321.4 × 5.6 = 1,799.84
4. 7.8 × 52.02 = 405.756
5. 21.09 × 9.26 = 195.2934
6. 843.1 × 0.2 = 168.62
7. 61.4 × 9.2 = 564.88
8. 7.612 × 5.143 = 39.148516
9. 8.12 × 0.04 = 0.3248
10. 9.14 × 3.6 = 32.904
11. 84.36 × 7.2 = 607.392
12. 7.04 × 4.65 = 32.736
13. 84.98 × 6.2 = 526.876
14. 6.40 × 5.8 = 37.12
15. 8.43 × 0.146 = 1.23078
16. 64.2 × 5.9 = 378.78
17. 0.14 × 8.35 = 1.169
18. 7.006 × 9.4 = 65.8564
19. 0.45 × 7.321 = 3.29445
20. 6.05 × 0.24 = 1.452
21. 7.106 × 0.9 = 6.3954
22. 64.2 × 3.02 = 193.884
23. 214.6 × 3.4 = 729.64
24. 41.254 × 6.1 = 251.6494
25. 51.6 × 8.43 = 434.988
26. 0.007 × 3.6 = 0.0252
27. 4.643 × 5.8 = 26.9294
28. 3.26 × 0.47 = 1.5322
29. 8.094 × 3.6 = 29.1384
30. 41.3 × 0.05 = 2.065
31. 392.6 × 50.4 = 19,787.04
32. 24.09 × 7.24 = 174.4116
33. 43.6 × 7.4 = 322.64
34. 3,214.9 × 8.1 = 26,040.69
35. 5.012 × 8.32 = 41.69984
36. 8.2 × 0.003 = 0.0246
37. 843.4 × 41.3 = 34,832.42
38. 8.64 × 9.2 = 79.488
39. 0.145 × 0.1342 = 0.019459
40. 1.368 × 0.03 = 0.04104
41. 49.7 × 3.64 = 180.908
42. 142.6 × 4.54 = 647.404
43. 64.8 × 0.004 = 0.2592
44. 564.9 × 38.2 = 21,579.18
45. 59.006 × 3.2 = 188.8192
46. 6,143.6 × 6.5 = 39,933.4
47. 3.0062 × 2.42 = 7.275004
48. 8.4 × 354.2 = 2,975.28
49. 0.43 × 0.2102 = 0.090386
50. 8.14 × 2.03 = 16.5242

Success ahoy! Just practice!

Page 39

Page 40

Skill: Division of Decimals by Whole Numbers

Decimals

Name ______________________

Show your work on another sheet. Write your answers here.

Total Problems 40

Problems Correct ______

1. 7.5 ÷ 6 = 1.25
2. 9.2 ÷ 4 = 2.3
3. 8.7 ÷ 3 = 2.9
4. 3.6 ÷ 9 = 0.4
5. 6.3 ÷ 7 = 0.9
6. 10.5 ÷ 5 = 2.1
7. 32.6 ÷ 2 = 16.3
8. 4.16 ÷ 8 = 0.52
9. 5.24 ÷ 4 = 1.31
10. 8.82 ÷ 9 = 0.98
11. 7.68 ÷ 3 = 2.56
12. 5.34 ÷ 6 = 0.89
13. 8.68 ÷ 4 = 2.17
14. 4.83 ÷ 7 = 0.69
15. 15.5 ÷ 5 = 3.1
16. 16.4 ÷ 2 = 8.2
17. 4.76 ÷ 7 = 0.68
18. 13.5 ÷ 3 = 4.5
19. 24.8 ÷ 8 = 3.1
20. 30.6 ÷ 9 = 3.4
21. 24.8 ÷ 4 = 6.2
22. 0.528 ÷ 6 = 0.088
23. 25.92 ÷ 8 = 3.24
24. 6.72 ÷ 7 = 0.96
25. 21.42 ÷ 3 = 7.14
26. 13.16 ÷ 2 = 6.58
27. 36.56 ÷ 4 = 9.14
28. 32.82 ÷ 6 = 5.47
29. 4.25 ÷ 5 = 0.85
30. 12.8 ÷ 4 = 3.2
31. 32.8 ÷ 8 = 4.1
32. 14.4 ÷ 3 = 4.8
33. 30.5 ÷ 5 = 6.1
34. 211.5 ÷ 9 = 23.5
35. 442.4 ÷ 7 = 63.2
36. 0.848 ÷ 4 = 0.212
37. 2.34 ÷ 6 = 0.39
38. 0.294 ÷ 3 = 0.098
39. 0.18 ÷ 2 = 0.09
40. 23.84 ÷ 8 = 2.98

Practice puts you on top!

Page 40

Answer Key

Page 41

Decimals

Skill: Division of Decimals by Whole Numbers

Name _____

Show your work on another sheet. Write your answers here.

Total Problems ___40___

Problems Correct _____

1. 4.12
23 | 94.76

2. 0.59
48 | 28.32

3. 5.74
13 | 74.62

4. 5.2
17 | 88.4

5. 0.69
52 | 35.88

6. 0.58
14 | 8.12

7. 3.4
12 | 40.8

8. 2.48
34 | 84.32

9. 4.27
23 | 98.21

10. 0.257
38 | 9.766

11. 3.01
45 | 135.45

12. 3.47
28 | 97.16

13. 0.57
43 | 24.51

14. 0.36
62 | 22.32

15. 0.25
27 | 6.75

16. 0.8
13 | 10.4

17. 3.69
24 | 88.56

18. 0.213
37 | 7.881

19. 1.2
84 | 100.8

20. 2.3
35 | 80.5

21. 0.356
22 | 7.832

22. 0.47
15 | 7.05

23. 2.4
39 | 93.6

24. 0.58
12 | 6.96

25. 3.47
16 | 55.52

26. 0.47
42 | 19.74

27. 1.3
94 | 122.2

28. 0.05
33 | 1.65

29. 1.25
47 | 58.75

30. 0.26
52 | 13.52

31. 1.2
62 | 74.4

32. 0.14
81 | 11.34

33. 0.39
25 | 9.75

34. 1.3
32 | 41.6

35. 2.89
17 | 49.13

36. 0.89
13 | 11.57

37. 3.49
45 | 157.05

Success ahoy! Just practice!

38. 0.04
72 | 2.88

39. 4.15
57 | 236.55

40. 0.24
74 | 17.76

Page 42

Decimals

Skill: Division of Decimals by Whole Numbers

Name _____

Show your work on another sheet. Write your answers here.

Total Problems ___45___

Problems Correct _____

1. 2.58
4 | 10.32

2. 1.39
6 | 8.34

3. 0.68
8 | 5.44

4. 6.87
2 | 13.74

5. 0.78
9 | 7.02

6. 1.46
7 | 10.22

7. 3.9
6 | 23.7

8. 0.654
3 | 1.962

9. 8.14
5 | 40.7

10. 4.28
8 | 34.24

11. 7.39
4 | 29.56

12. 9.37
2 | 18.74

13. 0.947
5 | 4.735

14. 6.97
7 | 48.79

15. 0.087
9 | 0.783

16. 2.54
8 | 20.32

17. 1.369
3 | 4.107

18. 0.198
6 | 1.188

19. 0.854
4 | 3.416

20. 2.47
7 | 17.29

21. 0.178
5 | 0.89

22. 0.874
3 | 2.622

23. 6.59
8 | 52.72

24. 12.3
9 | 110.7

25. 0.07
6 | 0.42

26. 9.27
4 | 37.08

27. 25.4
7 | 177.8

28. 4.39
3 | 13.17

29. 32.5
9 | 292.5

30. 3.17
8 | 25.36

31. 3.258
2 | 6.516

32. 0.365
6 | 2.19

33. 0.099
4 | 0.396

34. 23.8
8 | 190.4

35. 0.397
7 | 2.779

36. 6.57
4 | 26.28

37. 36.5
3 | 109.5

38. 0.09
6 | 0.54

39. 7.26
8 | 58.08

40. 7.89
2 | 15.78

41. 0.146
5 | 0.73

42. 3.48
7 | 24.36

43. 54.21
6 | 325.26

44. 37.14
4 | 148.56

45. 0.158
2 | 0.316

Practice! Practice! Practice!

Page 43

Decimals

Skill: Division of Decimals by Tenths

Name _____

Show your work on another sheet. Write your answers here.

Total Problems ___43___

Problems Correct _____

1. 3.14
0.7 | 2.198

2. 22
0.4 | 8.8

3. 6.4
0.5 | 3.2

4. 41.2
0.9 | 37.08

5. 7.05
1.2 | 8.46

6. 51.2
3.4 | 174.08

7. 4.9
0.8 | 3.92

8. 2.4
0.9 | 2.16

9. 7.36
1.6 | 11.776

10. 8.7
4.2 | 36.54

11. 7.6
4.4 | 33.44

12. 2.4
21.1 | 50.64

13. 62.14
0.2 | 12.428

14. 6.04
0.5 | 3.02

15. 8.5
1.3 | 11.05

16. 5.6
2.6 | 14.56

17. 78.4
3.2 | 250.88

18. 9.8
5.1 | 49.98

19. 32
0.2 | 6.4

20. 3.68
0.4 | 1.472

21. 9.4
0.8 | 7.52

22. 35.8
1.7 | 60.86

23. 6.47
3.4 | 21.998

24. 7.06
2.7 | 19.062

25. 5.4
1.3 | 7.02

26. 3.59
2.1 | 7.539

27. 8.9
0.7 | 6.23

28. 4.18
2.7 | 11.286

29. 6.4
1.4 | 8.96

30. 4.16
0.3 | 1.248

31. 0.415
0.6 | 0.249

32. 3.8
1.4 | 5.32

33. 7.4
2.3 | 17.02

34. 6.7
5.2 | 34.84

35. 5
0.5 | 2.5

36. 4.6
0.8 | 3.68

37. 9.5
1.8 | 17.1

38. 4.8
3.8 | 18.24

39. 3.04
5.6 | 17.024

40. 6.8
2.9 | 19.72

Practice makes perfect!

41. 3.17
3.4 | 10.778

42. 0.128
0.7 | 0.0896

43. 5.8
0.6 | 3.48

Page 44

Decimals

Skill: Division of Decimals by Hundredths

Name _____

Show your work on another sheet. Write your answers here.

Total Problems ___45___

Problems Correct _____

1. 23.4
0.14 | 3.276

2. 2.58
0.04 | 0.1032

3. 6.9
1.22 | 8.418

4. 3.24
0.06 | 0.1944

5. 8.4
0.36 | 3.024

6. 3.8
0.17 | 0.646

7. 9
0.26 | 2.34

8. 8.2
0.47 | 3.854

9. 2.14
0.32 | 0.6848

10. 25.4
0.22 | 5.588

11. 65
0.29 | 18.85

12. 84.2
0.03 | 2.526

13. 26.7
0.54 | 14.418

14. 88.2
0.35 | 30.87

15. 63.5
0.09 | 5.715

16. 8.9
1.24 | 11.036

17. 7.8
0.16 | 1.248

18. 4.7
5.03 | 23.641

19. 2.65
0.21 | 0.5565

20. 85.4
0.13 | 11.102

21. 78.6
0.07 | 5.502

22. 96
0.37 | 35.52

23. 60
0.11 | 6.6

24. 3.9
0.46 | 1.794

25. 360
0.18 | 64.8

26. 64.7
0.39 | 25.233

27. 89
0.25 | 22.25

28. 78.5
0.24 | 18.84

29. 5.2
0.12 | 0.624

30. 79.6
0.08 | 6.368

31. 64.5
0.38 | 24.51

32. 4.6
3.92 | 18.032

33. 3.6
2.53 | 9.108

34. 84
0.57 | 47.88

35. 23.9
0.43 | 10.277

36. 8.9
0.02 | 0.178

37. 6.80
0.24 | 1.632

38. 65
1.21 | 78.65

39. 74.8
0.23 | 17.204

40. 87
0.05 | 4.35

41. 9
6.04 | 54.36

42. 4.7
0.62 | 2.914

43. 63.7
0.15 | 9.555

44. 9.9
0.33 | 3.267

45. 7
0.29 | 2.03

Practice puts you on top!

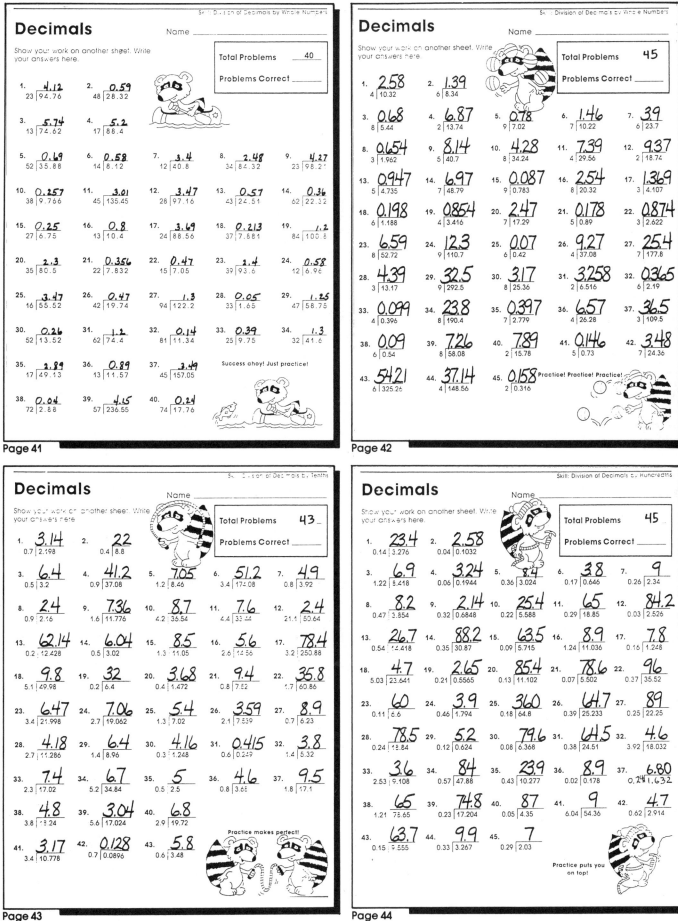

Answer Key

Decimals

Skill: Division of Decimals by Hundredths

Name ______________

Show your work on another sheet. Write your answers here.

Total Problems 43

Problems Correct ______

1. 0.12)10.68 = 89
2. 4.14)28.152 = 6.8
3. 0.62)4.154 = 6.7
4. 0.07)0.6552 = 9.36
5. 0.42)1.554 = 3.7
6. 0.17)13.634 = 80.2
7. 0.67)5.762 = 8.6
8. 0.05)4.93 = 98.6
9. 0.03)223.59 = 7,453
10. 0.15)13.05 = 87
11. 0.31)19.592 = 63.2
12. 0.24)2.544 = 10.6
13. 6.54)30.084 = 4.6
14. 0.26)14.56 = 56
15. 0.41)1.148 = 2.8
16. 0.18)3.852 = 21.4
17. 0.84)34.692 = 41.3
18. 0.19)3.857 = 20.3
19. 0.92)3.6984 = 4.02
20. 0.04)3.72 = 93
21. 0.28)0.756 = 2.7
22. 0.68)9.86 = 14.5
23. 0.39)2.262 = 5.8
24. 0.21)1.407 = 6.7
25. 0.08)50.4 = 630
26. 0.42)7.518 = 17.9
27. 0.74)5.18 = 7
28. 0.98)7.84 = 8
29. 0.17)0.816 = 4.8
30. 0.24)1.368 = 5.7
31. 0.14)0.476 = 3.4
32. 0.09)0.0027 = 0.03
33. 0.39)4.875 = 12.5
34. 0.64)4.864 = 7.6
35. 1.26)4.536 = 3.6
36. 5.03)24.144 = 4.8
37. 0.65)5.252 = 8.08
38. 0.38)1.14 = 3
39. 2.04)6.936 = 3.4
40. 2.94)14.406 = 4.9
41. 0.69)55.338 = 80.2
42. 3.02)175.16 = 58
43. 0.54)2.052 = 3.8

Practice brings success!

Page 45

Decimals

Skill: Division of Decimals by Thousandths

Name ______________

Show your work on another sheet. Write your answers here.

Total Problems 40

Problems Correct ______

1. 0.002)0.17 = 85
2. 0.415)3.735 = 9
3. 0.314)0.157 = 0.5
4. 0.006)0.282 = 47
5. 0.028)14.112 = 504
6. 0.054)0.3726 = 6.9
7. 0.329)2.632 = 8
8. 0.712)32.04 = 45
9. 0.742)471.17 = 635
10. 0.092)0.552 = 6
11. 0.184)0.6624 = 3.6
12. 0.003)0.2358 = 78.6
13. 0.246)11.808 = 48
14. 0.008)7.12 = 890
15. 0.623)34.888 = 56
16. 0.037)0.3552 = 9.6
17. 0.624)4.368 = 7
18. 0.108)6.804 = 63
19. 0.146)3.431 = 23.5
20. 0.609)4.872 = 8
21. 0.005)4.92 = 984
22. 0.424)22.896 = 54
23. 0.507)3.549 = 7
24. 0.319)6.38 = 20
25. 0.006)0.27 = 45
26. 0.031)2.3653 = 76.3
27. 0.506)376.97 = 745
28. 0.085)0.51 = 6
29. 0.046)24.104 = 524
30. 0.007)6.132 = 876
31. 0.024)2.304 = 96
32. 0.427)1.5372 = 3.6
33. 0.218)7.848 = 36
34. 0.611)5.499 = 9
35. 0.048)0.672 = 14
36. 0.009)6.705 = 745
37. 0.247)1.235 = 5
38. 0.329)29.281 = 89
39. 0.704)2.816 = 4
40. 0.162)3.4668 = 21.4

Practice brings success!

Page 46

Fractions

Skill: Finding Equivalent Fractions

Name ______________

Show your work on another sheet. Write your answers here.

Total Problems 40

Problems Correct ______

1. $\frac{1}{4} = \frac{4}{16}$
2. $\frac{3}{8} = \frac{9}{24}$
3. $\frac{1}{2} = \frac{4}{8}$
4. $\frac{2}{5} = \frac{4}{10}$
5. $\frac{3}{6} = \frac{6}{12}$
6. $\frac{2}{6} = \frac{6}{18}$
7. $\frac{3}{9} = \frac{6}{18}$
8. $\frac{1}{5} = \frac{3}{15}$
9. $\frac{2}{3} = \frac{4}{6}$
10. $\frac{7}{8} = \frac{14}{16}$
11. $\frac{1}{5} = \frac{4}{20}$
12. $\frac{1}{3} = \frac{5}{15}$
13. $\frac{2}{4} = \frac{4}{8}$
14. $\frac{3}{4} = \frac{21}{28}$
15. $\frac{3}{6} = \frac{9}{18}$
16. $\frac{4}{5} = \frac{16}{20}$
17. $\frac{6}{7} = \frac{12}{14}$
18. $\frac{2}{6} = \frac{8}{24}$
19. $\frac{2}{4} = \frac{6}{12}$
20. $\frac{1}{3} = \frac{9}{27}$
21. $\frac{2}{8} = \frac{6}{24}$
22. $\frac{1}{9} = \frac{2}{18}$
23. $\frac{2}{10} = \frac{4}{20}$
24. $\frac{3}{6} = \frac{12}{24}$
25. $\frac{9}{10} = \frac{27}{30}$
26. $\frac{2}{6} = \frac{10}{30}$
27. $\frac{3}{7} = \frac{21}{49}$
28. $\frac{11}{12} = \frac{110}{120}$
29. $\frac{4}{9} = \frac{16}{36}$
30. $\frac{3}{4} = \frac{24}{32}$
31. $\frac{2}{6} = \frac{12}{36}$
32. $\frac{8}{9} = \frac{16}{18}$
33. $\frac{2}{5} = \frac{14}{35}$
34. $\frac{2}{7} = \frac{12}{42}$
35. $\frac{3}{12} = \frac{9}{36}$
36. $\frac{6}{11} = \frac{72}{132}$
37. $\frac{1}{8} = \frac{12}{96}$
38. $\frac{5}{10} = \frac{60}{120}$
39. $\frac{2}{6} = \frac{8}{24}$
40. $\frac{6}{9} = \frac{48}{72}$

Practice brings success!

Page 47

Fractions

Skill: Reducing Fractions to Lowest Terms

Name ______________

Reduce these fractions to lowest terms. Show your work on another sheet. Write your answers here.

Total Problems 50

Problems Correct ______

1. $\frac{4}{8} = \frac{1}{2}$
2. $\frac{6}{12} = \frac{1}{2}$
3. $\frac{3}{9} = \frac{1}{3}$
4. $\frac{8}{12} = \frac{2}{3}$
5. $\frac{4}{16} = \frac{1}{4}$
6. $\frac{5}{15} = \frac{1}{3}$
7. $\frac{3}{12} = \frac{1}{4}$
8. $\frac{5}{10} = \frac{1}{2}$
9. $\frac{9}{18} = \frac{1}{2}$
10. $\frac{2}{6} = \frac{1}{3}$
11. $\frac{2}{10} = \frac{1}{5}$
12. $\frac{16}{18} = \frac{8}{9}$
13. $\frac{6}{9} = \frac{2}{3}$
14. $\frac{10}{25} = \frac{2}{5}$
15. $\frac{2}{4} = \frac{1}{2}$
16. $\frac{2}{14} = \frac{1}{7}$
17. $\frac{8}{16} = \frac{1}{2}$
18. $\frac{6}{10} = \frac{3}{5}$
19. $\frac{3}{6} = \frac{1}{2}$
20. $\frac{10}{20} = \frac{1}{2}$
21. $\frac{10}{12} = \frac{5}{6}$
22. $\frac{6}{30} = \frac{1}{5}$
23. $\frac{4}{24} = \frac{1}{6}$
24. $\frac{14}{16} = \frac{7}{8}$
25. $\frac{4}{20} = \frac{1}{5}$
26. $\frac{7}{14} = \frac{1}{2}$
27. $\frac{8}{8} = 1$
28. $\frac{5}{20} = \frac{1}{4}$
29. $\frac{2}{8} = \frac{1}{4}$
30. $\frac{4}{10} = \frac{2}{5}$
31. $\frac{14}{20} = \frac{7}{10}$
32. $\frac{8}{10} = \frac{4}{5}$
33. $\frac{4}{6} = \frac{2}{3}$
34. $\frac{8}{24} = \frac{1}{3}$
35. $\frac{3}{18} = \frac{1}{6}$
36. $\frac{20}{25} = \frac{4}{5}$
37. $\frac{6}{8} = \frac{3}{4}$
38. $\frac{10}{16} = \frac{5}{8}$
39. $\frac{10}{22} = \frac{5}{11}$
40. $\frac{6}{18} = \frac{1}{3}$
41. $\frac{12}{20} = \frac{3}{5}$
42. $\frac{5}{30} = \frac{1}{6}$
43. $\frac{4}{12} = \frac{1}{3}$
44. $\frac{12}{24} = \frac{1}{2}$
45. $\frac{16}{20} = \frac{4}{5}$
46. $\frac{3}{24} = \frac{1}{8}$
47. $\frac{5}{25} = \frac{1}{5}$
48. $\frac{18}{20} = \frac{9}{10}$
49. $\frac{13}{26} = \frac{1}{2}$
50. $\frac{12}{16} = \frac{3}{4}$

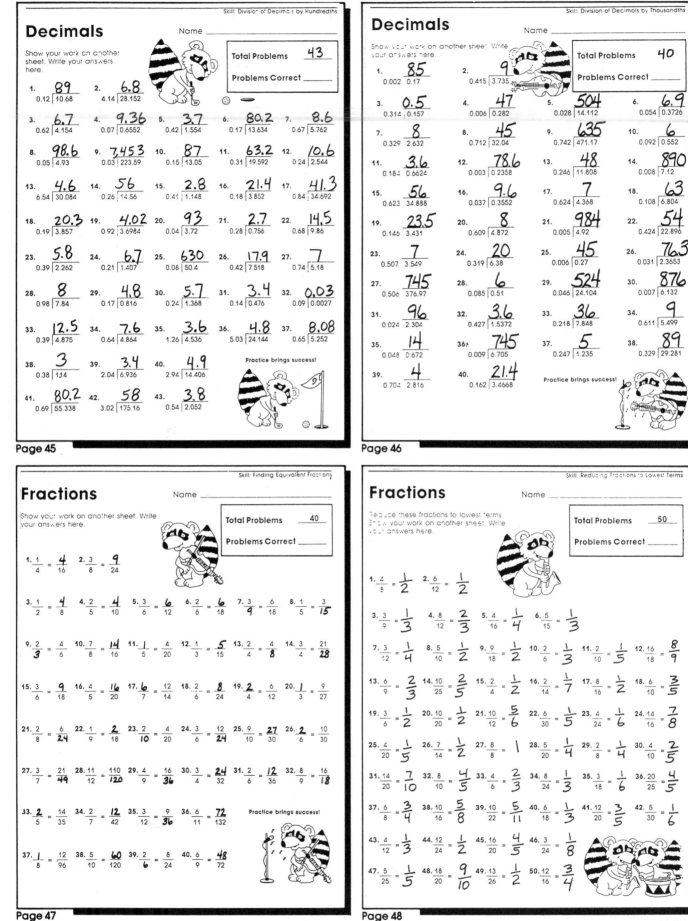

Page 48

Fractions

Change these fractions to mixed numbers in lowest terms. Show your work on another sheet. Write your answers here.

1. $\frac{10}{3} = 3\frac{1}{3}$ 2. $\frac{14}{6} = 2\frac{1}{3}$

3. $\frac{15}{8} = 1\frac{7}{8}$ 4. $\frac{17}{8} = 2\frac{1}{8}$

5. $\frac{9}{4} = 2\frac{1}{4}$ 6. $\frac{23}{5} = 4\frac{3}{5}$ 7. $\frac{18}{7} = 2\frac{4}{7}$ 8. $\frac{12}{10} = 1\frac{1}{5}$ 9. $\frac{7}{2} = 3\frac{1}{2}$ 10. $\frac{23}{7} = 3\frac{2}{7}$

11. $\frac{16}{5} = 3\frac{1}{5}$ 12. $\frac{26}{6} = 4\frac{1}{3}$ 13. $\frac{32}{5} = 6\frac{2}{5}$ 14. $\frac{25}{12} = 2\frac{1}{12}$ 15. $\frac{8}{3} = 2\frac{2}{3}$ 16. $\frac{17}{3} = 5\frac{2}{3}$

17. $\frac{14}{3} = 4\frac{2}{3}$ 18. $\frac{7}{3} = 2\frac{1}{3}$ 19. $\frac{27}{5} = 5\frac{2}{5}$ 20. $\frac{13}{4} = 3\frac{1}{4}$ 21. $\frac{20}{7} = 2\frac{6}{7}$ 22. $\frac{37}{9} = 4\frac{1}{9}$

23. $\frac{36}{7} = 5\frac{1}{7}$ 24. $\frac{19}{3} = 6\frac{1}{3}$ 25. $\frac{47}{8} = 5\frac{7}{8}$ 26. $\frac{32}{7} = 4\frac{4}{7}$ 27. $\frac{43}{8} = 5\frac{3}{8}$ 28. $\frac{13}{4} = 3\frac{1}{4}$

29. $\frac{53}{8} = 6\frac{5}{8}$ 30. $\frac{29}{9} = 3\frac{2}{9}$ 31. $\frac{26}{4} = 6\frac{1}{2}$ 32. $\frac{17}{7} = 2\frac{3}{7}$ 33. $\frac{64}{9} = 7\frac{1}{9}$ 34. $\frac{25}{6} = 4\frac{1}{6}$

35. $\frac{21}{8} = 2\frac{5}{8}$ 36. $\frac{26}{3} = 8\frac{2}{3}$ 37. $\frac{53}{9} = 5\frac{8}{9}$ 38. $\frac{85}{12} = 7\frac{1}{12}$

Practice hard. You'll win!

39. $\frac{29}{5} = 5\frac{4}{5}$ 40. $\frac{34}{9} = 3\frac{7}{9}$ 41. $\frac{19}{4} = 4\frac{3}{4}$ 42. $\frac{65}{9} = 7\frac{2}{9}$

Page 49

Skill: Changing Mixed Numbers to Improper Fractions

mbers

Name

mbers to improper … on another … here.

Total Problems 42

Problems Correct

1. $3\frac{2}{5} = \frac{17}{5}$ 2. $6\frac{2}{5} = \frac{32}{5}$

3. $2\frac{1}{4} = \frac{9}{4}$ 4. $7\frac{3}{8} = \frac{59}{8}$

5. $4\frac{2}{7} = \frac{30}{7}$ 6. $12\frac{3}{4} = \frac{51}{4}$ 7. $8\frac{2}{3} = \frac{26}{3}$ 8. $4\frac{1}{8} = \frac{33}{8}$ 9. $3\frac{2}{4} = \frac{14}{4}$ 10. $5\frac{2}{7} = \frac{37}{7}$

11. $8\frac{2}{5} = \frac{42}{5}$ 12. $4\frac{3}{7} = \frac{31}{7}$ 13. $2\frac{3}{8} = \frac{19}{8}$ 14. $9\frac{2}{3} = \frac{29}{3}$ 15. $4\frac{3}{9} = \frac{39}{9}$ 16. $8\frac{3}{5} = \frac{43}{5}$

17. $15\frac{1}{3} = \frac{46}{3}$ 18. $17\frac{1}{2} = \frac{35}{2}$ 19. $32\frac{1}{3} = \frac{97}{3}$ 20. $3\frac{2}{6} = \frac{20}{6}$ 21. $8\frac{2}{5} = \frac{42}{5}$ 22. $6\frac{2}{8} = \frac{50}{8}$

23. $7\frac{3}{5} = \frac{38}{5}$ 24. $4\frac{6}{7} = \frac{34}{7}$ 25. $8\frac{2}{7} = \frac{58}{7}$ 26. $9\frac{3}{4} = \frac{39}{4}$ 27. $6\frac{2}{8} = \frac{50}{8}$ 28. $8\frac{2}{6} = \frac{50}{6}$

29. $5\frac{2}{8} = \frac{42}{8}$ 30. $3\frac{7}{8} = \frac{31}{8}$ 31. $9\frac{2}{5} = \frac{47}{5}$ 32. $4\frac{3}{7} = \frac{31}{7}$ 33. $8\frac{3}{6} = \frac{51}{6}$ 34. $6\frac{2}{9} = \frac{56}{9}$

35. $8\frac{7}{12} = \frac{103}{12}$ 36. $5\frac{3}{9} = \frac{48}{9}$ 37. $3\frac{2}{11} = \frac{35}{11}$ 38. $9\frac{6}{12} = \frac{114}{12}$

39. $7\frac{2}{8} = \frac{58}{8}$ 40. $11\frac{2}{12} = \frac{134}{12}$ 41. $15\frac{2}{3} = \frac{47}{3}$ 42. $5\frac{3}{6} = \frac{33}{6}$

Page 50

Skill: Changing Improper Fractions to Mixed Numbers

Fractions

Name

Change these improper fractions to mixed numbers. Show your work on another sheet. Write your answers here.

Total Problems 50

Problems Correct

1. $\frac{36}{6} = 6$ 2. $\frac{14}{6} = 2\frac{1}{3}$

3. $\frac{28}{9} = 3\frac{1}{9}$ 4. $\frac{13}{5} = 2\frac{3}{5}$ 5. $\frac{17}{8} = 2\frac{1}{8}$ 6. $\frac{51}{10} = 5\frac{1}{10}$ 7. $\frac{13}{6} = 2\frac{1}{6}$

8. $\frac{43}{8} = 5\frac{3}{8}$ 9. $\frac{24}{5} = 4\frac{4}{5}$ 10. $\frac{34}{6} = 5\frac{2}{3}$ 11. $\frac{29}{4} = 7\frac{1}{4}$ 12. $\frac{91}{10} = 9\frac{1}{10}$

13. $\frac{37}{7} = 5\frac{2}{7}$ 14. $\frac{21}{4} = 5\frac{1}{4}$ 15. $\frac{83}{9} = 9\frac{2}{9}$ 16. $\frac{15}{6} = 2\frac{1}{2}$ 17. $\frac{37}{5} = 7\frac{2}{5}$

18. $\frac{49}{6} = 8\frac{1}{6}$ 19. $\frac{25}{4} = 6\frac{1}{4}$ 20. $\frac{48}{5} = 9\frac{3}{5}$ 21. $\frac{23}{7} = 3\frac{2}{7}$ 22. $\frac{15}{2} = 7\frac{1}{2}$

23. $\frac{39}{6} = 6\frac{1}{2}$ 24. $\frac{56}{9} = 6\frac{2}{9}$ 25. $\frac{47}{6} = 7\frac{5}{6}$ 26. $\frac{23}{3} = 7\frac{2}{3}$ 27. $\frac{63}{8} = 7\frac{7}{8}$

28. $\frac{75}{8} = 9\frac{3}{8}$ 29. $\frac{62}{7} = 8\frac{6}{7}$ 30. $\frac{42}{5} = 8\frac{2}{5}$ 31. $\frac{73}{9} = 8\frac{1}{9}$ 32. $\frac{47}{8} = 5\frac{7}{8}$

33. $\frac{59}{10} = 5\frac{9}{10}$ 34. $\frac{78}{9} = 8\frac{2}{3}$ 35. $\frac{46}{5} = 9\frac{1}{5}$ 36. $\frac{87}{12} = 7\frac{1}{4}$ 37. $\frac{95}{9} = 10\frac{5}{9}$

38. $\frac{111}{11} = 10\frac{1}{11}$ 39. $\frac{89}{11} = 8\frac{1}{11}$ 40. $\frac{123}{10} = 12\frac{3}{10}$ 41. $\frac{147}{12} = 12\frac{1}{4}$ 42. $\frac{113}{10} = 11\frac{3}{10}$

43. $\frac{135}{12} = 11\frac{1}{4}$ 44. $\frac{114}{10} = 11\frac{2}{5}$ 45. $\frac{59}{6} = 9\frac{5}{6}$

Anything's possible with practice!

46. $\frac{47}{4} = 11\frac{3}{4}$ 47. $\frac{134}{11} = 12\frac{2}{11}$ 48. $\frac{112}{10} = 11\frac{1}{5}$

49. $\frac{36}{5} = 7\frac{1}{5}$ 50. $\frac{88}{10} = 8\frac{4}{5}$

Page 51

Skill: Changing Mixed Numbers to Improper Fractions

Fractions

Name

Change these mixed numbers to improper fractions. Show your work on another sheet. Write your answers here.

Total Problems 50

Problems Correct

1. $3\frac{6}{7} = \frac{27}{7}$ 2. $4\frac{2}{8} = \frac{34}{8}$

3. $2\frac{1}{3} = \frac{7}{3}$ 4. $4\frac{5}{6} = \frac{29}{6}$ 5. $2\frac{2}{3} = \frac{8}{3}$ 6. $4\frac{1}{6} = \frac{25}{6}$ 7. $4\frac{3}{5} = \frac{23}{5}$

8. $3\frac{4}{6} = \frac{22}{6}$ 9. $5\frac{2}{3} = \frac{17}{3}$ 10. $6\frac{3}{7} = \frac{45}{7}$ 11. $2\frac{4}{9} = \frac{22}{9}$ 12. $6\frac{2}{5} = \frac{32}{5}$

13. $5\frac{2}{9} = \frac{47}{9}$ 14. $7\frac{3}{6} = \frac{45}{6}$ 15. $2\frac{3}{12} = \frac{27}{12}$ 16. $8\frac{4}{10} = \frac{84}{10}$ 17. $3\frac{4}{12} = \frac{40}{12}$

18. $2\frac{6}{14} = \frac{34}{14}$ 19. $6\frac{3}{9} = \frac{57}{9}$ 20. $5\frac{1}{9} = \frac{46}{9}$ 21. $12\frac{3}{11} = \frac{135}{11}$ 22. $4\frac{5}{8} = \frac{37}{8}$

23. $7\frac{6}{12} = \frac{90}{12}$ 24. $5\frac{7}{10} = \frac{57}{10}$ 25. $4\frac{6}{12} = \frac{54}{12}$ 26. $3\frac{2}{4} = \frac{14}{4}$ 27. $6\frac{1}{8} = \frac{49}{8}$

28. $7\frac{2}{5} = \frac{37}{5}$ 29. $3\frac{4}{8} = \frac{28}{8}$ 30. $9\frac{2}{12} = \frac{110}{12}$ 31. $8\frac{3}{7} = \frac{59}{7}$ 32. $4\frac{6}{11} = \frac{50}{11}$

33. $11\frac{3}{12} = \frac{135}{12}$ 34. $10\frac{4}{11} = \frac{114}{11}$ 35. $5\frac{6}{9} = \frac{51}{9}$ 36. $7\frac{8}{10} = \frac{78}{10}$ 37. $12\frac{4}{11} = \frac{136}{11}$

38. $14\frac{2}{3} = \frac{44}{3}$ 39. $15\frac{1}{4} = \frac{61}{4}$ 40. $3\frac{2}{6} = \frac{20}{6}$ 41. $4\frac{8}{15} = \frac{68}{15}$ 42. $2\frac{1}{11} = \frac{23}{11}$

43. $5\frac{1}{7} = \frac{36}{7}$ 44. $12\frac{6}{9} = \frac{114}{9}$ 45. $11\frac{3}{11} = \frac{124}{11}$

46. $30\frac{2}{10} = \frac{302}{10}$ 47. $13\frac{3}{4} = \frac{55}{4}$ 48. $20\frac{2}{4} = \frac{82}{4}$

49. $45\frac{1}{2} = \frac{91}{2}$ 50. $9\frac{5}{31} = \frac{284}{31}$

Practice!
Practice!
Practice!

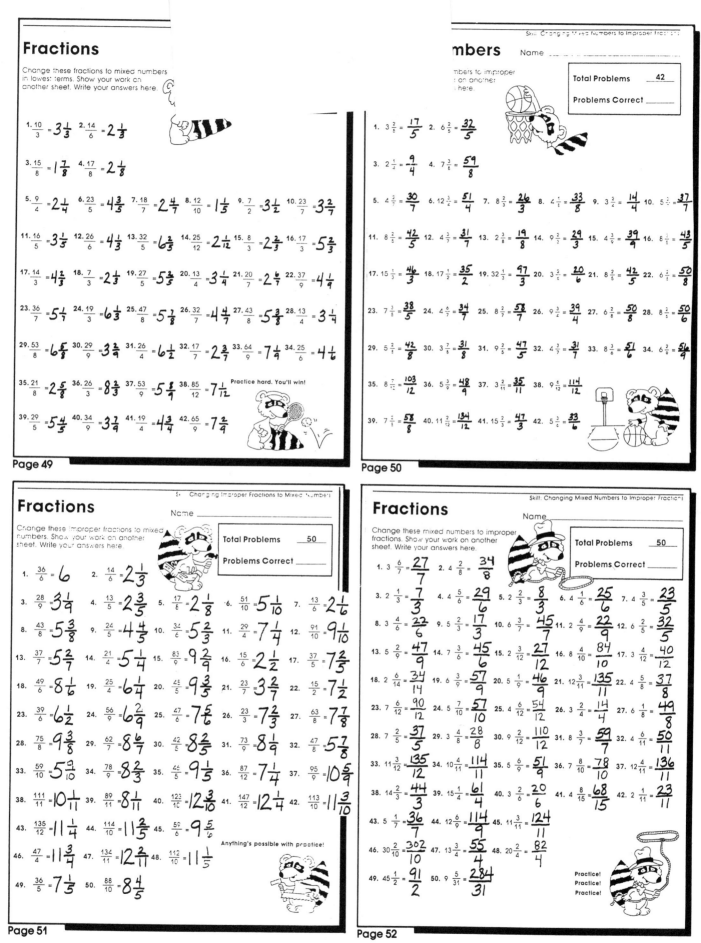

Page 52

Answer Key

Fractions

Skill: Addition of Like Fractions

Name ____________________

Show your work on another sheet. Reduce your answers to lowest terms and write them here.

Total Problems 40

Problems Correct ______

1. $\frac{2}{4} + \frac{1}{4} = \frac{3}{4}$
2. $\frac{3}{8} + \frac{4}{8} = \frac{7}{8}$
3. $\frac{3}{12} + \frac{8}{12} = \frac{11}{12}$
4. $\frac{1}{2} + \frac{1}{2} = 1$
5. $\frac{3}{7} + \frac{2}{7} = \frac{5}{7}$
6. $\frac{2}{3} + \frac{1}{3} = 1$
7. $\frac{8}{16} + \frac{3}{16} = \frac{11}{16}$
8. $\frac{1}{5} + \frac{2}{5} = \frac{3}{5}$
9. $\frac{5}{10} + \frac{2}{10} = \frac{7}{10}$
10. $\frac{2}{9} + \frac{4}{9} = \frac{2}{3}$
11. $\frac{3}{5} + \frac{1}{5} = \frac{4}{5}$
12. $\frac{2}{6} + \frac{2}{6} = \frac{2}{3}$
13. $\frac{2}{8} + \frac{1}{8} = \frac{3}{8}$
14. $\frac{5}{9} + \frac{1}{9} = \frac{2}{3}$
15. $\frac{6}{7} + \frac{1}{7} = 1$
16. $\frac{12}{20} + \frac{4}{20} = \frac{4}{5}$
17. $\frac{5}{8} + \frac{2}{8} = \frac{7}{8}$
18. $\frac{8}{18} + \frac{5}{18} = \frac{13}{18}$
19. $\frac{4}{11} + \frac{5}{11} = \frac{9}{11}$
20. $\frac{5}{16} + \frac{9}{16} = \frac{7}{8}$
21. $\frac{8}{24} + \frac{13}{24} = \frac{7}{8}$
22. $\frac{4}{12} + \frac{2}{12} = \frac{1}{2}$
23. $\frac{5}{9} + \frac{3}{9} = \frac{8}{9}$
24. $\frac{9}{21} + \frac{7}{21} = \frac{16}{21}$
25. $\frac{3}{10} + \frac{6}{10} = \frac{9}{10}$
26. $\frac{4}{9} + \frac{3}{9} = \frac{7}{9}$
27. $\frac{14}{24} + \frac{7}{24} = \frac{7}{8}$
28. $\frac{2}{7} + \frac{4}{7} = \frac{6}{7}$
29. $\frac{5}{16} + \frac{7}{16} = \frac{3}{4}$
30. $\frac{2}{5} + \frac{2}{5} = \frac{4}{5}$
31. $\frac{3}{6} + \frac{2}{6} = \frac{5}{6}$
32. $\frac{7}{20} + \frac{8}{20} = \frac{3}{4}$
33. $\frac{5}{8} + \frac{3}{8} = 1$
34. $\frac{8}{12} + \frac{3}{12} = \frac{11}{12}$
35. $\frac{11}{16} + \frac{5}{16} = 1$
36. $\frac{8}{24} + \frac{9}{24} = \frac{17}{24}$
37. $\frac{15}{30} + \frac{8}{30} = \frac{23}{30}$
38. $\frac{7}{21} + \frac{10}{21} = \frac{17}{21}$
39. $\frac{3}{14} + \frac{8}{14} = \frac{11}{14}$
40. $\frac{9}{15} + \frac{4}{15} = \frac{13}{15}$

Practice puts you on top!

Page 53

Fractions

Skill: Addition of Like Fractions

Name ____________________

Show your work on another sheet. Reduce your answers to lowest terms and write them here.

Total Problems 40

Problems Correct ______

1. $\frac{2}{3} + \frac{1}{3} = 1$
2. $\frac{2}{6} + \frac{3}{6} = \frac{5}{6}$
3. $\frac{4}{12} + \frac{3}{12} = \frac{7}{12}$
4. $\frac{8}{16} + \frac{4}{16} = \frac{3}{4}$
5. $\frac{3}{25} + \frac{18}{25} = \frac{21}{25}$
6. $\frac{7}{15} + \frac{4}{15} = \frac{11}{15}$
7. $\frac{2}{5} + \frac{2}{5} = \frac{4}{5}$
8. $\frac{6}{30} + \frac{17}{30} = \frac{23}{30}$
9. $\frac{4}{9} + \frac{3}{9} = \frac{7}{9}$
10. $\frac{7}{11} + \frac{3}{11} = \frac{10}{11}$
11. $\frac{6}{8} + \frac{2}{8} = 1$
12. $\frac{5}{16} + \frac{8}{16} = \frac{13}{16}$
13. $\frac{7}{10} + \frac{2}{10} = \frac{9}{10}$
14. $\frac{4}{8} + \frac{3}{8} = \frac{7}{8}$
15. $\frac{2}{17} + \frac{9}{17} = \frac{11}{17}$
16. $\frac{3}{9} + \frac{5}{9} = \frac{8}{9}$
17. $\frac{2}{7} + \frac{4}{7} = \frac{6}{7}$
18. $\frac{5}{12} + \frac{6}{12} = \frac{11}{12}$
19. $\frac{3}{48} + \frac{7}{48} = \frac{5}{24}$
20. $\frac{1}{6} + \frac{3}{6} = \frac{2}{3}$
21. $\frac{5}{28} + \frac{13}{28} = \frac{9}{14}$
22. $\frac{7}{30} + \frac{8}{30} = \frac{1}{2}$
23. $\frac{11}{22} + \frac{8}{22} = \frac{19}{22}$
24. $\frac{9}{14} + \frac{3}{14} = \frac{6}{7}$
25. $\frac{8}{64} + \frac{17}{64} = \frac{25}{64}$
26. $\frac{4}{7} + \frac{3}{7} = 1$
27. $\frac{2}{8} + \frac{3}{8} = \frac{5}{8}$
28. $\frac{3}{6} + \frac{1}{6} = \frac{2}{3}$
29. $\frac{6}{28} + \frac{17}{28} = \frac{23}{28}$
30. $\frac{14}{50} + \frac{7}{50} = \frac{21}{50}$
31. $\frac{6}{10} + \frac{3}{10} = \frac{9}{10}$
32. $\frac{8}{16} + \frac{4}{16} = \frac{3}{4}$
33. $\frac{5}{35} + \frac{17}{35} = \frac{22}{35}$
34. $\frac{5}{11} + \frac{2}{11} = \frac{7}{11}$
35. $\frac{2}{9} + \frac{5}{9} = \frac{7}{9}$
36. $\frac{8}{90} + \frac{23}{90} = \frac{31}{90}$
37. $\frac{8}{12} + \frac{2}{12} = \frac{5}{6}$
38. $\frac{4}{8} + \frac{1}{8} = \frac{5}{8}$
39. $\frac{8}{14} + \frac{5}{14} = \frac{13}{14}$
40. $\frac{17}{28} + \frac{6}{28} = \frac{23}{28}$

Practice brings success!

Page 54

Fractions

Skill: Addition of Unlike Fractions

Name ____________________

Show your work on another sheet. Reduce your answers to lowest terms and write them here.

Total Problems 40

Problems Correct ______

1. $\frac{1}{3} + \frac{3}{6} = \frac{5}{6}$
2. $\frac{1}{5} + \frac{3}{10} = \frac{1}{2}$
3. $\frac{1}{4} + \frac{5}{8} = \frac{7}{8}$
4. $\frac{1}{2} + \frac{2}{4} = 1$
5. $\frac{3}{7} + \frac{2}{14} = \frac{4}{7}$
6. $\frac{5}{6} + \frac{2}{12} = 1$
7. $\frac{2}{4} + \frac{5}{12} = \frac{11}{12}$
8. $\frac{2}{5} + \frac{4}{10} = \frac{4}{5}$
9. $\frac{1}{4} + \frac{2}{8} = \frac{1}{2}$
10. $\frac{1}{3} + \frac{4}{6} = 1$
11. $\frac{1}{7} + \frac{5}{14} = \frac{1}{2}$
12. $\frac{3}{6} + \frac{1}{12} = \frac{7}{12}$
13. $\frac{2}{5} + \frac{7}{15} = \frac{13}{15}$
14. $\frac{4}{8} + \frac{3}{16} = \frac{11}{16}$
15. $\frac{2}{9} + \frac{5}{18} = \frac{1}{2}$
16. $\frac{4}{7} + \frac{5}{21} = \frac{17}{21}$
17. $\frac{2}{3} + \frac{2}{6} = 1$
18. $\frac{4}{10} + \frac{5}{20} = \frac{13}{20}$
19. $\frac{1}{2} + \frac{1}{4} = \frac{3}{4}$
20. $\frac{1}{3} + \frac{2}{9} = \frac{5}{9}$
21. $\frac{3}{4} + \frac{1}{12} = \frac{5}{6}$
22. $\frac{6}{7} + \frac{2}{21} = \frac{20}{21}$
23. $\frac{6}{10} + \frac{6}{20} = \frac{9}{10}$
24. $\frac{4}{5} + \frac{1}{15} = \frac{13}{15}$
25. $\frac{2}{6} + \frac{7}{12} = \frac{11}{12}$
26. $\frac{2}{4} + \frac{3}{16} = \frac{11}{16}$
27. $\frac{2}{4} + \frac{3}{8} = \frac{7}{8}$
28. $\frac{4}{5} + \frac{1}{10} = \frac{9}{10}$
29. $\frac{4}{9} + \frac{3}{18} = \frac{11}{18}$
30. $\frac{1}{4} + \frac{6}{12} = \frac{3}{4}$
31. $\frac{4}{7} + \frac{3}{14} = \frac{11}{14}$
32. $\frac{2}{3} + \frac{2}{9} = \frac{8}{9}$
33. $\frac{3}{8} + \frac{7}{16} = \frac{13}{16}$
34. $\frac{2}{8} + \frac{5}{16} = \frac{9}{16}$
35. $\frac{1}{5} + \frac{9}{15} = \frac{4}{5}$
36. $\frac{3}{9} + \frac{7}{18} = \frac{13}{18}$
37. $\frac{5}{7} + \frac{4}{21} = \frac{19}{21}$
38. $\frac{8}{10} + \frac{1}{20} = \frac{17}{20}$
39. $\frac{1}{3} + \frac{5}{9} = \frac{8}{9}$
40. $\frac{3}{4} + \frac{2}{16} = \frac{7}{8}$

Practice brings success!

Page 55

Fractions

Skill: Addition of Unlike Fractions

Name ____________________

Show your work on another sheet. Reduce your answers to lowest terms and write them here.

Total Problems 40

Problems Correct ______

1. $\frac{1}{2} + \frac{3}{8} = \frac{7}{8}$
2. $\frac{1}{2} + \frac{2}{5} = \frac{9}{10}$
3. $\frac{2}{8} + \frac{2}{3} = \frac{11}{12}$
4. $\frac{4}{7} + \frac{1}{3} = \frac{19}{21}$
5. $\frac{2}{5} + \frac{2}{4} = \frac{9}{10}$
6. $\frac{1}{2} + \frac{2}{8} = \frac{3}{4}$
7. $\frac{2}{3} + \frac{1}{5} = \frac{13}{15}$
8. $\frac{2}{4} + \frac{7}{16} = \frac{15}{16}$
9. $\frac{3}{5} + \frac{2}{6} = \frac{14}{15}$
10. $\frac{5}{11} + \frac{1}{3} = \frac{26}{33}$
11. $\frac{3}{9} + \frac{1}{2} = \frac{5}{6}$
12. $\frac{6}{7} + \frac{2}{3} = 1\frac{11}{21}$
13. $\frac{2}{10} + \frac{1}{2} = \frac{7}{10}$
14. $\frac{1}{2} + \frac{4}{9} = \frac{17}{18}$
15. $\frac{1}{3} + \frac{6}{12} = \frac{5}{6}$
16. $\frac{1}{4} + \frac{3}{5} = \frac{17}{20}$
17. $\frac{2}{6} + \frac{1}{2} = \frac{5}{6}$
18. $\frac{1}{2} + \frac{1}{5} = \frac{7}{10}$
19. $\frac{1}{3} + \frac{3}{5} = \frac{14}{15}$
20. $\frac{4}{8} + \frac{1}{3} = \frac{5}{6}$
21. $\frac{1}{3} + \frac{5}{12} = \frac{3}{4}$
22. $\frac{1}{6} + \frac{1}{4} = \frac{5}{12}$
23. $\frac{5}{12} + \frac{1}{2} = \frac{11}{12}$
24. $\frac{2}{3} + \frac{5}{7} = 1\frac{8}{21}$
25. $\frac{3}{6} + \frac{2}{5} = 1\frac{1}{10}$
26. $\frac{2}{5} + \frac{1}{3} = \frac{11}{15}$
27. $\frac{2}{16} + \frac{3}{4} = \frac{7}{8}$
28. $\frac{4}{10} + \frac{1}{2} = \frac{9}{10}$
29. $\frac{2}{3} + \frac{3}{11} = \frac{31}{33}$
30. $\frac{5}{7} + \frac{1}{2} = 1\frac{3}{14}$
31. $\frac{1}{5} + \frac{3}{4} = \frac{19}{20}$
32. $\frac{1}{2} + \frac{1}{6} = \frac{2}{3}$
33. $\frac{1}{2} + \frac{3}{12} = \frac{3}{4}$
34. $\frac{1}{6} + \frac{4}{5} = \frac{29}{30}$
35. $\frac{4}{11} + \frac{1}{3} = \frac{23}{33}$
36. $\frac{3}{12} + \frac{2}{3} = \frac{11}{12}$
37. $\frac{1}{4} + \frac{9}{16} = \frac{13}{16}$
38. $\frac{5}{8} + \frac{1}{3} = \frac{23}{24}$
39. $\frac{3}{10} + \frac{1}{2} = \frac{4}{5}$
40. $\frac{3}{7} + \frac{1}{2} = \frac{13}{14}$

Practice and anything's possible!

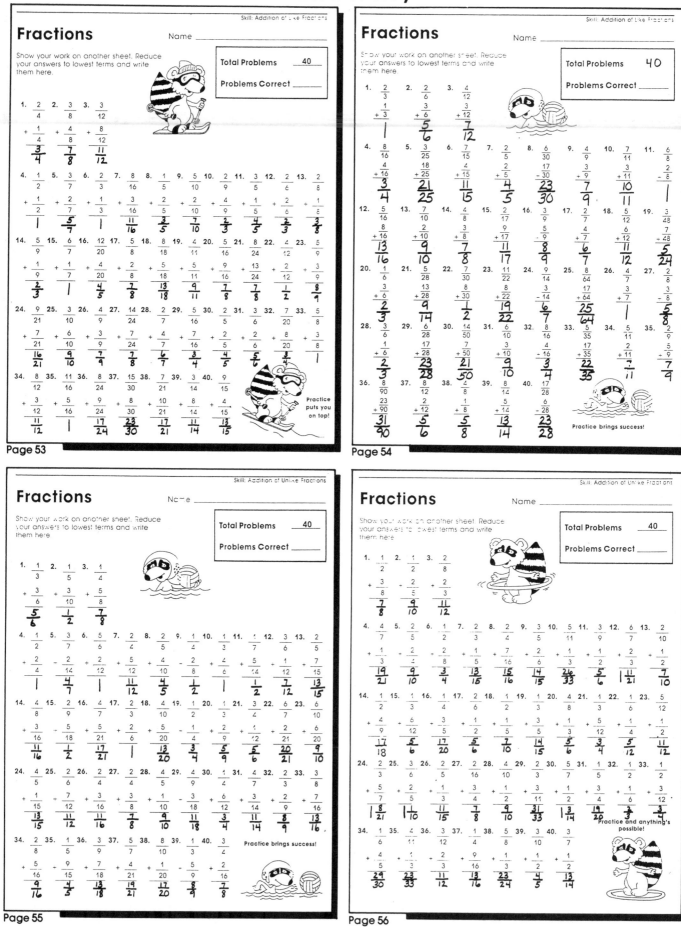

Page 56

Answer Key

Fractions

Skill: Addition of Unlike Fractions

Name ______________________

Show your work on another sheet. Reduce your answers to lowest terms and write them here.

Total Problems 40

Problems Correct ______

1. $\frac{2}{3} + \frac{1}{9} = \frac{7}{9}$
2. $\frac{3}{4} + \frac{2}{12} = \frac{11}{12}$
3. $\frac{1}{5} + \frac{3}{10} = \frac{1}{2}$
4. $\frac{1}{6} + \frac{2}{12} = \frac{1}{3}$
5. $\frac{3}{4} + \frac{1}{8} = \frac{7}{8}$
6. $\frac{2}{8} + \frac{1}{16} = \frac{5}{16}$
7. $\frac{3}{5} + \frac{2}{10} = \frac{4}{5}$
8. $\frac{7}{12} + \frac{2}{4} = 1\frac{1}{12}$
9. $\frac{6}{7} + \frac{2}{21} = \frac{20}{21}$
10. $\frac{3}{5} + \frac{2}{15} = \frac{11}{15}$
11. $\frac{7}{14} + \frac{2}{7} = \frac{11}{14}$
12. $\frac{3}{6} + \frac{2}{18} = \frac{11}{18}$
13. $\frac{2}{14} + \frac{1}{7} = \frac{2}{7}$
14. $\frac{1}{8} + \frac{1}{2} = \frac{5}{8}$
15. $\frac{6}{8} + \frac{1}{24} = \frac{19}{24}$
16. $\frac{4}{12} + \frac{1}{3} = \frac{2}{3}$
17. $\frac{8}{14} + \frac{3}{7} = 1$
18. $\frac{2}{3} + \frac{4}{12} = 1$
19. $\frac{6}{14} + \frac{1}{2} = \frac{13}{14}$
20. $\frac{3}{6} + \frac{4}{12} = \frac{5}{6}$
21. $\frac{3}{8} + \frac{5}{16} = \frac{11}{16}$
22. $\frac{7}{21} + \frac{2}{7} = \frac{13}{21}$
23. $\frac{5}{15} + \frac{1}{3} = \frac{2}{3}$
24. $\frac{4}{16} + \frac{1}{2} = \frac{3}{4}$
25. $\frac{3}{9} + \frac{1}{3} = \frac{2}{3}$
26. $\frac{1}{5} + \frac{6}{25} = \frac{11}{25}$
27. $\frac{1}{4} + \frac{2}{8} = \frac{1}{2}$
28. $\frac{1}{2} + \frac{4}{6} = 1\frac{1}{6}$
29. $\frac{10}{20} + \frac{3}{4} = 1\frac{1}{4}$
30. $\frac{7}{30} + \frac{1}{3} = \frac{17}{30}$
31. $\frac{4}{8} + \frac{1}{40} = \frac{21}{40}$
32. $\frac{1}{4} + \frac{3}{8} = \frac{5}{8}$
33. $\frac{2}{5} + \frac{4}{10} = \frac{4}{5}$
34. $\frac{1}{5} + \frac{1}{6} = \frac{11}{30}$
35. $\frac{2}{9} + \frac{1}{4} = \frac{17}{36}$
36. $\frac{3}{7} + \frac{1}{2} = \frac{13}{14}$
37. $\frac{2}{5} + \frac{1}{7} = \frac{19}{35}$
38. $\frac{4}{8} + \frac{1}{3} = \frac{5}{6}$
39. $\frac{5}{9} + \frac{1}{2} = 1\frac{1}{18}$
40. $\frac{2}{7} + \frac{1}{8} = \frac{23}{56}$

Anything's possible with practice

Page 57

Fractions

Skill: Addition of Unlike Fractions

Name ______________________

Show your work on another sheet. Reduce your answers to lowest terms and write them here.

Total Problems 40

Problems Correct ______

1. $\frac{2}{3} + \frac{2}{9} = \frac{8}{9}$
2. $\frac{1}{6} + \frac{2}{3} = \frac{5}{6}$
3. $\frac{1}{8} + \frac{4}{16} = \frac{3}{8}$
4. $\frac{4}{8} + \frac{1}{4} = \frac{3}{4}$
5. $\frac{5}{9} + \frac{3}{18} = \frac{13}{18}$
6. $\frac{5}{12} + \frac{1}{3} = \frac{3}{4}$
7. $\frac{8}{10} + \frac{1}{5} = 1$
8. $\frac{4}{5} + \frac{1}{20} = \frac{17}{20}$
9. $\frac{2}{8} + \frac{1}{2} = \frac{3}{4}$
10. $\frac{1}{10} + \frac{2}{5} = \frac{1}{2}$
11. $\frac{2}{11} + \frac{1}{22} = \frac{5}{22}$
12. $\frac{3}{10} + \frac{1}{2} = \frac{4}{5}$
13. $\frac{2}{6} + \frac{1}{3} = \frac{2}{3}$
14. $\frac{3}{8} + \frac{1}{4} = \frac{5}{8}$
15. $\frac{2}{5} + \frac{2}{15} = \frac{8}{15}$
16. $\frac{1}{9} + \frac{1}{18} = \frac{1}{6}$
17. $\frac{3}{4} + \frac{1}{16} = \frac{13}{16}$
18. $\frac{2}{7} + \frac{3}{21} = \frac{3}{7}$
19. $\frac{4}{6} + \frac{1}{12} = \frac{3}{4}$
20. $\frac{2}{3} + \frac{2}{12} = \frac{5}{6}$
21. $\frac{2}{8} + \frac{3}{16} = \frac{7}{16}$
22. $\frac{2}{21} + \frac{2}{7} = \frac{8}{21}$
23. $\frac{1}{4} + \frac{2}{12} = \frac{5}{12}$
24. $\frac{3}{6} + \frac{2}{18} = \frac{11}{18}$
25. $\frac{2}{7} + \frac{6}{21} = \frac{4}{7}$
26. $\frac{1}{2} + \frac{3}{18} = \frac{2}{3}$
27. $\frac{1}{3} + \frac{2}{15} = \frac{7}{15}$
28. $\frac{1}{8} + \frac{1}{4} = \frac{3}{8}$
29. $\frac{3}{6} + \frac{3}{12} = \frac{3}{4}$
30. $\frac{2}{5} + \frac{9}{15} = 1$
31. $\frac{3}{6} + \frac{5}{12} = \frac{11}{12}$
32. $\frac{1}{15} + \frac{1}{3} = \frac{2}{5}$
33. $\frac{2}{8} + \frac{1}{16} = \frac{5}{16}$
34. $\frac{3}{4} + \frac{1}{12} = \frac{5}{6}$
35. $\frac{1}{3} + \frac{5}{18} = \frac{11}{18}$
36. $\frac{1}{5} + \frac{4}{10} = \frac{3}{5}$
37. $\frac{2}{6} + \frac{4}{12} = \frac{2}{3}$
38. $\frac{3}{5} + \frac{2}{10} = \frac{4}{5}$
39. $\frac{1}{9} + \frac{3}{18} = \frac{5}{18}$
40. $\frac{4}{7} + \frac{2}{21} = \frac{2}{3}$

Anything's possible with practice!

Page 58

Mixed Numbers

Skill: Addition of Mixed Numbers With Like Denominators

Name ______________________

Show your work on another sheet. Reduce your answers to lowest terms and write them here.

Total Problems 40

Problems Correct ______

1. $3\frac{2}{4} + 7\frac{1}{4} = 10\frac{3}{4}$
2. $8\frac{2}{7} + 5\frac{3}{7} = 13\frac{5}{7}$
3. $4\frac{6}{9} + 8\frac{2}{9} = 12\frac{8}{9}$
4. $2\frac{4}{7} + 9\frac{2}{7} = 11\frac{6}{7}$
5. $4\frac{2}{5} + 5\frac{2}{5} = 9\frac{4}{5}$
6. $7\frac{2}{4} + 9\frac{1}{4} = 16\frac{3}{4}$
7. $5\frac{2}{7} + 8\frac{3}{7} = 13\frac{5}{7}$
8. $8\frac{3}{5} + 7\frac{1}{5} = 15\frac{4}{5}$
9. $3\frac{1}{4} + 8\frac{2}{4} = 11\frac{3}{4}$
10. $5\frac{3}{9} + 6\frac{4}{9} = 11\frac{7}{9}$
11. $9\frac{2}{4} + 6\frac{1}{4} = 15\frac{3}{4}$
12. $7\frac{2}{6} + 9\frac{3}{6} = 16\frac{5}{6}$
13. $6\frac{1}{7} + 4\frac{3}{7} = 10\frac{4}{7}$
14. $4\frac{1}{6} + 7\frac{4}{6} = 11\frac{5}{6}$
15. $9\frac{3}{7} + 8\frac{2}{7} = 17\frac{5}{7}$
16. $5\frac{1}{3} + 6\frac{1}{3} = 11\frac{2}{3}$
17. $8\frac{2}{14} + 9\frac{7}{14} = 17\frac{9}{14}$
18. $4\frac{3}{9} + 6\frac{4}{9} = 10\frac{7}{9}$
19. $6\frac{1}{5} + 8\frac{3}{5} = 14\frac{4}{5}$
20. $7\frac{1}{12} + 8\frac{6}{12} = 15\frac{7}{12}$
21. $3\frac{2}{8} + 9\frac{3}{8} = 12\frac{5}{8}$
22. $9\frac{6}{9} + 4\frac{1}{9} = 13\frac{7}{9}$
23. $5\frac{2}{7} + 8\frac{3}{7} = 13\frac{5}{7}$
24. $8\frac{3}{10} + 7\frac{4}{10} = 15\frac{7}{10}$
25. $9\frac{1}{4} + 7\frac{2}{4} = 16\frac{3}{4}$
26. $2\frac{6}{8} + 9\frac{1}{8} = 11\frac{7}{8}$
27. $6\frac{3}{5} + 9\frac{1}{5} = 15\frac{4}{5}$
28. $5\frac{1}{7} + 6\frac{1}{7} = 11\frac{2}{7}$
29. $4\frac{3}{8} + 7\frac{2}{8} = 11\frac{5}{8}$
30. $7\frac{3}{6} + 8\frac{2}{6} = 15\frac{5}{6}$
31. $7\frac{2}{9} + 4\frac{3}{9} = 11\frac{5}{9}$
32. $3\frac{4}{8} + 7\frac{3}{8} = 10\frac{7}{8}$
33. $9\frac{1}{5} + 4\frac{2}{5} = 13\frac{3}{5}$
34. $7\frac{1}{3} + 9\frac{1}{3} = 16\frac{2}{3}$
35. $6\frac{2}{9} + 4\frac{3}{9} = 10\frac{5}{9}$
36. $8\frac{2}{6} + 9\frac{3}{6} = 17\frac{5}{6}$
37. $4\frac{8}{10} + 7\frac{1}{10} = 11\frac{9}{10}$
38. $5\frac{1}{7} + 7\frac{3}{7} = 12\frac{4}{7}$
39. $3\frac{2}{12} + 8\frac{3}{12} = 11\frac{5}{12}$
40. $4\frac{3}{15} + 9\frac{8}{15} = 13\frac{11}{15}$

Practice hard. You'll win.

Page 59

Mixed Numbers

Skill: Addition of Mixed Numbers With Like Denominators

Name ______________________

Show your work on another sheet. Reduce your answers to lowest terms and write them here.

Total Problems 40

Problems Correct ______

1. $3\frac{2}{4} + 5\frac{3}{4} = 9\frac{1}{4}$
2. $8\frac{1}{6} + 4\frac{7}{6} = 13\frac{1}{3}$
3. $4\frac{2}{5} + 9\frac{3}{5} = 14$
4. $7\frac{2}{8} + 5\frac{7}{8} = 13\frac{1}{8}$
5. $9\frac{1}{3} + 8\frac{4}{3} = 18\frac{2}{3}$
6. $2\frac{4}{5} + 7\frac{3}{5} = 10\frac{2}{5}$
7. $4\frac{3}{8} + 7\frac{5}{8} = 12$
8. 6 [illegible] + 5 [illegible] $= 12\frac{4}{5}$
9. $3\frac{2}{4} + 7\frac{3}{4} = 11\frac{1}{4}$
10. 8 [illegible] + 9 [illegible] $= 18\frac{1}{2}$
11. $5\frac{2}{5} + 8\frac{4}{5} = 14\frac{1}{5}$
12. $7\frac{3}{8} + 3\frac{7}{8} = 11\frac{1}{4}$
13. $4\frac{5}{9} + 8\frac{7}{9} = 13\frac{1}{3}$
14. $6\frac{4}{5} + 6\frac{3}{5} = 13\frac{2}{5}$
15. 8 [illegible] + 9 [illegible] $= 18\frac{1}{7}$
16. $4\frac{2}{6} + 7\frac{5}{6} = 12\frac{1}{6}$
17. [illegible] + 9 [illegible] $= 16\frac{1}{4}$
18. $3\frac{2}{5} + 7\frac{4}{5} = 11\frac{1}{5}$
19. $7\frac{4}{6} + 5\frac{5}{6} = 13\frac{1}{2}$
20. $9\frac{2}{3} + 8\frac{2}{3} = 18\frac{1}{3}$
21. $6\frac{4}{5} + 8\frac{3}{5} = 15\frac{2}{5}$
22. 4 [illegible] + 5 [illegible] $= 10\frac{1}{9}$
23. $8\frac{4}{7} + 8\frac{6}{7} = 17\frac{3}{7}$
24. 2 [illegible] + [illegible] $= 4\frac{1}{3}$
25. $6\frac{4}{5} + 9\frac{4}{5} = 16\frac{3}{5}$
26. $4\frac{2}{5} + 8\frac{3}{5} = 13$
27. $8\frac{6}{10} + 3\frac{7}{10} = 12\frac{3}{10}$
28. $5\frac{2}{8} + 9\frac{7}{8} = 15\frac{1}{8}$
29. 12 [illegible] + 4 [illegible] $= 17\frac{2}{7}$
30. $9\frac{3}{6} + 8\frac{5}{6} = 18\frac{1}{3}$
31. 14 [illegible] + 7 [illegible] $= 22\frac{2}{5}$
32. $8\frac{2}{4} + 9\frac{3}{4} = 18\frac{1}{4}$
33. $7\frac{8}{10} + 9\frac{7}{10} = 17\frac{1}{2}$
34. $13\frac{2}{4} + 9\frac{3}{4} = 23\frac{1}{4}$
35. $5\frac{3}{7} + 8\frac{6}{7} = 14\frac{2}{7}$
36. 3 [illegible] + 7 [illegible] $= 11\frac{1}{9}$
37. $15\frac{2}{6} + 8\frac{5}{6} = 24\frac{1}{6}$
38. $21\frac{2}{8} + 8\frac{6}{8} = 30$
39. $4\frac{3}{5} + 7\frac{4}{5} = 12\frac{2}{5}$
40. $10\frac{2}{4} + 8\frac{3}{4} = 19\frac{1}{4}$

Practice hard. You'll win!

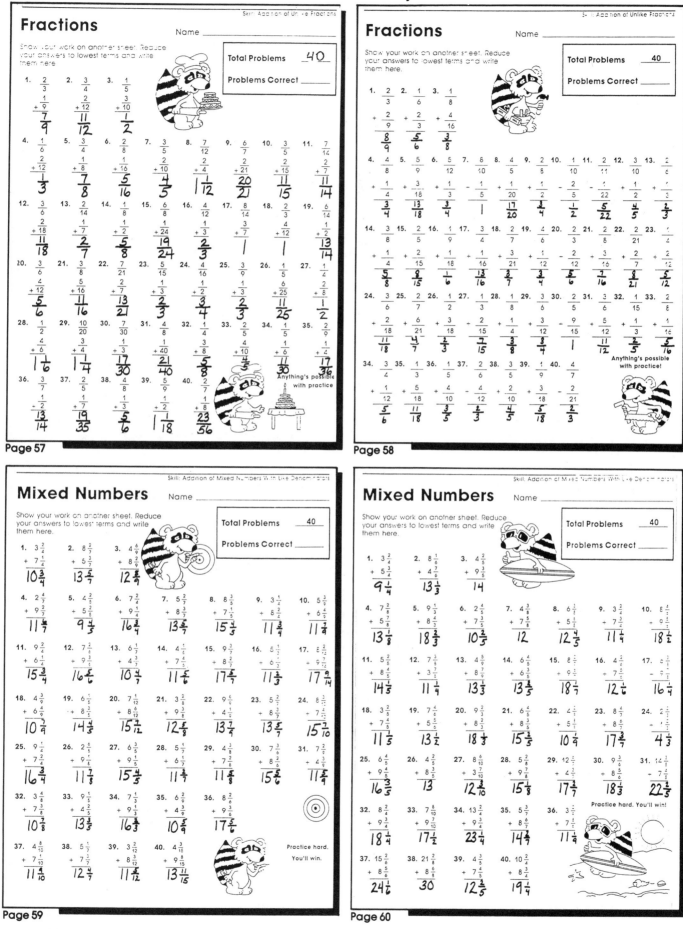

Page 60

Answer Key

Mixed Numbers

Name ______________________

Show your work on another sheet. Reduce your answers to lowest terms and write them here.

Total Problems 40

Problems Correct ______

1. $3\frac{2}{4} + 7\frac{3}{8}$ = $10\frac{7}{8}$
2. $5\frac{3}{5} + 9\frac{4}{10}$ = 15
3. $8\frac{1}{6} + 4\frac{3}{12}$ = $12\frac{5}{12}$
4. $6\frac{2}{10} + 5\frac{3}{5}$ = $11\frac{4}{5}$
5. 7 [illegible] + 6 [illegible] = $14\frac{1}{4}$
6. $2\frac{3}{10} + 6\frac{2}{5}$ = $8\frac{7}{10}$
7. $9\frac{3}{4}$ + 3 [illegible] = $12\frac{11}{12}$
8. 3 [illegible] − 8 [illegible] = $11\frac{2}{3}$
9. $7\frac{2}{6} + 8\frac{1}{2}$ = $15\frac{5}{6}$
10. $4\frac{2}{15}$ − 8 [illegible] = $12\frac{11}{15}$
11. $5\frac{2}{7} + 9\frac{3}{21}$ = $14\frac{3}{7}$
12. 2 [illegible] + $3\frac{1}{3}$ = 6
13. $8\frac{1}{2} + 9\frac{3}{4}$ = $18\frac{1}{4}$
14. 6 [illegible] + 8 [illegible] = $14\frac{7}{10}$
15. 4 [illegible] − 6 [illegible] = $10\frac{5}{8}$
16. $9\frac{2}{5} + 8\frac{3}{15}$ = $17\frac{3}{5}$
17. 7 [illegible] − 7 [illegible] = $14\frac{5}{6}$
18. $5\frac{3}{10} + 9\frac{2}{20}$ = $14\frac{2}{5}$
19. $2\frac{1}{8} + 8\frac{3}{24}$ = $10\frac{1}{4}$
20. $7\frac{3}{6} + 9\frac{1}{12}$ = $16\frac{7}{12}$
21. 8 [illegible] + $7\frac{1}{2}$ = $16\frac{1}{6}$
22. 3 [illegible] − 6 [illegible] = 10
23. $9\frac{3}{9}$ + 7 [illegible] = $16\frac{2}{3}$
24. $2\frac{3}{5}$ − 8 [illegible] = $10\frac{7}{10}$
25. $11\frac{3}{6} + 8\frac{4}{12}$ = $19\frac{5}{6}$
26. $9\frac{2}{7} + 7\frac{3}{21}$ = $16\frac{3}{7}$
27. $6\frac{2}{5} + 8\frac{3}{15}$ = $14\frac{3}{5}$
28. $8\frac{1}{6} + 9\frac{2}{3}$ = $17\frac{5}{6}$
29. 15 [illegible] − 8 [illegible] = $23\frac{5}{6}$
30. $4\frac{2}{3} + 7\frac{1}{9}$ = $11\frac{7}{9}$
31. $13\frac{2}{8} + 8\frac{1}{2}$ = $21\frac{3}{4}$
32. $5\frac{3}{8} + 9\frac{6}{16}$ = $14\frac{3}{4}$
33. $4\frac{1}{2} + 8\frac{3}{12}$ = $12\frac{3}{4}$
34. $12\frac{1}{3} + 8\frac{3}{6}$ = $20\frac{5}{6}$
35. $8\frac{1}{5}$ + 9 [illegible] = $17\frac{3}{5}$
36. 18 [illegible] − 5 [illegible] = 24
37. $4\frac{3}{6} + 5\frac{2}{12}$ = $9\frac{2}{3}$
38. 2 [illegible] + $3\frac{2}{32}$ = $5\frac{9}{16}$
39. $5\frac{2}{12} + 8\frac{4}{36}$ = $13\frac{5}{18}$
40. $9\frac{2}{7} + 6\frac{3}{21}$ = $15\frac{3}{7}$

Practice hard.

You'll win!

Page 61

Mixed Numbers

Name ______________________

Show your work on another sheet. Reduce your answers to lowest terms and write them here.

Total Problems 40

Problems Correct ______

1. $2\frac{1}{8} + 3\frac{2}{4}$ = $5\frac{5}{8}$
2. $3\frac{4}{6} + 7\frac{2}{12}$ = $10\frac{5}{6}$
3. $9\frac{3}{7} + 4\frac{2}{21}$ = $13\frac{11}{21}$
4. $5\frac{1}{20} + 3\frac{2}{4}$ = $8\frac{11}{20}$
5. $10\frac{1}{2} + 3\frac{2}{6}$ = $13\frac{5}{6}$
6. $4\frac{2}{6} + 8\frac{7}{12}$ = $12\frac{11}{12}$
7. $6\frac{2}{4} + 3\frac{1}{8}$ = $9\frac{5}{8}$
8. 7 [illegible] − 2 [illegible] = $10\frac{1}{4}$
9. 8 [illegible] + 7 [illegible] = $16\frac{1}{4}$
10. $2\frac{4}{9} + 3\frac{2}{3}$ = $6\frac{1}{9}$
11. $5\frac{3}{4} + 8\frac{2}{8}$ = 14
12. $3\frac{1}{4} + 2\frac{8}{12}$ = $5\frac{11}{12}$
13. $2\frac{4}{5} + 3\frac{5}{10}$ = $6\frac{3}{10}$
14. $8\frac{4}{5} + 7\frac{2}{15}$ = $15\frac{14}{15}$
15. 9 [illegible] − 3 [illegible] = $12\frac{13}{16}$
16. 8 [illegible] + 8 [illegible] = 17
17. $6\frac{2}{5} + 8\frac{1}{10}$ = $14\frac{1}{2}$
18. $7\frac{1}{8} + 7\frac{9}{16}$ = $14\frac{11}{16}$
19. $3\frac{1}{21} + 7\frac{6}{7}$ = $10\frac{19}{21}$
20. $5\frac{1}{15} + 6\frac{1}{3}$ = $11\frac{6}{15}$
21. $2\frac{3}{5} + 9\frac{2}{10}$ = $11\frac{4}{5}$
22. $6\frac{2}{4}$ − 8 [illegible] = $15\frac{1}{4}$
23. 7 [illegible] + 6 [illegible] = $13\frac{5}{12}$
24. $2\frac{1}{4} + 6\frac{3}{12}$ = $8\frac{1}{2}$
25. $9\frac{2}{6} + 8\frac{2}{3}$ = 18
26. $4\frac{1}{16} + 8\frac{3}{4}$ = $12\frac{13}{16}$
27. $8\frac{2}{7} + 7\frac{9}{14}$ = $15\frac{13}{14}$
28. $6\frac{1}{4} + 3\frac{4}{16}$ = $9\frac{1}{2}$
29. 8 [illegible] + 3 [illegible] = $11\frac{1}{2}$
30. 5 [illegible] + 8 [illegible] = 14
31. $2\frac{6}{7} + 3\frac{2}{14}$ = 6
32. $9\frac{2}{16} + 6\frac{1}{4}$ = $15\frac{3}{8}$
33. $4\frac{2}{5} + 8\frac{1}{10}$ = $12\frac{1}{2}$
34. $12\frac{2}{7} + 6\frac{1}{14}$ = $18\frac{5}{14}$
35. $16\frac{2}{5} + 2\frac{1}{15}$ = $18\frac{7}{15}$
36. $3\frac{2}{12}$ − $4\frac{1}{24}$ = $7\frac{5}{24}$
37. $4\frac{1}{8} + 7\frac{2}{4}$ = $11\frac{5}{8}$
38. $2\frac{6}{9} + 3\frac{1}{3}$ = 6
39. $4\frac{2}{9} + 8\frac{2}{3}$ = $12\frac{8}{9}$
40. $7\frac{4}{21} + 2\frac{1}{3}$ = $9\frac{11}{21}$

Practice! Practice! Practice

Page 62

Mixed Numbers

Name ______________________

Show your work on another sheet. Reduce your answers to lowest terms and write them here.

Total Problems 40

Problems Correct ______

1. $5\frac{2}{6} + \frac{1}{3}$ = $5\frac{2}{3}$
2. $8\frac{3}{4} + \frac{3}{4}$ = $9\frac{1}{2}$
3. 4 [illegible] + [illegible] = $4\frac{5}{8}$
4. $12\frac{3}{6} + \frac{4}{12}$ = $12\frac{5}{6}$
5. $9\frac{2}{5} + \frac{2}{5}$ = $9\frac{4}{5}$
6. 5 [illegible] + [illegible] = $6\frac{1}{14}$
7. $10\frac{3}{8} + \frac{2}{8}$ = $10\frac{5}{8}$
8. 4 [illegible] + [illegible] = $4\frac{5}{6}$
9. $8\frac{2}{4} + \frac{1}{4}$ = $8\frac{3}{4}$
10. $16\frac{3}{9} + \frac{4}{18}$ = $16\frac{5}{9}$
11. $12\frac{3}{8} + \frac{2}{8}$ = $12\frac{5}{8}$
12. $3\frac{6}{12} + \frac{2}{12}$ = $3\frac{2}{3}$
13. [illegible] − [illegible] = $11\frac{7}{8}$
14. $3\frac{2}{7} + \frac{3}{14}$ = $3\frac{1}{2}$
15. 9 [illegible] + [illegible] = $9\frac{9}{16}$
16. $8\frac{3}{4} + \frac{1}{2}$ = $9\frac{1}{4}$
17. $6\frac{2}{5} + \frac{3}{10}$ = $6\frac{7}{10}$
18. $8\frac{4}{7} + \frac{2}{7}$ = $8\frac{6}{7}$
19. $2\frac{1}{3} + \frac{7}{9}$ = $3\frac{1}{9}$
20. $8\frac{2}{3}$ + [illegible] = $9\frac{1}{2}$
21. $12\frac{2}{5} + \frac{2}{10}$ = $12\frac{3}{5}$
22. 14 [illegible] + [illegible] = $14\frac{3}{5}$
23. $8\frac{1}{3} + \frac{2}{6}$ = $8\frac{2}{3}$
24. $9\frac{3}{5} + \frac{3}{10}$ = $9\frac{9}{10}$
25. $6\frac{2}{8} + \frac{1}{2}$ = $6\frac{3}{4}$
26. $8\frac{6}{9} + \frac{1}{3}$ = 9
27. 12 [illegible] + $\frac{3}{6}$ = $12\frac{5}{6}$
28. $8\frac{9}{12} + \frac{2}{3}$ = $9\frac{5}{12}$
29. $7\frac{3}{5} + \frac{2}{15}$ = $7\frac{11}{15}$
30. $3\frac{2}{5} + \frac{5}{10}$ = $3\frac{9}{10}$
31. $16\frac{2}{16} + \frac{3}{8}$ = $16\frac{1}{2}$
32. $8\frac{2}{10} + \frac{3}{10}$ = $8\frac{1}{2}$
33. $6\frac{3}{7} + \frac{4}{21}$ = $6\frac{13}{21}$
34. $19\frac{4}{12} + \frac{7}{12}$ = $19\frac{11}{12}$
35. $7\frac{3}{4} + \frac{2}{8}$ = 8
36. $14\frac{2}{9}$ + [illegible] = $14\frac{5}{9}$
37. $6\frac{8}{10} + \frac{4}{5}$ = $7\frac{3}{5}$
38. $9\frac{4}{8} + \frac{2}{4}$ = 10
39. 3 [illegible] + $\frac{2}{4}$ = $3\frac{11}{16}$
40. $4\frac{8}{12} + \frac{2}{6}$ = 5

Practice puts you on top!

Page 63

Fractions

Name ______________________

Show your work on another sheet. Reduce your answers to lowest terms and write them here.

Total Problems 40

Problems Correct ______

1. $\frac{8}{10} - \frac{3}{10}$ = $\frac{1}{2}$
2. $\frac{3}{6} - \frac{1}{6}$ = $\frac{1}{3}$
3. $\frac{6}{8} - \frac{4}{8}$ = $\frac{1}{4}$
4. $\frac{8}{9} - \frac{5}{9}$ = $\frac{1}{3}$
5. $\frac{4}{5} - \frac{2}{5}$ = $\frac{2}{5}$
6. $\frac{1}{2} - \frac{1}{2}$ = 0
7. $\frac{2}{3} - \frac{1}{3}$ = $\frac{1}{3}$
8. $\frac{11}{12} - \frac{8}{12}$ = $\frac{1}{4}$
9. $\frac{5}{7} - \frac{3}{7}$ = $\frac{2}{7}$
10. $\frac{4}{6} - \frac{3}{6}$ = $\frac{1}{6}$
11. $\frac{11}{14} - \frac{9}{14}$ = $\frac{1}{7}$
12. $\frac{15}{20} - \frac{7}{20}$ = $\frac{2}{5}$
13. $\frac{9}{16} - \frac{5}{16}$ = $\frac{1}{4}$
14. $\frac{9}{12} - \frac{4}{12}$ = $\frac{5}{12}$
15. $\frac{13}{15} - \frac{4}{15}$ = $\frac{3}{5}$
16. $\frac{3}{4} - \frac{1}{4}$ = $\frac{1}{2}$
17. $\frac{5}{10} - \frac{2}{10}$ = $\frac{3}{10}$
18. $\frac{16}{24} - \frac{8}{24}$ = $\frac{1}{3}$
19. $\frac{6}{9} - \frac{2}{9}$ = $\frac{4}{9}$
20. $\frac{17}{20} - \frac{9}{20}$ = $\frac{2}{5}$
21. $\frac{3}{5} - \frac{1}{5}$ = $\frac{2}{5}$
22. $\frac{10}{12} - \frac{7}{12}$ = $\frac{1}{4}$
23. $\frac{4}{7} - \frac{3}{7}$ = $\frac{1}{7}$
24. $\frac{7}{8} - \frac{2}{8}$ = $\frac{5}{8}$
25. $\frac{11}{20} - \frac{10}{20}$ = $\frac{1}{20}$
26. $\frac{13}{14} - \frac{8}{14}$ = $\frac{5}{14}$
27. $\frac{20}{24} - \frac{15}{24}$ = $\frac{5}{24}$
28. $\frac{5}{6} - \frac{3}{6}$ = $\frac{1}{3}$
29. $\frac{3}{4} - \frac{2}{4}$ = $\frac{1}{4}$
30. $\frac{7}{9} - \frac{6}{9}$ = $\frac{1}{9}$
31. $\frac{12}{16} - \frac{4}{16}$ = $\frac{1}{2}$
32. $\frac{14}{15} - \frac{8}{15}$ = $\frac{2}{5}$
33. $\frac{6}{8} - \frac{2}{8}$ = $\frac{1}{2}$
34. $\frac{6}{7} - \frac{2}{7}$ = $\frac{4}{7}$
35. $\frac{9}{10} - \frac{6}{10}$ = $\frac{3}{10}$
36. $\frac{12}{14} - \frac{9}{14}$ = $\frac{3}{14}$
37. $\frac{10}{15} - \frac{6}{15}$ = $\frac{4}{15}$
38. $\frac{5}{8} - \frac{1}{8}$ = $\frac{1}{2}$
39. $\frac{13}{16} - \frac{9}{16}$ = $\frac{1}{4}$
40. $\frac{11}{22} - \frac{5}{22}$ = $\frac{3}{11}$

Practice hard. You'll win

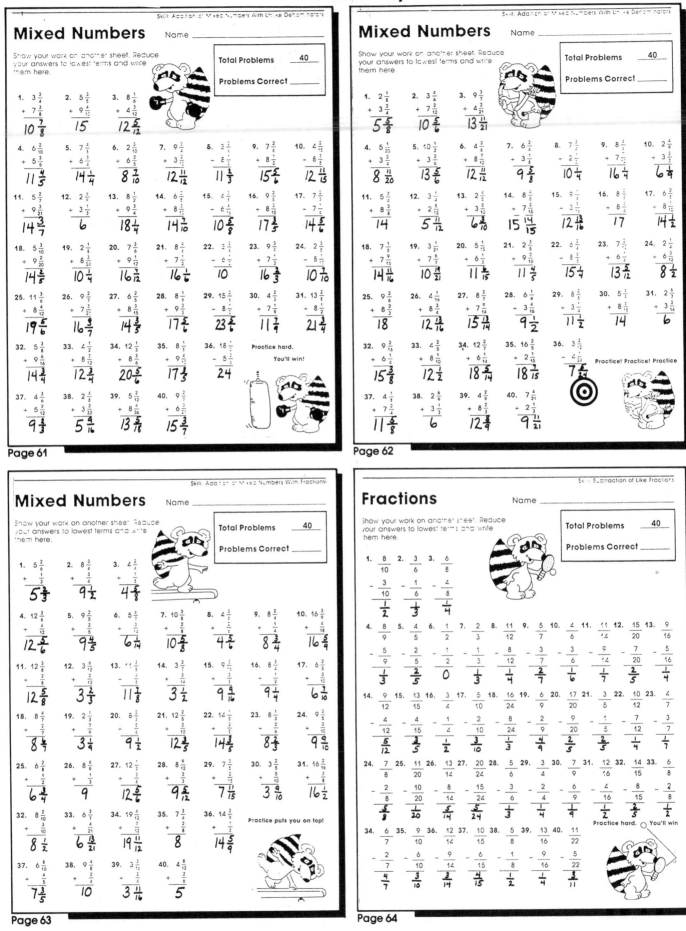

Page 64

Answer Key

Fractions

Name ____________

Show your work on another sheet. Reduce your answers to lowest terms and write them here.

Total Problems 40

Problems Correct ______

1. $\frac{8}{10} - \frac{3}{10} = \frac{1}{2}$
2. $\frac{4}{6} - \frac{3}{6} = \frac{1}{6}$
3. $\frac{5}{12} - \frac{3}{12} = \frac{1}{6}$
4. $\frac{7}{14} - \frac{5}{14} = \frac{1}{7}$
5. $\frac{9}{21} - \frac{6}{21} = \frac{1}{7}$
6. $\frac{14}{17} - \frac{8}{17} = \frac{6}{17}$
7. $\frac{5}{6} - \frac{3}{6} = \frac{1}{3}$
8. $\frac{8}{9} - \frac{5}{9} = \frac{1}{3}$
9. $\frac{10}{20} - \frac{7}{20} = \frac{3}{20}$
10. $\frac{5}{8} - \frac{2}{8} = \frac{3}{8}$
11. $\frac{14}{30} - \frac{7}{30} = \frac{7}{30}$
12. $\frac{2}{4} - \frac{1}{4} = \frac{1}{4}$
13. $\frac{7}{8} - \frac{3}{8} = \frac{1}{2}$
14. $\frac{9}{15} - \frac{3}{15} = \frac{2}{5}$
15. $\frac{24}{26} - \frac{15}{26} = \frac{9}{26}$
16. $\frac{8}{20} - \frac{3}{20} = \frac{1}{4}$
17. $\frac{13}{24} - \frac{7}{24} = \frac{1}{4}$
18. $\frac{5}{21} - \frac{2}{21} = \frac{1}{7}$
19. $\frac{3}{6} - \frac{1}{6} = \frac{1}{3}$
20. $\frac{5}{7} - \frac{4}{7} = \frac{1}{7}$
21. $\frac{18}{32} - \frac{7}{32} = \frac{11}{32}$
22. $\frac{14}{15} - \frac{8}{15} = \frac{2}{5}$
23. $\frac{21}{50} - \frac{15}{50} = \frac{3}{25}$
24. $\frac{11}{12} - \frac{4}{12} = \frac{7}{12}$
25. $\frac{5}{8} - \frac{4}{8} = \frac{1}{8}$
26. $\frac{7}{10} - \frac{3}{10} = \frac{2}{5}$
27. $\frac{6}{15} - \frac{3}{15} = \frac{1}{5}$
28. $\frac{3}{9} - \frac{1}{9} = \frac{2}{9}$
29. $\frac{6}{11} - \frac{2}{11} = \frac{4}{11}$
30. $\frac{7}{12} - \frac{5}{12} = \frac{1}{6}$
31. $\frac{19}{20} - \frac{12}{20} = \frac{7}{20}$
32. $\frac{5}{13} - \frac{2}{13} = \frac{3}{13}$
33. $\frac{6}{15} - \frac{2}{15} = \frac{4}{15}$
34. $\frac{4}{5} - \frac{2}{5} = \frac{2}{5}$
35. $\frac{3}{9} - \frac{2}{9} = \frac{1}{9}$
36. $\frac{17}{21} - \frac{8}{21} = \frac{3}{7}$
37. $\frac{42}{50} - \frac{13}{50} = \frac{29}{50}$
38. $\frac{71}{100} - \frac{40}{100} = \frac{31}{100}$
39. $\frac{7}{10} - \frac{1}{10} = \frac{3}{5}$
40. $\frac{8}{19} - \frac{3}{19} = \frac{5}{19}$

Success ahoy! Just practice!

Page 65

Fractions

Name ____________

Show your work on another sheet. Reduce your answers to lowest terms and write them here.

Total Problems 35

Problems Correct ______

1. $\frac{3}{8} - \frac{1}{4} = \frac{1}{8}$
2. $\frac{2}{5} - \frac{2}{15} = \frac{4}{15}$
3. $\frac{3}{4} - \frac{1}{12} = \frac{2}{3}$
4. $\frac{5}{6} - \frac{1}{3} = \frac{1}{2}$
5. $\frac{3}{5} - \frac{2}{10} = \frac{2}{5}$
6. $\frac{6}{7} - \frac{3}{14} = \frac{9}{14}$
7. $\frac{5}{8} - \frac{5}{16} = \frac{5}{16}$
8. $\frac{7}{10} - \frac{2}{20} = \frac{3}{5}$
9. $\frac{2}{4} - \frac{1}{12} = \frac{5}{12}$
10. $\frac{5}{15} - \frac{1}{5} = \frac{2}{15}$
11. $\frac{7}{16} - \frac{2}{8} = \frac{3}{16}$
12. $\frac{4}{9} - \frac{1}{3} = \frac{1}{9}$
13. $\frac{5}{7} - \frac{2}{14} = \frac{4}{7}$
14. $\frac{9}{10} - \frac{2}{5} = \frac{1}{2}$
15. $\frac{2}{3} - \frac{1}{9} = \frac{5}{9}$
16. $\frac{5}{8} - \frac{1}{4} = \frac{3}{8}$
17. $\frac{2}{4} - \frac{1}{2} = 0$
18. $\frac{3}{6} - \frac{1}{3} = \frac{1}{6}$
19. $\frac{1}{2} - \frac{2}{8} = \frac{1}{4}$
20. $\frac{8}{9} - \frac{3}{18} = \frac{13}{18}$
21. $\frac{6}{8} - \frac{2}{16} = \frac{5}{8}$
22. $\frac{3}{4} - \frac{5}{16} = \frac{7}{16}$
23. $\frac{7}{16} - \frac{3}{8} = \frac{1}{16}$
24. $\frac{5}{6} - \frac{2}{18} = \frac{13}{18}$
25. $\frac{7}{21} - \frac{1}{7} = \frac{4}{21}$
26. $\frac{8}{24} - \frac{2}{12} = \frac{1}{6}$
27. $\frac{5}{8} - \frac{3}{16} = \frac{7}{16}$
28. $\frac{7}{10} - \frac{1}{5} = \frac{1}{2}$
29. $\frac{1}{2} - \frac{3}{18} = \frac{1}{3}$
30. $\frac{7}{9} - \frac{2}{27} = \frac{19}{27}$
31. $\frac{1}{2} - \frac{7}{16} = \frac{1}{16}$
32. $\frac{3}{4} - \frac{2}{12} = \frac{7}{12}$
33. $\frac{9}{10} - \frac{3}{20} = \frac{3}{4}$
34. $\frac{8}{10} - \frac{5}{20} = \frac{11}{20}$
35. $\frac{3}{15} - \frac{1}{5} = 0$

Page 66

Fractions

Name ____________

Show your work on another sheet. Reduce your answers to lowest terms and write them here.

Total Problems 40

Problems Correct ______

1. $\frac{1}{2} - \frac{3}{8} = \frac{1}{8}$
2. $\frac{2}{5} - \frac{3}{10} = \frac{1}{10}$
3. $\frac{2}{3} - \frac{2}{9} = \frac{4}{9}$
4. $\frac{1}{2} - \frac{1}{4} = \frac{1}{4}$
5. $\frac{2}{3} - \frac{1}{6} = \frac{1}{2}$
6. $\frac{7}{8} - \frac{2}{4} = \frac{3}{8}$
7. $\frac{4}{5} - \frac{3}{10} = \frac{1}{2}$
8. $\frac{8}{10} - \frac{1}{2} = \frac{3}{10}$
9. $\frac{6}{9} - \frac{1}{3} = \frac{1}{3}$
10. $\frac{3}{4} - \frac{1}{12} = \frac{2}{3}$
11. $\frac{1}{4} - \frac{1}{8} = \frac{1}{8}$
12. $\frac{5}{6} - \frac{2}{3} = \frac{1}{6}$
13. $\frac{8}{12} - \frac{2}{6} = \frac{1}{3}$
14. $\frac{3}{4} - \frac{2}{8} = \frac{1}{2}$
15. $\frac{1}{2} - \frac{2}{4} = 0$
16. $\frac{5}{9} - \frac{3}{18} = \frac{7}{18}$
17. $\frac{6}{8} - \frac{1}{4} = \frac{1}{2}$
18. $\frac{1}{2} - \frac{2}{8} = \frac{1}{4}$
19. $\frac{3}{5} - \frac{2}{10} = \frac{2}{5}$
20. $\frac{12}{16} - \frac{5}{8} = \frac{1}{8}$
21. $\frac{9}{14} - \frac{3}{7} = \frac{3}{14}$
22. $\frac{5}{10} - \frac{1}{2} = 0$
23. $\frac{2}{3} - \frac{1}{6} = \frac{1}{2}$
24. $\frac{3}{5} - \frac{6}{15} = \frac{1}{5}$
25. $\frac{9}{10} - \frac{4}{5} = \frac{1}{10}$
26. $\frac{13}{14} - \frac{5}{7} = \frac{3}{14}$
27. $\frac{1}{2} - \frac{2}{6} = \frac{1}{6}$
28. $\frac{7}{9} - \frac{2}{18} = \frac{2}{3}$
29. $\frac{3}{4} - \frac{2}{8} = \frac{1}{2}$
30. $\frac{7}{8} - \frac{3}{4} = \frac{1}{8}$
31. $\frac{8}{9} - \frac{1}{3} = \frac{5}{9}$
32. $\frac{9}{16} - \frac{2}{8} = \frac{5}{16}$
33. $\frac{4}{7} - \frac{3}{14} = \frac{5}{14}$
34. $\frac{11}{18} - \frac{4}{9} = \frac{1}{6}$
35. $\frac{7}{8} - \frac{3}{16} = \frac{11}{16}$
36. $\frac{7}{10} - \frac{2}{5} = \frac{3}{10}$
37. $\frac{4}{5} - \frac{9}{15} = \frac{1}{5}$
38. $\frac{6}{7} - \frac{5}{14} = \frac{1}{2}$
39. $\frac{10}{12} - \frac{4}{6} = \frac{1}{6}$
40. $\frac{6}{10} - \frac{1}{5} = \frac{2}{5}$

Practice hard. You'll win.

Page 67

Fractions

Name ____________

Show your work on another sheet. Reduce your answers to lowest terms and write them here.

Total Problems 40

Problems Correct ______

1. $\frac{3}{4} - \frac{2}{5} = \frac{7}{20}$
2. $\frac{7}{9} - \frac{1}{2} = \frac{5}{18}$
3. $\frac{11}{16} - \frac{2}{4} = \frac{3}{16}$
4. $\frac{16}{20} - \frac{5}{10} = \frac{3}{10}$
5. $\frac{2}{3} - \frac{6}{11} = \frac{4}{33}$
6. $\frac{4}{5} - \frac{2}{4} = \frac{3}{10}$
7. $\frac{7}{8} - \frac{2}{3} = \frac{5}{24}$
8. $\frac{3}{4} - \frac{4}{16} = \frac{1}{2}$
9. $\frac{5}{6} - \frac{12}{18} = \frac{1}{6}$
10. $\frac{3}{4} - \frac{2}{6} = \frac{5}{12}$
11. $\frac{1}{3} - \frac{2}{11} = \frac{5}{33}$
12. $\frac{5}{6} - \frac{2}{4} = \frac{1}{3}$
13. $\frac{3}{4} - \frac{4}{9} = \frac{11}{36}$
14. $\frac{5}{6} - \frac{3}{5} = \frac{7}{30}$
15. $\frac{3}{4} - \frac{4}{6} = \frac{1}{12}$
16. $\frac{8}{10} - \frac{9}{20} = \frac{7}{20}$
17. $\frac{2}{3} - \frac{1}{6} = \frac{1}{2}$
18. $\frac{5}{9} - \frac{1}{2} = \frac{1}{18}$
19. $\frac{2}{3} - \frac{4}{8} = \frac{1}{6}$
20. $\frac{4}{5} - \frac{1}{6} = \frac{19}{30}$
21. $\frac{5}{8} - \frac{1}{3} = \frac{7}{24}$
22. $\frac{6}{7} - \frac{2}{5} = \frac{16}{35}$
23. $\frac{1}{2} - \frac{5}{14} = \frac{1}{7}$
24. $\frac{1}{2} - \frac{2}{9} = \frac{5}{18}$
25. $\frac{4}{5} - \frac{2}{6} = \frac{7}{15}$
26. $\frac{5}{7} - \frac{1}{2} = \frac{3}{14}$
27. $\frac{3}{5} - \frac{1}{4} = \frac{7}{20}$
28. $\frac{4}{6} - \frac{9}{18} = \frac{1}{6}$
29. $\frac{5}{7} - \frac{3}{5} = \frac{4}{35}$
30. $\frac{11}{15} - \frac{5}{30} = \frac{17}{30}$
31. $\frac{7}{16} - \frac{1}{4} = \frac{3}{16}$
32. $\frac{9}{14} - \frac{1}{2} = \frac{1}{7}$
33. $\frac{1}{2} - \frac{3}{7} = \frac{1}{14}$
34. $\frac{4}{6} - \frac{2}{5} = \frac{4}{15}$
35. $\frac{2}{3} - \frac{5}{8} = \frac{1}{24}$
36. $\frac{17}{18} - \frac{3}{6} = \frac{4}{9}$
37. $\frac{7}{9} - \frac{2}{4} = \frac{5}{18}$
38. $\frac{5}{9} - \frac{8}{27} = \frac{7}{27}$
39. $\frac{4}{5} - \frac{3}{7} = \frac{13}{35}$
40. $\frac{6}{12} - \frac{7}{36} = \frac{11}{36}$

Practice = Success!

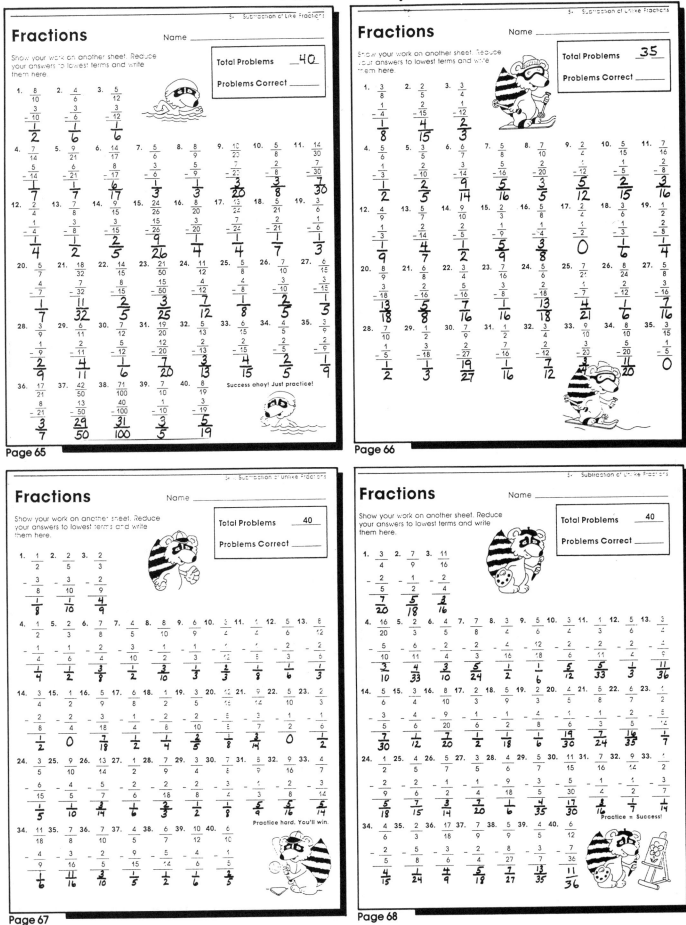

Page 68

Answer Key

Skill: Subtraction of Fractions From Whole Numbers

Fractions

Name ____________________

Show your work on another sheet. Reduce your answers to lowest terms and write them here.

Total Problems 40

Problems Correct ______

1. $5 - \frac{3}{4} = 4\frac{1}{4}$
2. $8 - \frac{7}{8} = 7\frac{1}{8}$
3. $4 - \frac{3}{6} = 3\frac{1}{2}$
4. $10 - \frac{3}{8} = 9\frac{5}{8}$
5. $14 - \frac{2}{5} = 13\frac{3}{5}$
6. $11 - \frac{7}{9} = 10\frac{2}{9}$
7. $4 - \frac{3}{5} = 3\frac{2}{5}$
8. $7 - \frac{5}{8} = 6\frac{3}{8}$
9. $6 - \frac{2}{4} = 5\frac{1}{2}$
10. $12 - \frac{3}{6} = 11\frac{1}{2}$
11. $9 - \frac{5}{8} = 8\frac{3}{8}$
12. $3 - \frac{6}{10} = 2\frac{2}{5}$
13. $7 - \frac{3}{4} = 6\frac{1}{4}$
14. $40 - \frac{3}{7} = 39\frac{4}{7}$
15. $5 - \frac{2}{3} = 4\frac{1}{3}$
16. $8 - \frac{5}{9} = 7\frac{4}{9}$
17. $11 - \frac{6}{12} = 10\frac{1}{2}$
18. $4 - \frac{3}{8} = 3\frac{5}{8}$
19. $6 - \frac{5}{7} = 5\frac{2}{7}$
20. $9 - \frac{3}{4} = 8\frac{1}{4}$
21. $12 - \frac{3}{9} = 11\frac{2}{3}$
22. $4 - \frac{6}{11} = 3\frac{5}{11}$
23. $7 - \frac{5}{10} = 6\frac{1}{2}$
24. $32 - \frac{5}{7} = 31\frac{2}{7}$
25. $25 - \frac{3}{4} = 24\frac{1}{4}$
26. $20 - \frac{5}{8} = 19\frac{3}{8}$
27. $5 - \frac{3}{6} = 4\frac{1}{2}$
28. $8 - \frac{2}{5} = 7\frac{3}{5}$
29. $4 - \frac{3}{9} = 3\frac{2}{3}$
30. $11 - \frac{2}{4} = 10\frac{1}{2}$
31. $14 - \frac{3}{7} = 13\frac{4}{7}$
32. $23 - \frac{6}{8} = 22\frac{1}{4}$
33. $56 - \frac{3}{5} = 55\frac{2}{5}$
34. $12 - \frac{5}{7} = 11\frac{2}{7}$
35. $30 - \frac{8}{9} = 29\frac{1}{9}$
36. $10 - \frac{14}{20} = 9\frac{3}{10}$
37. $9 - \frac{5}{6} = 8\frac{1}{6}$
38. $4 - \frac{1}{4} = 3\frac{3}{4}$
39. $6 - \frac{7}{8} = 5\frac{1}{8}$
40. $9 - \frac{7}{12} = 8\frac{5}{12}$

Practice hard. You'll win.

Page 69

Skill: Subtraction of Fractions From Mixed Numbers With Like and Unlike Denominators

Mixed Numbers

Name ____________________

Show your work on another sheet. Reduce your answers to lowest terms and write them here.

Total Problems 40

Problems Correct ______

1. $5\frac{3}{5} - \frac{1}{5} = 5\frac{2}{5}$
2. $11\frac{5}{8} - \frac{4}{8} = 11\frac{1}{8}$
3. $14\frac{6}{7} - \frac{4}{7} = 14\frac{2}{7}$
4. $10\frac{3}{6} - \frac{1}{6} = 10\frac{1}{3}$
5. $8\frac{5}{8} - \frac{3}{8} = 8\frac{1}{4}$
6. $14\frac{3}{4} - \frac{6}{8} = 14$
7. $3\frac{6}{8} - \frac{5}{8} = 3\frac{1}{8}$
8. $7\frac{4}{5} - \frac{3}{5} = 7\frac{1}{5}$
9. $9\frac{2}{3} - \frac{2}{6} = 9\frac{1}{3}$
10. 5 [illegible] − [illegible] = $5\frac{1}{2}$
11. $15\frac{4}{7} - \frac{1}{7} = 15\frac{3}{7}$
12. $8\frac{2}{3} - \frac{5}{18} = 8\frac{7}{18}$
13. $12\frac{3}{7} - \frac{1}{7} = 12\frac{2}{7}$
14. $8\frac{3}{4} - \frac{2}{8} = 8\frac{1}{2}$
15. $10\frac{5}{7} - \frac{3}{14} = 10\frac{1}{2}$
16. $4\frac{6}{8} - \frac{1}{2} = 4\frac{1}{4}$
17. 7 [illegible] − [illegible] = $7\frac{1}{5}$
18. $3\frac{6}{9} - \frac{2}{3} = 3$
19. $6\frac{7}{8} - \frac{2}{4} = 6\frac{3}{8}$
20. $9\frac{5}{6} - \frac{1}{3} = 9\frac{1}{2}$
21. $5\frac{4}{6} - \frac{1}{2} = 5\frac{1}{6}$
22. $7\frac{5}{8} - \frac{2}{4} = 7\frac{1}{8}$
23. $15\frac{7}{10} - \frac{3}{5} = 15\frac{1}{10}$
24. 10 [illegible] − [illegible] = $10\frac{1}{5}$
25. $5\frac{3}{7} - \frac{4}{14} = 5\frac{1}{7}$
26. $7\frac{5}{8} - \frac{1}{2} = 7\frac{1}{8}$
27. $4\frac{6}{10} - \frac{2}{5} = 4\frac{1}{5}$
28. $8\frac{6}{7} - \frac{5}{14} = 8\frac{1}{2}$
29. $2\frac{6}{8} - \frac{3}{4} = 2$
30. $9\frac{8}{10} - \frac{3}{5} = 9\frac{1}{5}$
31. $4\frac{5}{7} - \frac{3}{21} = 4\frac{4}{7}$
32. $10\frac{3}{5} - \frac{1}{10} = 10\frac{1}{2}$
33. $22\frac{8}{9} - \frac{2}{3} = 22\frac{2}{9}$
34. $7\frac{5}{6} - \frac{2}{3} = 7\frac{1}{6}$
35. $10\frac{5}{8} - \frac{3}{8} = 10\frac{1}{4}$
36. $8\frac{9}{10} - \frac{4}{5} = 8\frac{1}{10}$
37. $11\frac{3}{10} - \frac{1}{5} = 11\frac{1}{10}$
38. $4\frac{4}{7} - \frac{1}{7} = 4\frac{3}{7}$
39. $6\frac{5}{6} - \frac{1}{3} = 6\frac{1}{2}$
40. $12\frac{7}{8} - \frac{5}{8} = 12\frac{1}{4}$

Practice = Success!

Page 70

Skill: Subtraction of Mixed Numbers With Like Denominators

Mixed Numbers

Name ____________________

Show your work on another sheet. Reduce your answers to lowest terms and write them here.

Total Problems 40

Problems Correct ______

1. $2\frac{5}{8} - 1\frac{2}{8} = 1\frac{3}{8}$
2. $6\frac{6}{10} - 2\frac{4}{10} = 4\frac{1}{5}$
3. $8\frac{3}{6} - 1\frac{1}{6} = 7\frac{1}{3}$
4. $5\frac{2}{8} - 3\frac{1}{8} = 2\frac{1}{8}$
5. $16\frac{2}{4} - 8\frac{1}{4} = 8\frac{1}{4}$
6. $12\frac{4}{6} - 3\frac{2}{6} = 9\frac{1}{3}$
7. $9\frac{6}{7} - 3\frac{4}{7} = 6\frac{2}{7}$
8. $8\frac{3}{6} - 4\frac{2}{6} = 4\frac{1}{6}$
9. $4\frac{3}{8} - 2\frac{3}{8} = 2$
10. $15\frac{2}{7} - 8\frac{1}{7} = 7\frac{1}{7}$
11. $9\frac{6}{8} - 4\frac{2}{8} = 5\frac{1}{2}$
12. $7\frac{6}{8} - 4\frac{5}{8} = 3\frac{1}{8}$
13. $14\frac{2}{5} - 8\frac{1}{5} = 6\frac{1}{5}$
14. $3\frac{2}{6} - 1\frac{1}{6} = 2\frac{1}{6}$
15. $8\frac{11}{12} - 4\frac{8}{12} = 4\frac{1}{4}$
16. $9\frac{2}{6} - 4\frac{1}{6} = 5\frac{1}{6}$
17. 12 [illegible] − 8 [illegible] = $4\frac{1}{4}$
18. $4\frac{3}{6} - 3\frac{1}{6} = 1\frac{1}{3}$
19. $8\frac{2}{5} - 4\frac{1}{5} = 4\frac{1}{5}$
20. $9\frac{6}{11} - 4\frac{5}{11} = 5\frac{1}{11}$
21. $6\frac{3}{8} - 4\frac{1}{8} = 2\frac{1}{4}$
22. $12\frac{4}{6} - 9\frac{2}{6} = 3\frac{1}{3}$
23. $5\frac{2}{8} - 3\frac{1}{8} = 2\frac{1}{8}$
24. 20 [illegible] − 6 [illegible] = 14
25. $14\frac{2}{6} - 9\frac{1}{6} = 5\frac{1}{6}$
26. $7\frac{2}{9} - 5\frac{1}{9} = 2\frac{1}{9}$
27. $8\frac{6}{7} - 4\frac{2}{7} = 4\frac{4}{7}$
28. $5\frac{4}{10} - 3\frac{2}{10} = 2\frac{1}{5}$
29. $8\frac{5}{6} - 4\frac{2}{6} = 4\frac{1}{2}$
30. $2\frac{3}{6} - 1\frac{2}{6} = 1\frac{1}{6}$
31. $9\frac{4}{10} - 3\frac{3}{10} = 6\frac{1}{10}$
32. $5\frac{4}{6} - 4\frac{2}{6} = 1\frac{1}{3}$
33. $7\frac{3}{8} - 6\frac{1}{8} = 1\frac{1}{4}$
34. $4\frac{11}{20} - 2\frac{4}{20} = 2\frac{7}{20}$
35. $9\frac{6}{14} - 3\frac{2}{14} = 6\frac{2}{7}$
36. 7 [illegible] − 4 [illegible] = $3\frac{1}{4}$
37. $3\frac{6}{10} - 1\frac{3}{10} = 2\frac{3}{10}$
38. $6\frac{3}{7} - 4\frac{2}{7} = 2\frac{1}{7}$
39. $10\frac{2}{5} - 5\frac{1}{5} = 5\frac{1}{5}$
40. $12\frac{4}{6} - 8\frac{2}{6} = 4\frac{1}{3}$

Through practice you learn!

Page 71

Skill: Subtraction of Mixed Numbers With Like Denominators-Regrouping

Mixed Numbers

Name ____________________

Show your work on another sheet. Reduce your answers to lowest terms and write them here.

Total Problems 40

Problems Correct ______

1. $8\frac{3}{5} - 2\frac{4}{5} = 5\frac{4}{5}$
2. $6\frac{1}{8} - 4\frac{5}{8} = 1\frac{1}{2}$
3. $3\frac{2}{7} - 1\frac{5}{7} = 1\frac{4}{7}$
4. $5\frac{1}{4} - 2\frac{3}{4} = 2\frac{1}{2}$
5. $7\frac{1}{5} - 4\frac{3}{5} = 2\frac{3}{5}$
6. $4\frac{2}{10} - 2\frac{3}{10} = 1\frac{9}{10}$
7. $8\frac{3}{6} - 2\frac{5}{6} = 5\frac{2}{3}$
8. $2\frac{1}{4} - 1\frac{3}{4} = \frac{1}{2}$
9. $12\frac{1}{6} - 8\frac{3}{6} = 3\frac{2}{3}$
10. 5 [illegible] − 2 [illegible] = $2\frac{2}{3}$
11. $6\frac{4}{12} - 2\frac{8}{12} = 3\frac{2}{3}$
12. $4\frac{2}{5} - 1\frac{4}{5} = 2\frac{3}{5}$
13. $8\frac{2}{7} - 2\frac{5}{7} = 5\frac{4}{7}$
14. $7\frac{2}{8} - 5\frac{4}{8} = 1\frac{3}{4}$
15. $12\frac{2}{5} - 8\frac{4}{5} = 3\frac{3}{5}$
16. $14\frac{3}{9} - 9\frac{5}{9} = 4\frac{7}{9}$
17. 3 [illegible] − 1 [illegible] = $1\frac{3}{5}$
18. $8\frac{4}{10} - 6\frac{8}{10} = 1\frac{3}{5}$
19. $10\frac{3}{7} - 5\frac{6}{7} = 4\frac{4}{7}$
20. $4\frac{2}{6} - 3\frac{5}{6} = \frac{1}{2}$
21. $2\frac{1}{4} - 1\frac{3}{4} = \frac{1}{2}$
22. $7\frac{3}{8} - 2\frac{4}{8} = 4\frac{7}{8}$
23. $20\frac{1}{10} - 8\frac{4}{10} = 11\frac{7}{10}$
24. 9 [illegible] − 6 [illegible] = $2\frac{5}{8}$
25. $2\frac{4}{7} - 1\frac{5}{7} = \frac{6}{7}$
26. $6\frac{3}{9} - 4\frac{8}{9} = 1\frac{4}{9}$
27. $8\frac{4}{6} - 3\frac{5}{6} = 4\frac{5}{6}$
28. $5\frac{3}{7} - 2\frac{5}{7} = 2\frac{5}{7}$
29. $12\frac{2}{11} - 8\frac{4}{11} = 3\frac{9}{11}$
30. $9\frac{3}{8} - 4\frac{7}{8} = 4\frac{1}{2}$
31. 8 [illegible] − 7 [illegible] = $\frac{9}{10}$
32. $11\frac{2}{6} - 4\frac{5}{6} = 6\frac{1}{2}$
33. $4\frac{5}{7} - 1\frac{6}{7} = 2\frac{6}{7}$
34. $14\frac{2}{6} - 8\frac{4}{6} = 5\frac{2}{3}$
35. $3\frac{1}{4} - 1\frac{2}{4} = 1\frac{3}{4}$
36. $15\frac{1}{3} - 7\frac{2}{3} = 7\frac{2}{3}$
37. $8\frac{1}{6} - 4\frac{5}{6} = 3\frac{1}{3}$
38. $3\frac{2}{12} - 2\frac{6}{12} = \frac{2}{3}$
39. $4\frac{1}{8} - 2\frac{5}{8} = 1\frac{1}{2}$
40. $21\frac{2}{5} - 13\frac{3}{5} = 7\frac{4}{5}$

Practice! Practice! Practice!

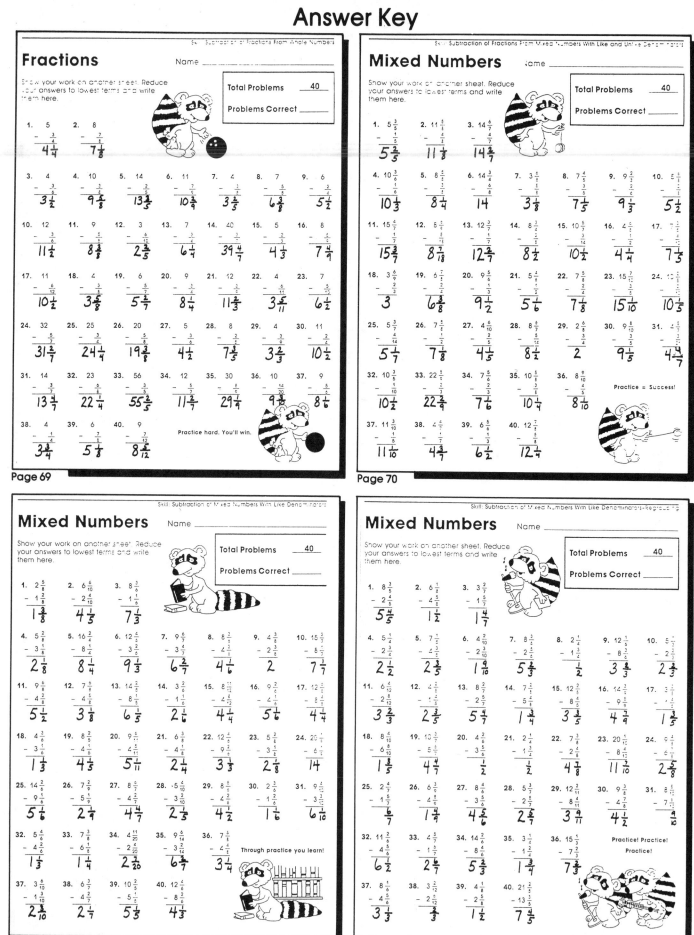

Page 72

Answer Key

Skill: Subtraction of Mixed Numbers With Unlike Denominators

Mixed Numbers

Name ____________________

Show your work on another sheet. Reduce your answers to lowest terms and write them here.

Total Problems 40

Problems Correct ______

1. $3\frac{1}{3} - 2\frac{1}{6} = 1\frac{1}{6}$
2. $8\frac{3}{4} - 3\frac{5}{8} = 5\frac{1}{8}$
3. $12\frac{3}{6} - 8\frac{1}{3} = 4\frac{1}{6}$
4. $5\frac{4}{6} - 2\frac{1}{2} = 3\frac{1}{6}$
5. $8\frac{5}{10} - 3\frac{1}{2} = 5$
6. $12\frac{3}{4} - 5\frac{1}{2} = 7\frac{1}{4}$
7. $6\frac{5}{7} - 4\frac{2}{14} = 2\frac{4}{7}$
8. $9\frac{4}{6} - 3\frac{1}{3} = 6\frac{1}{3}$
9. $7\frac{8}{12} - 4\frac{1}{3} = 3\frac{1}{3}$
10. $4\frac{8}{10} - 2\frac{2}{5} = 2\frac{2}{5}$
11. $6\frac{3}{7} - 5\frac{1}{14} = 1\frac{5}{14}$
12. $12\frac{6}{8} - 6\frac{3}{4} = 6$
13. $5\frac{2}{3} - 4\frac{1}{6} = 1\frac{1}{2}$
14. $12\frac{5}{8} - 8\frac{2}{4} = 4\frac{1}{8}$
15. $3\frac{2}{11} - 1\frac{1}{22} = 2\frac{3}{22}$
16. $5\frac{3}{9} - 3\frac{1}{18} = 2\frac{5}{18}$
17. $10\frac{3}{5} - 8\frac{1}{10} = 2\frac{1}{2}$
18. $14\frac{2}{3} - 8\frac{1}{6} = 6\frac{1}{2}$
19. $4\frac{3}{6} - 2\frac{1}{3} = 2\frac{1}{6}$
20. $8\frac{6}{7} - 4\frac{2}{14} = 4\frac{5}{7}$
21. $10\frac{2}{4} - 6\frac{1}{8} = 4\frac{3}{8}$
22. $12\frac{3}{5} - 8\frac{2}{10} = 4\frac{2}{5}$
23. $2\frac{6}{8} - 1\frac{1}{2} = 1\frac{1}{4}$
24. $5\frac{3}{4} - 3\frac{1}{12} = 2\frac{2}{3}$
25. $8\frac{3}{5} - 4\frac{2}{10} = 4\frac{2}{5}$
26. $3\frac{2}{4} - 1\frac{1}{8} = 2\frac{3}{8}$
27. $10\frac{2}{3} - 4\frac{2}{6} = 6\frac{1}{3}$
28. $2\frac{11}{12} - 1\frac{4}{6} = 1\frac{1}{4}$
29. $9\frac{2}{3} - 6\frac{1}{9} = 3\frac{5}{9}$
30. $2\frac{4}{8} - 1\frac{1}{4} = 1\frac{1}{4}$
31. $15\frac{2}{7} - 8\frac{1}{14} = 7\frac{3}{14}$
32. $8\frac{3}{5} - 7\frac{2}{15} = 1\frac{7}{15}$
33. $7\frac{8}{9} - 4\frac{2}{3} = 3\frac{2}{9}$
34. $7\frac{2}{3} - 4\frac{2}{9} = 3\frac{4}{9}$
35. $14\frac{8}{10} - 6\frac{4}{20} = 8\frac{3}{5}$
36. $25\frac{6}{7} - 14\frac{3}{21} = 11\frac{5}{7}$
37. $3\frac{5}{8} - 2\frac{4}{16} = 1\frac{3}{8}$
38. $9\frac{2}{4} - 6\frac{2}{12} = 3\frac{1}{3}$
39. $15\frac{3}{5} - 8\frac{2}{10} = 7\frac{2}{5}$
40. $20\frac{4}{7} - 8\frac{2}{14} = 12\frac{3}{7}$

Practice hard. You'll win.

Page 73

Skill: Multiplication of Fractions

Fractions

Name ____________________

Show your work on another sheet. Reduce your answers to lowest terms and write them here.

Total Problems 28

Problems Correct ______

1. $\frac{1}{3} \times \frac{2}{4} = \frac{1}{6}$
2. $\frac{1}{4} \times \frac{3}{6} = \frac{1}{8}$
3. $\frac{1}{2} \times \frac{3}{4} = \frac{3}{8}$
4. $\frac{1}{3} \times \frac{1}{5} = \frac{1}{15}$
5. $\frac{1}{6} \times \frac{3}{7} = \frac{1}{14}$
6. $\frac{2}{6} \times \frac{1}{8} = \frac{1}{24}$
7. $\frac{3}{5} \times \frac{2}{4} = \frac{3}{10}$
8. $\frac{2}{3} \times \frac{1}{5} = \frac{2}{15}$
9. $\frac{3}{8} \times \frac{1}{6} = \frac{1}{16}$
10. $\frac{1}{2} \times \frac{2}{3} = \frac{1}{3}$
11. $\frac{1}{4} \times \frac{2}{5} = \frac{1}{10}$
12. $\frac{4}{6} \times \frac{1}{7} = \frac{2}{21}$
13. $\frac{1}{3} \times \frac{4}{5} = \frac{4}{15}$
14. $\frac{1}{5} \times \frac{3}{6} = \frac{1}{10}$
15. $\frac{1}{4} \times \frac{5}{6} = \frac{5}{24}$
16. $\frac{2}{6} \times \frac{3}{5} = \frac{1}{5}$
17. $\frac{1}{3} \times \frac{1}{4} = \frac{1}{12}$
18. $\frac{3}{5} \times \frac{6}{7} = \frac{18}{35}$
19. $\frac{3}{8} \times \frac{1}{9} = \frac{1}{24}$
20. $\frac{1}{5} \times \frac{4}{6} = \frac{2}{15}$
21. $\frac{1}{2} \times \frac{4}{7} = \frac{2}{7}$
22. $\frac{1}{5} \times \frac{3}{5} = \frac{3}{25}$
23. $\frac{2}{3} \times \frac{4}{5} = \frac{8}{15}$
24. $\frac{1}{4} \times \frac{2}{8} = \frac{1}{16}$
25. $\frac{1}{2} \times \frac{3}{7} = \frac{3}{14}$
26. $\frac{2}{3} \times \frac{2}{6} = \frac{2}{9}$
27. $\frac{1}{6} \times \frac{2}{3} = \frac{1}{9}$
28. $\frac{1}{3} \times \frac{1}{6} = \frac{1}{18}$

Practice = Success!

Page 74

Skill: Multiplication of Fractions

Fractions

Name ____________________

Show your work on another sheet. Reduce your answers to lowest terms and write them here.

Total Problems 28

Problems Correct ______

1. $\frac{3}{4} \times \frac{5}{6} = \frac{5}{8}$
2. $\frac{2}{9} \times \frac{1}{4} = \frac{1}{18}$
3. $\frac{4}{5} \times \frac{1}{5} = \frac{4}{25}$
4. $\frac{3}{7} \times \frac{2}{6} = \frac{1}{7}$
5. $\frac{3}{4} \times \frac{1}{6} = \frac{1}{8}$
6. $\frac{5}{7} \times \frac{3}{5} = \frac{3}{7}$
7. $\frac{4}{6} \times \frac{2}{4} = \frac{1}{3}$
8. $\frac{3}{4} \times \frac{4}{5} = \frac{3}{5}$
9. $\frac{2}{7} \times \frac{4}{6} = \frac{4}{21}$
10. $\frac{8}{9} \times \frac{1}{3} = \frac{8}{27}$
11. $\frac{2}{4} \times \frac{5}{7} = \frac{5}{14}$
12. $\frac{6}{8} \times \frac{3}{7} = \frac{9}{28}$
13. $\frac{2}{3} \times \frac{4}{5} = \frac{8}{15}$
14. $\frac{7}{8} \times \frac{3}{4} = \frac{21}{32}$
15. $\frac{5}{8} \times \frac{2}{6} = \frac{5}{24}$
16. $\frac{4}{7} \times \frac{2}{3} = \frac{8}{21}$
17. $\frac{1}{12} \times \frac{4}{9} = \frac{1}{27}$
18. $\frac{6}{8} \times \frac{3}{5} = \frac{9}{20}$
19. $\frac{5}{8} \times \frac{1}{3} = \frac{5}{24}$
20. $\frac{5}{10} \times \frac{2}{4} = \frac{1}{4}$
21. $\frac{6}{7} \times \frac{2}{3} = \frac{4}{7}$
22. $\frac{1}{2} \times \frac{3}{8} = \frac{3}{16}$
23. $\frac{4}{7} \times \frac{3}{6} = \frac{2}{7}$
24. $\frac{3}{4} \times \frac{2}{3} = \frac{1}{2}$
25. $\frac{5}{11} \times \frac{2}{3} = \frac{10}{33}$
26. $\frac{6}{7} \times \frac{4}{5} = \frac{24}{35}$
27. $\frac{3}{8} \times \frac{2}{9} = \frac{1}{12}$
28. $\frac{3}{12} \times \frac{2}{4} = \frac{1}{8}$

Practice and anything'. possible!

Page 75

Skill: Multiplication of Fractions

Fractions

Name ____________________

Show your work on another sheet. Reduce your answers to lowest terms and write them here.

Total Problems 45

Problems Correct ______

1. $\frac{2}{3} \times \frac{4}{7} = \frac{8}{21}$
2. $\frac{5}{6} \times \frac{2}{4} = \frac{5}{12}$
3. $\frac{3}{9} \times \frac{2}{3} = \frac{2}{9}$
4. $\frac{6}{8} \times \frac{1}{4} = \frac{3}{16}$
5. $\frac{4}{7} \times \frac{1}{8} = \frac{1}{14}$
6. $\frac{2}{7} \times \frac{3}{6} = \frac{1}{7}$
7. $\frac{5}{8} \times \frac{2}{9} = \frac{5}{36}$
8. $\frac{4}{10} \times \frac{3}{8} = \frac{3}{20}$
9. $\frac{8}{11} \times \frac{3}{6} = \frac{4}{11}$
10. $\frac{4}{5} \times \frac{2}{9} = \frac{8}{45}$
11. $\frac{6}{10} \times \frac{5}{7} = \frac{3}{7}$
12. $\frac{3}{6} \times \frac{2}{4} = \frac{1}{4}$
13. $\frac{3}{11} \times \frac{4}{12} = \frac{1}{11}$
14. $\frac{5}{9} \times \frac{3}{7} = \frac{5}{21}$
15. $\frac{1}{20} \times \frac{2}{10} = \frac{1}{100}$
16. $\frac{2}{5} \times \frac{3}{15} = \frac{2}{25}$
17. $\frac{4}{7} \times \frac{8}{12} = \frac{8}{21}$
18. $\frac{4}{13} \times \frac{2}{3} = \frac{8}{39}$
19. $\frac{5}{6} \times \frac{3}{9} = \frac{5}{18}$
20. $\frac{2}{13} \times \frac{4}{5} = \frac{8}{65}$
21. $\frac{2}{3} \times \frac{1}{2} = \frac{1}{3}$
22. $\frac{4}{5} \times \frac{2}{7} = \frac{8}{35}$
23. $\frac{8}{9} \times \frac{3}{7} = \frac{8}{21}$
24. $\frac{2}{5} \times \frac{1}{6} = \frac{1}{15}$
25. $\frac{9}{10} \times \frac{3}{14} = \frac{27}{140}$
26. $\frac{2}{3} \times \frac{2}{16} = \frac{1}{12}$
27. $\frac{5}{8} \times \frac{2}{9} = \frac{5}{36}$
28. $\frac{1}{5} \times \frac{2}{17} = \frac{2}{85}$
29. $\frac{3}{4} \times \frac{2}{3} = \frac{1}{2}$
30. $\frac{2}{7} \times \frac{5}{10} = \frac{1}{7}$
31. $\frac{2}{3} \times \frac{6}{16} = \frac{1}{4}$
32. $\frac{2}{8} \times \frac{4}{7} = \frac{1}{7}$
33. $\frac{2}{30} \times \frac{2}{4} = \frac{1}{30}$
34. $\frac{3}{6} \times \frac{2}{8} = \frac{1}{8}$
35. $\frac{6}{9} \times \frac{2}{8} = \frac{1}{6}$
36. $\frac{2}{3} \times \frac{3}{30} = \frac{1}{15}$
37. $\frac{4}{7} \times \frac{2}{8} = \frac{1}{7}$
38. $\frac{5}{6} \times \frac{2}{12} = \frac{5}{36}$
39. $\frac{2}{10} \times \frac{3}{15} = \frac{1}{25}$
40. $\frac{3}{8} \times \frac{4}{9} = \frac{1}{6}$
41. $\frac{2}{6} \times \frac{5}{13} = \frac{5}{39}$
42. $\frac{4}{6} \times \frac{8}{9} = \frac{16}{27}$
43. $\frac{5}{30} \times \frac{2}{4} = \frac{1}{12}$
44. $\frac{11}{12} \times \frac{2}{11} = \frac{1}{6}$
45. $\frac{5}{8} \times \frac{4}{9} = \frac{5}{18}$

Through practice you learn!

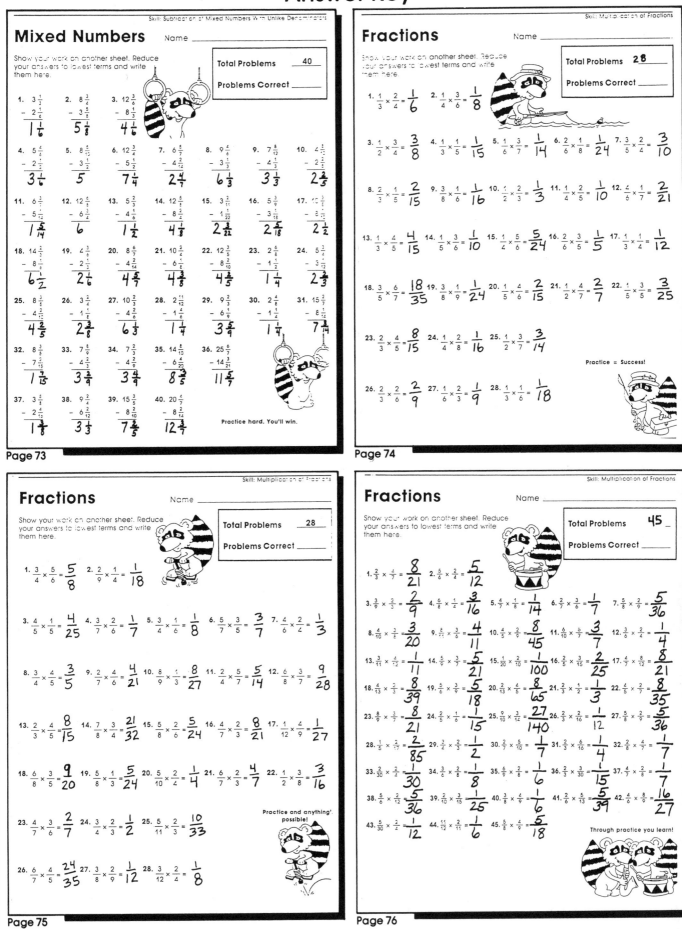

Page 76

Answer Key

Skill: Multiplication of Fractions

Fractions

Name ______________________

Show your work on another sheet. Reduce your answers to lowest terms and write them here.

Total Problems 46

Problems Correct ______

1. $\frac{4}{7} \times \frac{3}{4} = \frac{3}{7}$
2. $\frac{2}{5} \times \frac{4}{8} = \frac{1}{5}$
3. $\frac{3}{12} \times \frac{4}{6} = \frac{1}{6}$
4. $\frac{5}{8} \times \frac{1}{6} = \frac{5}{48}$
5. $\frac{2}{9} \times \frac{3}{5} = \frac{2}{15}$
6. $\frac{4}{6} \times \frac{4}{5} = \frac{8}{15}$
7. $\frac{3}{6} \times \frac{4}{5} = \frac{2}{5}$
8. $\frac{2}{7} \times \frac{3}{8} = \frac{3}{28}$
9. $\frac{2}{7} \times \frac{4}{14} = \frac{4}{49}$
10. $\frac{5}{12} \times \frac{2}{4} = \frac{5}{24}$
11. $\frac{3}{7} \times \frac{4}{5} = \frac{12}{35}$
12. $\frac{3}{7} \times \frac{5}{8} = \frac{15}{56}$
13. $\frac{5}{7} \times \frac{2}{5} = \frac{2}{7}$
14. $\frac{3}{8} \times \frac{2}{5} = \frac{3}{20}$
15. $\frac{4}{5} \times \frac{1}{4} = \frac{1}{5}$
16. $\frac{2}{3} \times \frac{5}{6} = \frac{5}{9}$
17. $\frac{1}{4} \times \frac{6}{12} = \frac{1}{8}$
18. $\frac{3}{8} \times \frac{5}{9} = \frac{5}{24}$
19. $\frac{2}{8} \times \frac{1}{12} = \frac{1}{48}$
20. $\frac{2}{8} \times \frac{4}{5} = \frac{1}{5}$
21. $\frac{5}{8} \times \frac{6}{7} = \frac{15}{28}$
22. $\frac{4}{5} \times \frac{3}{7} = \frac{12}{35}$
23. $\frac{6}{18} \times \frac{2}{3} = \frac{2}{9}$
24. $\frac{5}{7} \times \frac{4}{8} = \frac{5}{14}$
25. $\frac{3}{6} \times \frac{1}{2} = \frac{1}{4}$
26. $\frac{4}{8} \times \frac{3}{7} = \frac{3}{14}$
27. $\frac{8}{9} \times \frac{2}{5} = \frac{16}{45}$
28. $\frac{4}{6} \times \frac{3}{4} = \frac{1}{2}$
29. $\frac{3}{6} \times \frac{1}{2} = \frac{1}{4}$
30. $\frac{8}{12} \times \frac{5}{8} = \frac{5}{12}$
31. $\frac{10}{11} \times \frac{1}{10} = \frac{1}{11}$
32. $\frac{11}{12} \times \frac{2}{3} = \frac{11}{18}$
33. $\frac{7}{8} \times \frac{2}{3} = \frac{7}{12}$
34. $\frac{2}{7} \times \frac{1}{10} = \frac{1}{35}$
35. $\frac{3}{5} \times \frac{6}{9} = \frac{2}{5}$
36. $\frac{3}{6} \times \frac{2}{4} = \frac{1}{4}$
37. $\frac{5}{6} \times \frac{2}{4} = \frac{5}{12}$
38. $\frac{8}{10} \times \frac{2}{20} = \frac{2}{25}$
39. $\frac{4}{8} \times \frac{5}{12} = \frac{5}{24}$
40. $\frac{3}{6} \times \frac{8}{9} = \frac{4}{9}$
41. $\frac{7}{11} \times \frac{4}{5} = \frac{28}{55}$
42. $\frac{7}{8} \times \frac{2}{14} = \frac{1}{8}$
43. $\frac{3}{8} \times \frac{11}{12} = \frac{11}{32}$
44. $\frac{11}{12} \times \frac{4}{8} = \frac{11}{24}$
45. $\frac{2}{7} \times \frac{4}{8} = \frac{1}{7}$
46. $\frac{3}{6} \times \frac{5}{10} = \frac{1}{4}$

Practice!
Practice!
Practice!

Page 77

Skill: Multiplication of Fractions and Whole Numbers

Fractions

Name ______________________

Show your work on another sheet. Reduce your answers to lowest terms and write them here.

Total Problems 28

Problems Correct ______

1. $3 \times \frac{4}{6} = 2$
2. $8 \times \frac{2}{4} = 4$
3. $\frac{2}{8} \times 2 = \frac{1}{2}$
4. $3 \times \frac{1}{7} = \frac{3}{7}$
5. $6 \times \frac{3}{6} = 3$
6. $9 \times \frac{2}{9} = 2$
7. $\frac{2}{5} \times 2 = \frac{4}{5}$
8. $\frac{2}{3} \times 9 = 6$
9. $\frac{2}{10} \times 3 = \frac{3}{5}$
10. $\frac{3}{6} \times 4 = 2$
11. $\frac{3}{8} \times 3 = 1\frac{1}{8}$
12. $5 \times \frac{1}{11} = \frac{5}{11}$
13. $10 \times \frac{2}{4} = 5$
14. $8 \times \frac{1}{12} = \frac{2}{3}$
15. $\frac{3}{12} \times 3 = \frac{3}{4}$
16. $8 \times \frac{1}{2} = 4$
17. $\frac{4}{12} \times 6 = 2$
18. $14 \times \frac{2}{30} = \frac{14}{15}$
19. $\frac{6}{10} \times 5 = 3$
20. $6 \times \frac{2}{14} = \frac{6}{7}$
21. $\frac{3}{12} \times 2 = \frac{1}{2}$
22. $16 \times \frac{2}{40} = \frac{4}{5}$
23. $\frac{1}{3} \times 1 = \frac{1}{3}$
24. $8 \times \frac{3}{6} = 4$
25. $\frac{2}{4} \times 12 = 6$
26. $15 \times \frac{1}{18} = \frac{5}{6}$
27. $4 \times \frac{2}{11} = \frac{8}{11}$
28. $\frac{1}{3} \times 2 = \frac{2}{3}$

Practice hard. You'll win!

Page 78

Skill: Multiplication of Whole and Mixed Numbers

Mixed Numbers

Name ______________________

Show your work on another sheet. Reduce your answers to lowest terms and write them here.

Total Problems 50

Problems Correct ______

1. $3 \times 2\frac{1}{3} = 7$
2. $2\frac{1}{4} \times 8 = 18$
3. $5 \times 1\frac{1}{9} = 5\frac{5}{9}$
4. $3\frac{1}{2} \times 6 = 21$
5. $2 \times 3\frac{2}{4} = 7$
6. $14 \times 2\frac{1}{2} = 35$
7. $5 \times 3\frac{1}{4} = 16\frac{1}{4}$
8. $7 \times 2\frac{2}{4} = 17\frac{1}{2}$
9. $3 \times 2\frac{4}{5} = 8\frac{2}{5}$
10. $2 \times 2\frac{4}{6} = 5\frac{1}{3}$
11. $2\frac{1}{4} \times 9 = 20\frac{1}{4}$
12. $5 \times 3\frac{1}{4} = 16\frac{1}{4}$
13. $6\frac{2}{4} \times 5 = 32\frac{1}{2}$
14. $3\frac{1}{5} \times 6 = 19\frac{1}{5}$
15. $12 \times 1\frac{1}{4} = 15$
16. $7\frac{1}{2} \times 4 = 30$
17. $3\frac{2}{6} \times 2 = 6\frac{2}{3}$
18. $4\frac{2}{3} \times 2 = 9\frac{1}{3}$
19. $2 \times 1\frac{1}{3} = 2\frac{2}{3}$
20. $3\frac{1}{6} \times 10 = 31\frac{2}{3}$
21. $3 \times 1\frac{1}{8} = 3\frac{3}{8}$
22. $2\frac{4}{5} \times 4 = 11\frac{1}{5}$
23. $4\frac{1}{4} \times 3 = 12\frac{3}{4}$
24. $5 \times 6\frac{2}{3} = 33\frac{1}{3}$
25. $3 \times 1\frac{1}{2} = 4\frac{1}{2}$
26. $4 \times 2\frac{1}{2} = 10$
27. $1\frac{1}{4} \times 3 = 3\frac{3}{4}$
28. $2\frac{1}{3} \times 5 = 11\frac{2}{3}$
29. $3 \times 1\frac{1}{8} = 3\frac{3}{8}$
30. $1\frac{1}{5} \times 4 = 4\frac{4}{5}$
31. $14 \times 1\frac{1}{2} = 21$
32. $6\frac{1}{2} \times 2 = 13$
33. $4\frac{1}{6} \times 2 = 8\frac{1}{3}$
34. $5\frac{2}{4} \times 6 = 33$
35. $2\frac{1}{2} \times 4 = 10$
36. $1\frac{1}{3} \times 4 = 5\frac{1}{3}$
37. $7 \times 1\frac{1}{5} = 8\frac{2}{5}$
38. $15 \times 1\frac{1}{3} = 20$
39. $2\frac{1}{4} \times 4 = 9$
40. $5\frac{1}{3} \times 3 = 16$
41. $6\frac{1}{3} \times 6 = 38$
42. $5\frac{1}{2} \times 8 = 44$
43. $2 \times 3\frac{1}{8} = 6\frac{1}{4}$
44. $4 \times 2\frac{1}{5} = 8\frac{4}{5}$
45. $9 \times 1\frac{1}{4} = 11\frac{1}{4}$
46. $1\frac{1}{5} \times 3 = 3\frac{3}{5}$
47. $6\frac{1}{8} \times 4 = 24\frac{1}{2}$
48. $3 \times 2\frac{1}{5} = 6\frac{3}{5}$
49. $7\frac{1}{4} \times 2 = 14\frac{1}{2}$
50. $20 \times 1\frac{1}{2} = 30$

With practice, you can do it!

Page 79

Skill: Multiplication of Mixed Numbers and Proper Fractions

Mixed Numbers

Name ______________________

Show your work on another sheet. Reduce your answers to lowest terms and write them here.

Total Problems 50

Problems Correct ______

1. $1\frac{1}{3} \times 2\frac{1}{2} = 3\frac{1}{3}$
2. $1\frac{1}{8} \times 2\frac{1}{3} = 2\frac{5}{8}$
3. $2\frac{1}{4} \times \frac{3}{4} = 1\frac{11}{16}$
4. $1\frac{1}{3} \times 1\frac{1}{5} = 1\frac{3}{5}$
5. $2\frac{2}{3} \times 1\frac{1}{6} = 3\frac{1}{9}$
6. $4\frac{1}{2} \times 2\frac{1}{3} = 10\frac{1}{2}$
7. $1\frac{1}{9} \times 1\frac{1}{3} = 1\frac{13}{27}$
8. $2\frac{1}{4} \times 3\frac{1}{3} = 7\frac{1}{2}$
9. $3\frac{1}{6} \times 1\frac{1}{2} = 4\frac{3}{4}$
10. $4\frac{1}{2} \times \frac{2}{4} = 2\frac{1}{4}$
11. $\frac{1}{6} \times 1\frac{1}{3} = \frac{2}{9}$
12. $3\frac{2}{4} \times \frac{3}{8} = 1\frac{5}{16}$
13. $2\frac{1}{12} \times 1\frac{1}{3} = 2\frac{7}{9}$
14. $\frac{6}{8} \times 3\frac{1}{2} = 2\frac{5}{8}$
15. $\frac{3}{5} \times 1\frac{1}{5} = \frac{18}{25}$
16. $\frac{4}{8} \times 2\frac{1}{4} = 1\frac{1}{8}$
17. $1\frac{1}{10} \times \frac{3}{4} = \frac{33}{40}$
18. $3\frac{2}{4} \times 1\frac{1}{5} = 4\frac{1}{5}$
19. $1\frac{1}{8} \times 1\frac{3}{7} = 1\frac{17}{28}$
20. $1\frac{2}{5} \times \frac{6}{8} = 1\frac{1}{20}$
21. $4\frac{2}{4} \times \frac{3}{5} = 2\frac{7}{10}$
22. $1\frac{3}{4} \times 3\frac{1}{5} = 5\frac{3}{5}$
23. $1\frac{1}{6} \times 3\frac{2}{4} = 4\frac{1}{12}$
24. $1\frac{4}{5} \times 2\frac{1}{6} = 3\frac{9}{10}$
25. $2\frac{1}{6} \times 1\frac{4}{8} = 3\frac{1}{4}$
26. $3\frac{2}{5} \times 2\frac{1}{6} = 7\frac{11}{30}$
27. $5\frac{1}{4} \times \frac{2}{3} = 3\frac{1}{2}$
28. $2\frac{1}{4} \times \frac{4}{6} = 1\frac{1}{2}$
29. $\frac{2}{7} \times 3\frac{1}{6} = \frac{19}{21}$
30. $4\frac{1}{3} \times \frac{6}{7} = 3\frac{5}{7}$
31. $3\frac{1}{4} \times 2\frac{3}{5} = 8\frac{9}{20}$
32. $1\frac{1}{8} \times 3\frac{2}{6} = 3\frac{3}{4}$
33. $2\frac{1}{6} \times \frac{4}{5} = 1\frac{11}{15}$
34. $1\frac{1}{4} \times \frac{6}{8} = \frac{15}{16}$
35. $3\frac{1}{2} \times \frac{2}{5} = 1\frac{2}{5}$
36. $1\frac{1}{6} \times 2\frac{1}{3} = 2\frac{13}{18}$
37. $4\frac{1}{3} \times \frac{2}{3} = 2\frac{8}{9}$
38. $\frac{4}{5} \times 2\frac{1}{4} = 1\frac{4}{5}$
39. $1\frac{5}{7} \times \frac{2}{3} = 1\frac{1}{7}$
40. $1\frac{1}{2} \times \frac{4}{5} = 1\frac{1}{5}$
41. $2\frac{3}{10} \times \frac{4}{5} = 1\frac{21}{25}$
42. $5\frac{4}{6} \times 1\frac{1}{3} = 7\frac{5}{9}$
43. $3\frac{1}{4} \times 2\frac{1}{3} = 7\frac{7}{12}$
44. $\frac{3}{7} \times 4\frac{3}{5} = 1\frac{34}{35}$
45. $1\frac{2}{4} \times \frac{3}{5} = \frac{9}{10}$
46. $2\frac{4}{5} \times 3\frac{1}{6} = 8\frac{13}{15}$
47. $1\frac{2}{4} \times \frac{2}{3} = 1$
48. $3\frac{2}{5} \times \frac{4}{8} = 1\frac{7}{10}$
49. $\frac{6}{7} \times 2\frac{1}{3} = 2$
50. $8\frac{2}{3} \times \frac{1}{6} = 1\frac{4}{9}$

Practice!
Practice!
Practice!

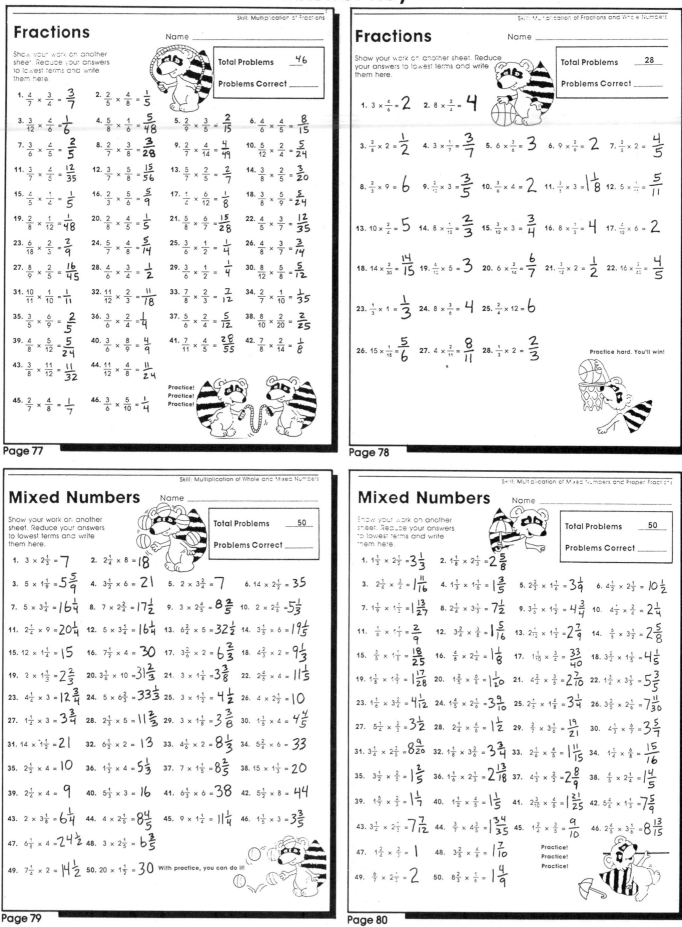

Page 80

Answer Key

Fractions

Name ____________________

Show your work on another sheet. Reduce your answers to lowest terms and write them here.

Total Problems 28
Problems Correct ______

1. $6 \div \frac{1}{2} = 12$
2. $5 \div \frac{1}{3} = 15$
3. $7 \div \frac{1}{6} = 42$
4. $3 \div \frac{1}{9} = 27$
5. $7 \div \frac{1}{8} = 56$
6. $4 \div \frac{1}{6} = 24$
7. $8 \div \frac{1}{10} = 80$
8. $5 \div \frac{1}{6} = 30$
9. $12 \div \frac{1}{6} = 72$
10. $5 \div \frac{2}{4} = 10$
11. $15 \div \frac{1}{2} = 30$
12. $3 \div \frac{2}{6} = 9$
13. $5 \div \frac{1}{8} = 40$
14. $12 \div \frac{1}{3} = 36$
15. $10 \div \frac{1}{9} = 90$
16. $7 \div \frac{2}{4} = 14$
17. $6 \div \frac{2}{5} = 15$
18. $12 \div \frac{3}{4} = 16$
19. $6 \div \frac{1}{8} = 48$
20. $7 \div \frac{3}{6} = 14$
21. $12 \div \frac{1}{4} = 48$
22. $7 \div \frac{2}{6} = 21$
23. $4 \div \frac{2}{7} = 14$
24. $8 \div \frac{3}{6} = 16$
25. $10 \div \frac{2}{5} = 25$
26. $15 \div \frac{1}{3} = 45$
27. $8 \div \frac{1}{2} = 16$
28. $14 \div \frac{2}{4} = 28$

Practice = Success!

Page 81

Fractions

Name ____________________

Show your work on another sheet. Reduce your answers to lowest terms and write them here.

Total Problems 28
Problems Correct ______

1. $\frac{2}{5} \div \frac{3}{6} = \frac{4}{5}$
2. $\frac{3}{8} \div \frac{2}{5} = \frac{15}{16}$
3. $\frac{2}{8} \div \frac{3}{6} = \frac{1}{2}$
4. $\frac{1}{5} \div \frac{2}{7} = \frac{7}{10}$
5. $\frac{3}{7} \div \frac{4}{5} = \frac{15}{28}$
6. $\frac{2}{8} \div \frac{3}{9} = \frac{3}{4}$
7. $\frac{4}{6} \div \frac{3}{7} = 1\frac{5}{9}$
8. $\frac{6}{8} \div \frac{7}{8} = \frac{6}{7}$
9. $\frac{7}{9} \div \frac{7}{8} = \frac{8}{9}$
10. $\frac{4}{8} \div \frac{3}{7} = 1\frac{1}{6}$
11. $\frac{4}{5} \div \frac{6}{7} = \frac{14}{15}$
12. $\frac{8}{9} \div \frac{3}{4} = 1\frac{5}{27}$
13. $\frac{6}{8} \div \frac{5}{12} = 1\frac{4}{5}$
14. $\frac{3}{5} \div \frac{4}{8} = 1\frac{1}{5}$
15. $\frac{11}{12} \div \frac{5}{6} = 1\frac{1}{10}$
16. $\frac{4}{6} \div \frac{3}{9} = 2$
17. $\frac{7}{9} \div \frac{4}{5} = \frac{35}{36}$
18. $\frac{6}{8} \div \frac{4}{11} = 2\frac{1}{16}$
19. $\frac{4}{5} \div \frac{2}{7} = 2\frac{4}{5}$
20. $\frac{8}{9} \div \frac{5}{6} = 1\frac{1}{15}$
21. $\frac{4}{5} \div \frac{10}{12} = \frac{24}{25}$
22. $\frac{7}{9} \div \frac{3}{4} = 1\frac{1}{27}$
23. $\frac{8}{9} \div \frac{3}{7} = 2\frac{2}{27}$
24. $\frac{8}{9} \div \frac{2}{4} = 1\frac{7}{9}$
25. $\frac{4}{6} \div \frac{2}{9} = 3$
26. $\frac{3}{4} \div \frac{1}{7} = 5\frac{1}{4}$
27. $\frac{6}{8} \div \frac{3}{9} = 2\frac{1}{4}$
28. $\frac{3}{7} \div \frac{5}{12} = 1\frac{1}{35}$

Page 82

Fractions

Name ____________________

Show your work on another sheet. Reduce your answers to lowest terms and write them here.

Total Problems 50
Problems Correct ______

1. $\frac{2}{8} \div \frac{3}{4} = \frac{1}{3}$
2. $\frac{4}{7} \div \frac{1}{2} = 1\frac{1}{7}$
3. $\frac{2}{6} \div \frac{8}{9} = \frac{3}{8}$
4. $\frac{3}{9} \div \frac{3}{5} = \frac{5}{9}$
5. $\frac{7}{8} \div \frac{2}{4} = 1\frac{3}{4}$
6. $\frac{3}{9} \div \frac{2}{6} = 1$
7. $\frac{4}{8} \div \frac{1}{7} = 3\frac{1}{2}$
8. $\frac{2}{3} \div \frac{5}{8} = 1\frac{1}{15}$
9. $\frac{2}{10} \div \frac{3}{4} = \frac{4}{15}$
10. $\frac{2}{6} \div \frac{5}{8} = \frac{8}{15}$
11. $\frac{3}{6} \div \frac{2}{8} = 2$
12. $\frac{7}{8} \div \frac{2}{5} = 2\frac{3}{16}$
13. $\frac{11}{12} \div \frac{2}{3} = 1\frac{3}{8}$
14. $\frac{1}{8} \div \frac{9}{12} = \frac{1}{6}$
15. $\frac{1}{6} \div \frac{5}{7} = \frac{7}{30}$
16. $\frac{3}{10} \div \frac{2}{6} = \frac{9}{10}$
17. $\frac{2}{7} \div \frac{8}{12} = \frac{3}{7}$
18. $\frac{2}{9} \div \frac{3}{8} = \frac{16}{27}$
19. $\frac{3}{4} \div \frac{6}{9} = 1\frac{1}{8}$
20. $\frac{1}{11} \div \frac{7}{9} = \frac{9}{77}$
21. $\frac{4}{5} \div \frac{3}{4} = 1\frac{1}{15}$
22. $\frac{6}{8} \div \frac{7}{10} = 1\frac{1}{14}$
23. $\frac{10}{12} \div \frac{3}{4} = 1\frac{1}{9}$
24. $\frac{1}{2} \div \frac{4}{5} = \frac{5}{8}$
25. $\frac{6}{7} \div \frac{4}{5} = 1\frac{1}{14}$
26. $\frac{3}{8} \div \frac{4}{7} = \frac{21}{32}$
27. $\frac{3}{5} \div \frac{4}{6} = \frac{9}{10}$
28. $\frac{7}{8} \div \frac{5}{6} = 1\frac{1}{20}$
29. $\frac{2}{4} \div \frac{3}{5} = \frac{5}{6}$
30. $\frac{6}{10} \div \frac{3}{5} = 1$
31. $\frac{7}{9} \div \frac{2}{6} = 2\frac{1}{3}$
32. $\frac{11}{12} \div \frac{3}{6} = 1\frac{5}{6}$
33. $\frac{11}{15} \div \frac{4}{8} = 1\frac{7}{15}$
34. $\frac{9}{12} \div \frac{8}{10} = \frac{15}{16}$
35. $\frac{4}{6} \div \frac{5}{8} = 1\frac{1}{15}$
36. $\frac{7}{9} \div \frac{4}{6} = 1\frac{1}{6}$
37. $\frac{8}{9} \div \frac{3}{5} = 1\frac{13}{27}$
38. $\frac{6}{7} \div \frac{8}{12} = 1\frac{2}{7}$
39. $\frac{6}{12} \div \frac{7}{10} = \frac{5}{7}$
40. $\frac{8}{12} \div \frac{3}{4} = \frac{8}{9}$
41. $\frac{7}{10} \div \frac{8}{12} = 1\frac{1}{20}$
42. $\frac{4}{15} \div \frac{6}{7} = \frac{14}{45}$
43. $\frac{16}{20} \div \frac{3}{4} = 1\frac{1}{15}$
44. $\frac{10}{12} \div \frac{5}{8} = 1\frac{1}{3}$
45. $\frac{7}{8} \div \frac{10}{11} = \frac{77}{80}$
46. $\frac{3}{12} \div \frac{4}{11} = \frac{11}{16}$
47. $\frac{6}{10} \div \frac{8}{13} = \frac{39}{40}$
48. $\frac{5}{6} \div \frac{6}{7} = \frac{35}{36}$
49. $\frac{4}{5} \div \frac{11}{12} = \frac{48}{55}$
50. $\frac{7}{8} \div \frac{12}{14} = 1\frac{1}{48}$

Through practice you learn!

Page 83

Mixed Numbers

Name ____________________

Show your work on another sheet. Reduce your answers to lowest terms and write them here.

Total Problems 50
Problems Correct ______

1. $3 \div 2\frac{1}{4} = 1\frac{1}{3}$
2. $3\frac{1}{4} \div 6 = \frac{13}{24}$
3. $2 \div 4\frac{1}{3} = \frac{6}{13}$
4. $5\frac{2}{3} \div 6 = \frac{17}{18}$
5. $4 \div 2\frac{1}{5} = 1\frac{9}{11}$
6. $3\frac{1}{4} \div 8 = \frac{13}{32}$
7. $2\frac{3}{6} \div 5 = \frac{1}{2}$
8. $4\frac{1}{2} \div 8 = \frac{9}{16}$
9. $6\frac{1}{4} \div 7 = \frac{25}{28}$
10. $3\frac{2}{3} \div 9 = \frac{11}{27}$
11. $2\frac{1}{3} \div 4 = \frac{7}{12}$
12. $4\frac{2}{6} \div 2 = 2\frac{1}{6}$
13. $5\frac{2}{3} \div 2 = 2\frac{5}{6}$
14. $4 \div 6\frac{1}{3} = \frac{12}{19}$
15. $2\frac{1}{5} \div 6 = \frac{11}{30}$
16. $10 \div 1\frac{1}{8} = 8\frac{8}{9}$
17. $5\frac{2}{6} \div 4 = 1\frac{1}{3}$
18. $3 \div 1\frac{4}{7} = 1\frac{10}{11}$
19. $5 \div 1\frac{1}{3} = 3\frac{3}{4}$
20. $9 \div 3\frac{2}{4} = 2\frac{4}{7}$
21. $4 \div 1\frac{3}{6} = 2\frac{2}{3}$
22. $2 \div 5\frac{1}{3} = \frac{3}{8}$
23. $5 \div 2\frac{3}{5} = 1\frac{12}{13}$
24. $4\frac{1}{2} \div 7 = \frac{9}{14}$
25. $6\frac{2}{3} \div 3 = 2\frac{2}{9}$
26. $8 \div 2\frac{4}{5} = 2\frac{6}{7}$
27. $9 \div 2\frac{2}{4} = 3\frac{3}{5}$
28. $4\frac{2}{3} \div 8 = \frac{7}{12}$
29. $6\frac{2}{4} \div 4 = 1\frac{5}{8}$
30. $2\frac{1}{3} \div 6 = \frac{7}{18}$
31. $8\frac{1}{3} \div 3 = 2\frac{7}{9}$
32. $7\frac{2}{4} \div 9 = \frac{5}{6}$
33. $1\frac{3}{7} \div 4 = \frac{5}{14}$
34. $7\frac{1}{2} \div 3 = 2\frac{1}{2}$
35. $1\frac{2}{4} \div 7 = \frac{3}{14}$
36. $9 \div 2\frac{1}{5} = 4\frac{1}{11}$
37. $2\frac{4}{6} \div 8 = \frac{1}{3}$
38. $1\frac{8}{9} \div 4 = \frac{17}{36}$
39. $3\frac{2}{4} \div 6 = \frac{7}{12}$
40. $8 \div 1\frac{1}{4} = 6\frac{2}{5}$
41. $3\frac{2}{6} \div 5 = \frac{2}{3}$
42. $2 \div 3\frac{1}{2} = \frac{4}{7}$
43. $8\frac{1}{2} \div 7 = 1\frac{3}{14}$
44. $15 \div 2\frac{1}{4} = 6\frac{2}{3}$
45. $4 \div 2\frac{1}{6} = 1\frac{11}{13}$
46. $10 \div 2\frac{4}{8} = 4$
47. $7 \div 2\frac{2}{3} = 2\frac{5}{8}$
48. $3\frac{2}{4} \div 8 = \frac{7}{16}$
49. $4\frac{1}{6} \div 2 = 2\frac{1}{12}$
50. $3 \div 1\frac{1}{4} = 2\frac{2}{5}$

Practice = Success!

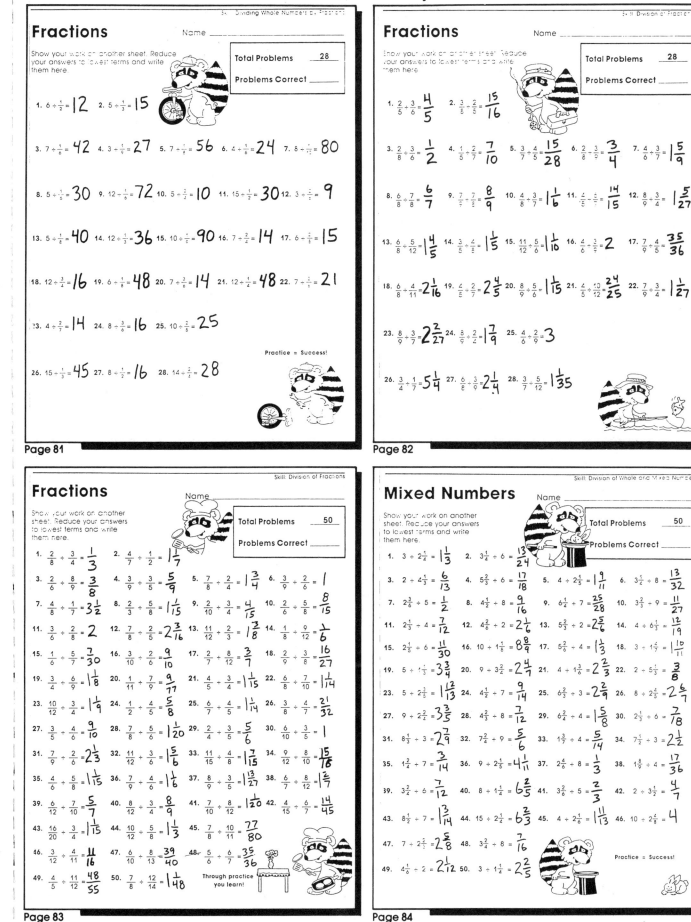

Page 84

Answer Key

Skill: Changing Proper Fractions and Mixed Numbers to Decimals

Fractions

Name ____________

Change these proper fractions and mixed numbers to decimals. Round to the nearest hundredth. Show your work on another sheet. Write your answers here.

Total Problems 48

Problems Correct ______

1. $\frac{3}{4}$ = 0.75
2. $\frac{2}{5}$ = 0.40
3. $\frac{8}{9}$ = 0.89
4. $\frac{3}{5}$ = 0.60
5. $2\frac{1}{4}$ = 2.25
6. $7\frac{2}{3}$ = 7.67
7. $\frac{14}{15}$ = 0.93
8. $\frac{3}{50}$ = 0.06
9. $\frac{5}{6}$ = 0.83
10. $\frac{7}{8}$ = 0.88
11. $\frac{2}{9}$ = 0.22
12. $32\frac{1}{8}$ = 32.13
13. $4\frac{4}{5}$ = 4.8
14. $\frac{1}{8}$ = 0.13
15. $\frac{7}{12}$ = 0.58
16. $\frac{2}{15}$ = 0.13
17. $42\frac{1}{3}$ = 42.33
18. $\frac{21}{30}$ = 0.70
19. $15\frac{2}{3}$ = 15.67
20. $4\frac{2}{9}$ = 4.22
21. $\frac{1}{4}$ = 0.25
22. $\frac{21}{25}$ = 0.84
23. $\frac{1}{2}$ = 0.50
24. $3\frac{2}{6}$ = 3.33
25. $\frac{1}{5}$ = 0.20
26. $16\frac{1}{4}$ = 16.25
27. $3\frac{3}{8}$ = 3.38
28. $\frac{4}{5}$ = 0.80
29. $\frac{7}{40}$ = 0.18
30. $\frac{23}{25}$ = 0.92
31. $\frac{9}{25}$ = 0.36
32. $8\frac{1}{5}$ = 8.20
33. $6\frac{3}{5}$ = 6.60
34. $\frac{39}{40}$ = 0.98
35. $6\frac{1}{3}$ = 6.33
36. $17\frac{4}{5}$ = 17.80
37. $\frac{5}{8}$ = 0.63
38. $\frac{4}{25}$ = 0.16
39. $84\frac{3}{8}$ = 84.38
40. $\frac{7}{20}$ = 0.35
41. $\frac{7}{16}$ = 0.44
42. $\frac{6}{25}$ = 0.24
43. $\frac{13}{20}$ = 0.65
44. $\frac{16}{33}$ = 0.48
45. $1\frac{3}{5}$ = 1.60
46. $8\frac{2}{3}$ = 8.67
47. $6\frac{3}{5}$ = 6.60
48. $\frac{4}{9}$ = 0.44

Practice! Practice! Practice!

Page 85

Skill: Changing Decimals to Proper Fractions and Mixed Numbers

Fractions

Name ____________

Change these decimals to proper fractions or mixed numbers in lowest terms. Show your work on another sheet. Write your answers here.

Total Problems 50

Problems Correct ______

1. 0.75 = $\frac{3}{4}$
2. 3.4 = $3\frac{2}{5}$
3. 0.5 = $\frac{1}{2}$
4. 3.25 = $3\frac{1}{4}$
5. 0.875 = $\frac{7}{8}$
6. 5.05 = $5\frac{1}{20}$
7. 6.10 = $6\frac{1}{10}$
8. 0.315 = $\frac{63}{200}$
9. 0.45 = $\frac{9}{20}$
10. 0.6 = $\frac{3}{5}$
11. 0.2 = $\frac{1}{5}$
12. 9.125 = $9\frac{1}{8}$
13. 7.4 = $7\frac{2}{5}$
14. 6.875 = $6\frac{7}{8}$
15. 0.84 = $\frac{21}{25}$
16. 0.319 = $\frac{319}{1000}$
17. 8.09 = $8\frac{9}{100}$
18. 0.405 = $\frac{81}{200}$
19. 0.73 = $\frac{73}{100}$
20. 0.17 = $\frac{17}{100}$
21. 16.8 = $16\frac{4}{5}$
22. 32.05 = $32\frac{1}{20}$
23. 4.3 = $4\frac{3}{10}$
24. 10.84 = $10\frac{21}{25}$
25. 3.6 = $3\frac{3}{5}$
26. 0.56 = $\frac{14}{25}$
27. 9.02 = $9\frac{1}{50}$
28. 8.25 = $8\frac{1}{4}$
29. 6.4 = $6\frac{2}{5}$
30. 7.5 = $7\frac{1}{2}$
31. 24.03 = $24\frac{3}{100}$
32. 0.93 = $\frac{93}{100}$
33. 0.36 = $\frac{9}{25}$
34. 0.24 = $\frac{6}{25}$
35. 2.875 = $2\frac{7}{8}$
36. 8.2 = $8\frac{1}{5}$
37. 5.1 = $5\frac{1}{10}$
38. 14.05 = $14\frac{1}{20}$
39. 7.25 = $7\frac{1}{4}$
40. 0.029 = $\frac{29}{1000}$
41. 0.749 = $\frac{749}{1000}$
42. 0.237 = $\frac{237}{1000}$
43. 1.07 = $1\frac{7}{100}$
44. 4.375 = $4\frac{3}{8}$
45. 2.23 = $2\frac{23}{100}$
46. 5.125 = $5\frac{1}{8}$
47. 16.9 = $16\frac{9}{10}$
48. 3.05 = $3\frac{1}{20}$
49. 0.006 = $\frac{3}{500}$
50. 4.25 = $4\frac{1}{4}$

Practice makes perfect!

Page 86

Skill: Determining Fractions of Whole Numbers

Fractions

Name ____________

Show your work on another sheet. Write your answers here.

Total Problems 48

Problems Correct ______

1. $\frac{2}{3}$ of 9 = 6
2. $\frac{7}{8}$ of 16 = 14
3. $\frac{4}{5}$ of 20 = 16
4. $\frac{5}{7}$ of 49 = 35
5. $\frac{3}{7}$ of 21 = 9
6. $\frac{4}{6}$ of 18 = 12
7. $\frac{3}{8}$ of 24 = 9
8. $\frac{5}{9}$ of 18 = 10
9. $\frac{4}{7}$ of 28 = 16
10. $\frac{5}{10}$ of 20 = 10
11. $\frac{6}{8}$ of 24 = 18
12. $\frac{5}{6}$ of 18 = 15
13. $\frac{7}{9}$ of 36 = 28
14. $\frac{5}{8}$ of 24 = 15
15. $\frac{2}{9}$ of 27 = 6
16. $\frac{10}{12}$ of 24 = 20
17. $\frac{5}{8}$ of 48 = 30
18. $\frac{2}{3}$ of 24 = 16
19. $\frac{2}{5}$ of 10 = 4
20. $\frac{4}{6}$ of 36 = 24
21. $\frac{3}{9}$ of 36 = 12
22. $\frac{7}{8}$ of 72 = 63
23. $\frac{6}{9}$ of 63 = 42
24. $\frac{8}{10}$ of 90 = 72
25. $\frac{4}{11}$ of 121 = 44
26. $\frac{5}{9}$ of 90 = 50
27. $\frac{3}{12}$ of 60 = 15
28. $\frac{6}{12}$ of 72 = 36
29. $\frac{1}{2}$ of 18 = 9
30. $\frac{2}{3}$ of 21 = 14
31. $\frac{4}{7}$ of 56 = 32
32. $\frac{3}{9}$ of 63 = 21
33. $\frac{1}{4}$ of 24 = 6
34. $\frac{3}{8}$ of 72 = 27
35. $\frac{5}{9}$ of 108 = 60
36. $\frac{4}{7}$ of 84 = 48
37. $\frac{2}{8}$ of 88 = 22
38. $\frac{8}{10}$ of 100 = 80
39. $\frac{9}{10}$ of 120 = 108
40. $\frac{4}{12}$ of 144 = 48
41. $\frac{8}{10}$ of 30 = 24
42. $\frac{4}{11}$ of 132 = 48
43. $\frac{3}{11}$ of 132 = 36
44. $\frac{8}{9}$ of 108 = 96
45. $\frac{4}{7}$ of 35 = 20
46. $\frac{8}{11}$ of 121 = 88
47. $\frac{9}{10}$ of 110 = 99
48. $\frac{6}{9}$ of 81 = 54

Page 87

Skill: Changing Decimals to Percents

Percents

Name ____________

Change these decimals to percents. Show your work on another sheet. Write your answers here.

Total Problems 50

Problems Correct ______

1. 0.07 = 7%
2. 0.82 = 82%
3. 0.01 = 1%
4. 0.74 = 74%
5. 0.85 = 85%
6. 0.32 = 32%
7. 0.02 = 2%
8. 0.18 = 18%
9. 0.7 = 70%
10. 0.9 = 90%
11. 0.37 = 37%
12. 0.69 = 69%
13. 0.08 = 8%
14. 0.72 = 72%
15. 0.48 = 48%
16. 0.3 = 30%
17. 0.6 = 60%
18. 0.05 = 5%
19. 7.36 = 736%
20. 0.83 = 83%
21. 0.4 = 40%
22. 0.21 = 21%
23. 0.1 = 10%
24. 0.24 = 24%
25. 0.91 = 91%
26. 0.79 = 79%
27. 0.81 = 81%
28. 8.92 = 892%
29. 0.38 = 38%
30. 3.24 = 324%
31. 0.83 = 83%
32. 0.42 = 42%
33. 0.45 = 45%
34. 9.27 = 927%
35. 0.5 = 50%
36. 0.47 = 47%
37. 0.78 = 78%
38. 0.03 = 3%
39. 0.76 = 76%
40. 0.12 = 12%
41. 0.88 = 88%
42. 0.03 = 3%
43. 0.8 = 80%
44. 0.87 = 87%
45. 0.04 = 4%
46. 0.94 = 94%
47. 0.27 = 27%
48. 0.93 = 93%
49. 0.27 = 27%
50. 0.71 = 71%

With practice, you can do it!

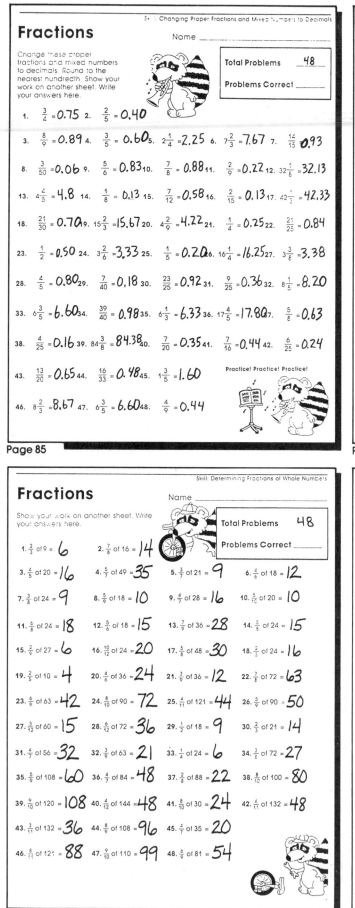

Page 88

Answer Key

Percents

Skill: Changing Percents to Proper Fractions or Mixed Numbers

Name ____________

Change these percents to proper fractions or mixed numbers. Show your work on another sheet. Reduce your answers to lowest terms and write them here.

Total Problems 50

Problems Correct ______

1. 7% = $\frac{7}{100}$
2. 48% = $\frac{12}{25}$
3. 120% = $1\frac{1}{5}$
4. 12% = $\frac{3}{25}$
5. 1% = $\frac{1}{100}$
6. 160% = $1\frac{3}{5}$
7. 2% = $\frac{1}{50}$
8. 21% = $\frac{21}{100}$
9. 750% = $7\frac{1}{2}$
10. 59% = $\frac{59}{100}$
11. 43% = $\frac{43}{100}$
12. 250% = $2\frac{1}{2}$
13. 3% = $\frac{3}{100}$
14. 140% = $1\frac{2}{5}$
15. 4% = $\frac{1}{25}$
16. 260% = $2\frac{3}{5}$
17. 9% = $\frac{9}{100}$
18. 675% = $6\frac{3}{4}$
19. 850% = $8\frac{1}{2}$
20. 36% = $\frac{9}{25}$
21. 75% = $\frac{3}{4}$
22. 85% = $\frac{17}{20}$
23. 27% = $\frac{27}{100}$
24. 73% = $\frac{73}{100}$
25. 230% = $2\frac{3}{10}$
26. 5% = $\frac{1}{20}$
27. 180% = $1\frac{4}{5}$
28. 37% = $\frac{37}{100}$
29. 6% = $\frac{3}{50}$
30. 12% = $\frac{3}{25}$
31. 290% = $2\frac{9}{10}$
32. 15% = $\frac{3}{20}$
33. 87% = $\frac{87}{100}$
34. 53% = $\frac{53}{100}$
35. 95% = $\frac{19}{20}$
36. 125% = $1\frac{1}{4}$
37. 420% = $4\frac{1}{5}$
38. 19% = $\frac{19}{100}$
39. 79% = $\frac{79}{100}$
40. 23% = $\frac{23}{100}$
41. 825% = $8\frac{1}{4}$
42. 77% = $\frac{77}{100}$
43. 61% = $\frac{61}{100}$
44. 29% = $\frac{29}{100}$
45. 80% = $\frac{4}{5}$
46. 28% = $\frac{7}{25}$
47. 25% = $\frac{1}{4}$
48. 93% = $\frac{93}{100}$
49. 83% = $\frac{83}{100}$
50. 39% = $\frac{39}{100}$

Through practice you learn!

Page 89

Percents

Skill: Changing Percents to Decimals

Name ____________

Change these percents to decimals. Show your work on another sheet. Write your answers here.

Total Problems 50

Problems Correct ______

1. 50% = 0.5
2. 42% = 0.42
3. 8% = 0.08
4. 43% = 0.43
5. 12% = 0.12
6. 32% = 0.32
7. 79% = 0.79
8. 49% = 0.49
9. 31% = 0.31
10. 68% = 0.68
11. 3% = 0.03
12. 41% = 0.41
13. 40% = 0.40
14. 23% = 0.23
15. 75% = 0.75
16. 24% = 0.24
17. 89% = 0.89
18. 98% = 0.98
19. 8% = 0.08
20. 2% = 0.02
21. 17% = 0.17
22. 18% = 0.18
23. 6% = 0.06
24. 49% = 0.49
25. 73% = 0.73
26. 64% = 0.64
27. 1% = 0.01
28. 58% = 0.58
29. 96% = 0.96
30. 16% = 0.16
31. 25% = 0.25
32. 82% = 0.82
33. 14% = 0.14
34. 22% = 0.22
35. 71% = 0.71
36. 4% = 0.04
37. 27% = 0.27
38. 61% = 0.61
39. 83% = 0.83
40. 7% = 0.07
41. 28% = 0.28
42. 13% = 0.13
43. 81% = 0.81
44. 99% = 0.99
45. 91% = 0.91
46. 5% = 0.05
47. 39% = 0.39
48. 28% = 0.28
49. 94% = 0.94
50. 88% = 0.88

Practice = Success!

Page 90

Percents

Skill: Changing Proper Fractions and Mixed Numbers to Percents

Name ____________

Change these proper fractions and mixed numbers to percents. Show your work on another sheet. Write your answers here.

Total Problems 50

Problems Correct ______

1. $\frac{37}{100}$ = 37%
2. $\frac{3}{100}$ = 3%
3. $\frac{65}{100}$ = 65%
4. $\frac{49}{100}$ = 49%
5. $\frac{1}{4}$ = 25%
6. $\frac{12}{100}$ = 12%
7. $\frac{11}{50}$ = 22%
8. $\frac{71}{100}$ = 71%
9. $4\frac{1}{2}$ = 450%
10. $3\frac{1}{4}$ = 325%
11. $1\frac{3}{4}$ = 175%
12. $\frac{2}{5}$ = 40%
13. $\frac{3}{10}$ = 30%
14. $\frac{63}{100}$ = 63%
15. $\frac{1}{20}$ = 5%
16. $\frac{1}{5}$ = 20%
17. $\frac{17}{20}$ = 85%
18. $\frac{57}{100}$ = 57%
19. $\frac{3}{5}$ = 60%
20. $\frac{1}{25}$ = 4%
21. $\frac{7}{10}$ = 70%
22. $5\frac{1}{4}$ = 525%
23. $\frac{37}{50}$ = 74%
24. $\frac{23}{100}$ = 23%
25. $\frac{1}{2}$ = 50%
26. $\frac{9}{10}$ = 90%
27. $\frac{81}{100}$ = 81%
28. $\frac{39}{100}$ = 39%
29. $3\frac{3}{4}$ = 375%
30. $\frac{73}{100}$ = 73%
31. $\frac{7}{20}$ = 35%
32. $9\frac{1}{2}$ = 950%
33. $\frac{4}{5}$ = 80%
34. $\frac{1}{10}$ = 10%
35. $\frac{13}{20}$ = 65%
36. $\frac{91}{100}$ = 91%
37. $\frac{51}{100}$ = 51%
38. $5\frac{1}{4}$ = 525%
39. $\frac{11}{100}$ = 11%
40. $\frac{3}{20}$ = 15%
41. $8\frac{1}{2}$ = 850%
42. $\frac{47}{50}$ = 94%
43. $2\frac{1}{5}$ = 220%
44. $1\frac{4}{5}$ = 180%
45. $\frac{7}{100}$ = 7%
46. $6\frac{1}{2}$ = 650%
47. $\frac{21}{50}$ = 42%
48. $\frac{21}{100}$ = 21%
49. $\frac{53}{100}$ = 53%
50. $\frac{67}{100}$ = 67%

Practice! Practice! Practice!

Page 91

Percents

Skill: Finding Percents of Numbers

Name ____________

Show your work on another sheet. Write your answers here.

Total Problems 50

Problems Correct ______

1. 10% of 80 = 8
2. 35% of 60 = 21
3. 50% of 20 = 10
4. 15% of 20 = 3
5. 10% of 60 = 6
6. 20% of 50 = 10
7. 30% of 60 = 18
8. 5% of 100 = 5
9. 25% of 100 = 25
10. 5% of 25 = 1.25
11. 15% of 40 = 6
12. 20% of 45 = 9
13. 24% of 60 = 14.4
14. 20% of 10 = 2
15. 50% of 32 = 16
16. 28% of 35 = 9.8
17. 18% of 25 = 4.5
18. 50% of 36 = 18
19. 18% of 32 = 5.76
20. 30% of 70 = 21
21. 30% of 40 = 12
22. 44% of 34 = 14.96
23. 25% of 20 = 5
24. 5% of 60 = 3
25. 10% of 70 = 7
26. 25% of 64 = 16
27. 8% of 21 = 1.68
28. 50% of 48 = 24
29. 4% of 20 = 0.8
30. 75% of 200 = 150
31. 28% of 40 = 11.2
32. 35% of 80 = 28
33. 26% of 50 = 13
34. 32% of 18 = 5.76
35. 19% of 25 = 4.75
36. 10% of 90 = 9
37. 80% of 30 = 24
38. 66% of 40 = 26.4
39. 45% of 60 = 27
40. 95% of 30 = 28.5
41. 46% of 80 = 36.8
42. 10% of 50 = 5
43. 95% of 20 = 19
44. 31% of 40 = 12.4
45. 36% of 22 = 7.92
46. 40% of 30 = 12
47. 20% of 80 = 16
48. 10% of 76 = 7.6
49. 86% of 40 = 34.4
50. 56% of 20 = 11.2

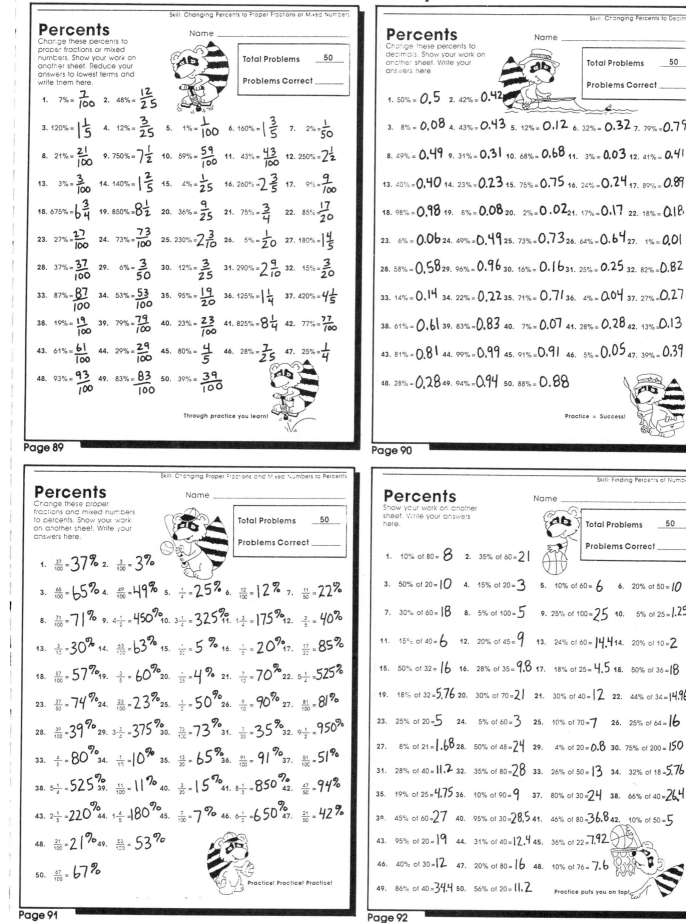

Practice puts you on top!

Page 92

Answer Key

Skill: Finding Percents

Percents

Show your work on another sheet. Write your answers here.

Name ________________

Total Problems 50

Problems Correct ______

1. 5 is 25% of 20
2. 6 is 15% of 40
3. 8 is 20% of 40
4. 10 is 20% of 50
5. 2 is 50% of 4
6. 5 is 20% of 25
7. 14 is 70% of 20
8. 6 is 20% of 30
9. 18 is 50% of 36
10. 7 is 70% of 10
11. 24 is 80% of 30
12. 22 is 22% of 100
13. 36 is 90% of 40
14. 12 is 30% of 40
15. 2 is 25% of 8
16. 5 is 10% of 50
17. 38 is 76% of 50
18. 6 is 40% of 15
19. 6 is 25% of 24
20. 26 is 65% of 40
21. 9 is 45% of 20
22. 26 is 52% of 50
23. 48 is 48% of 100
24. 27 is 90% of 30
25. 68 is 34% of 200
26. 7 is 10% of 70
27. 12 is 20% of 60
28. 16 is 40% of 40
29. 36 is 45% of 80
30. 14 is 28% of 50
31. 74 is 74% of 100
32. 39 is 78% of 50
33. 38 is 50% of 76
34. 36 is 18% of 200
35. 48 is 24% of 200
36. 72 is 90% of 80
37. 43 is 86% of 50
38. 89 is 89% of 100
39. 28 is 35% of 80
40. 24 is 25% of 96
41. 8 is 5% of 160
42. 16 is 50% of 32
43. 10 is 10% of 100
44. 8 is 10% of 80
45. 15 is 25% of 60
46. 9 is 25% of 36
47. 36 is 50% of 72
48. 6 is 12% of 50
49. 4 is 5% of 80
50. 9 is 5% of 180

Practice brings success!

Page 93

Skill: Solving Proportions

Proportions

Show your work on another sheet. Write your answers here.

Name ________________

Total Problems 50

Problems Correct ______

1. $\frac{2}{4}=\frac{n}{8}$ n = 4
2. $\frac{3}{x}=\frac{9}{15}$ x = 5
3. $\frac{n}{20}=\frac{5}{4}$ n = 25
4. $\frac{5}{6}=\frac{30}{n}$ n = 36
5. $\frac{27}{n}=\frac{9}{10}$ n = 30
6. $\frac{3}{14}=\frac{n}{42}$ n = 9
7. $\frac{2}{n}=\frac{24}{72}$ n = 6
8. $\frac{3}{9}=\frac{x}{54}$ x = 18
9. $\frac{3}{7}=\frac{x}{42}$ x = 18
10. $\frac{6}{12}=\frac{12}{n}$ n = 24
11. $\frac{7}{8}=\frac{42}{x}$ x = 48
12. $\frac{3}{8}=\frac{n}{48}$ n = 18
13. $\frac{12}{13}=\frac{24}{x}$ x = 26
14. $\frac{7}{9}=\frac{21}{n}$ n = 27
15. $\frac{7}{4}=\frac{x}{28}$ x = 49
16. $\frac{n}{30}=\frac{5}{3}$ n = 50
17. $\frac{5}{40}=\frac{2}{m}$ m = 16
18. $\frac{6}{2}=\frac{t}{20}$ t = 60
19. $\frac{3}{9}=\frac{x}{15}$ x = 5
20. $\frac{6}{n}=\frac{4}{8}$ n = 12
21. $\frac{7}{4}=\frac{49}{y}$ y = 28
22. $\frac{6}{8}=\frac{n}{48}$ n = 36
23. $\frac{y}{15}=\frac{1}{3}$ y = 5
24. $\frac{40}{120}=\frac{4}{n}$ n = 12
25. $\frac{9}{3}=\frac{27}{y}$ y = 9
26. $\frac{14}{6}=\frac{n}{3}$ n = 7
27. $\frac{12}{3}=\frac{12}{n}$ n = 3
28. $\frac{1}{8}=\frac{24}{m}$ m = 192
29. $\frac{25}{6}=\frac{75}{n}$ n = 18
30. $\frac{3}{12}=\frac{x}{48}$ x = 12
31. $\frac{2}{30}=\frac{y}{60}$ y = 4
32. $\frac{6}{t}=\frac{4}{6}$ t = 9
33. $\frac{n}{44}=\frac{2}{4}$ n = 22
34. $\frac{7}{21}=\frac{m}{9}$ m = 3
35. $\frac{42}{4}=\frac{t}{22}$ t = 231
36. $\frac{18}{3}=\frac{x}{2}$ x = 12
37. $\frac{y}{10}=\frac{4}{5}$ y = 8
38. $\frac{n}{24}=\frac{4}{12}$ n = 8
39. $\frac{5}{2}=\frac{20}{x}$ x = 8
40. $\frac{6}{24}=\frac{3}{n}$ n = 12
41. $\frac{13}{2}=\frac{39}{x}$ x = 6
42. $\frac{2}{8}=\frac{14}{m}$ m = 56
43. $\frac{6}{t}=\frac{24}{12}$ t = 3
44. $\frac{9}{2}=\frac{y}{4}$ y = 18
45. $\frac{n}{55}=\frac{2}{11}$ n = 10
46. $\frac{5}{7}=\frac{10}{m}$ m = 14
47. $\frac{8}{10}=\frac{64}{y}$ y = 80
48. $\frac{3}{4}=\frac{12}{n}$ n = 16
49. $\frac{5}{25}=\frac{t}{20}$ t = 4
50. $\frac{16}{2}=\frac{32}{x}$ x = 4

Practice = Success!

Page 94

Skill: Addition of Integers

Integers

Show your work on another sheet. Write your answers here.

Name ________________

Total Problems 50

Problems Correct ______

1. 4 + -5 = -1
2. 6 + -8 = -2
3. -3 + -4 = -7
4. 8 + 9 = 17
5. -4 + 8 = 4
6. 3 + -9 = -6
7. 13 + -14 = -1
8. -8 + 0 = -8
9. -5 + -5 = -10
10. -6 + 8 = 2
11. -12 + 1 = -11
12. -7 + 9 = 2
13. -2 + 10 = 8
14. -5 + 6 = 1
15. -14 + 7 = -7
16. -12 + 12 = 0
17. -14 + 3 = -11
18. -10 + -10 = -20
19. -5 + 0 = -5
20. 12 + -11 = 1
21. -6 + 9 = 3
22. -8 + 14 = 6
23. -6 + 5 = -1
24. -5 + 3 = -2
25. -1 + 12 = 11
26. 15 + -10 = 5
27. -2 + 8 = 6
28. -30 + 2 = -28
29. -4 + 5 = 1
30. 7 + 8 = 15
31. 14 + -12 = 2
32. -14 + 8 = -6
33. -12 + 6 = -6
34. -4 + 12 = 8
35. -24 + 14 = -10
36. -3 + 15 = 12
37. -5 + 10 = 5
38. -15 + 5 = -10
39. -18 + 25 = 7
40. -15 + 16 = 1
41. -16 + 16 = 0
42. -7 + 14 = 7
43. -14 + 30 = 16
44. -30 + 15 = -15
45. -10 + -7 = -17
46. -2 + 12 = 10
47. -3 + 10 = 7
48. 20 + -10 = 10
49. -5 + 21 = 16
50. -13 + 2 = -11

Practice makes perfect!

Page 95

Skill: Subtraction of Integers

Integers

Show your work on another sheet. Write your answers here.

Name ________________

Total Problems 50

Problems Correct ______

1. 10 - -2 = 12
2. 7 - -4 = 11
3. -6 - 8 = -14
4. 8 - -9 = 17
5. -4 - 2 = -6
6. -6 - 9 = -15
7. -18 - 9 = -27
8. -5 - -8 = 3
9. 15 - 20 = -5
10. -32 - -10 = -22
11. -7 - 10 = -17
12. 10 - -14 = 24
13. 14 - -7 = 21
14. 10 - -3 = 13
15. -10 - 6 = -16
16. -5 - -5 = 0
17. -8 - -9 = 1
18. 20 - -6 = 26
19. -6 - 3 = -9
20. -8 - 3 = -11
21. 30 - -8 = 38
22. -14 - 9 = -23
23. 16 - -4 = 20
24. 20 - 30 = -10
25. -10 - 4 = -14
26. 15 - -8 = 23
27. -15 - 7 = -22
28. -21 - -1 = -20
29. 20 - -5 = 25
30. -3 - -8 = 5
31. -9 - 3 = -12
32. 14 - -3 = 17
33. -8 - -8 = 0
34. 15 - -5 = 20
35. -3 - -3 = 0
36. -5 - -6 = 1
37. 25 - -5 = 30
38. 18 - -4 = 22
39. 60 - -5 = 65
40. 12 - 15 = -3
41. 18 - -3 = 21
42. 21 - 40 = -19
43. 83 - -21 = 104
44. 35 - -5 = 40
45. -10 - -7 = -3
46. 39 - -18 = 57
47. 12 - -42 = 54
48. 25 - -10 = 35
49. -20 - 5 = -25
50. -28 - 30 = -58

Practice hard. You'll win.

Page 96

Answer Key

Equations

Skill: Order of Operations

Name ______________________

Show your work on another sheet. Write your answers here.

Total Problems	50
Problems Correct	______

1. 2 + 7 − 3 = 6
2. 16 ÷ 4 + 3 = 7
3. 4 + 6 − 7 = 3
4. 2 × 6 ÷ 3 = 4
5. 6 × 4 ÷ 12 = 2
6. 10 − 7 + 6 = 9
7. 36 ÷ 6 + 4 = 10
8. 7 × 4 + 2 = 30
9. 5 × 5 − 5 = 20
10. 12 ÷ 4 + 7 = 10
11. 6 + 9 − 3 = 12
12. 13 + 6 − 7 = 12
13. 14 ÷ 2 × 3 = 21
14. 4 + 8 − 7 = 5
15. (16 + 9) ÷ 5 = 5
16. 9 × 4 ÷ 6 = 6
17. 3 × 9 − 17 = 10
18. 5 + 5 × 3 = 20
19. 6 × 6 ÷ 12 = 3
20. 12 + 7 − 9 = 10
21. 6 + 12 ÷ 2 = 12
22. 9 × 3 + 4 = 31
23. 9 + 6 − 8 = 7
24. 64 ÷ 8 + 9 = 17
25. 16 ÷ 2 + 9 = 17
26. 18 ÷ 2 × 3 = 27
27. 16 + 18 − 8 = 26
28. 14 − 7 + 3 = 10
29. 6 × 7 − 6 = 36
30. 24 ÷ 6 × 7 = 28
31. 32 ÷ 8 × 5 = 20
32. 16 + 4 ÷ 2 = 18
33. 9 × 9 + 6 = 87
34. 13 + 5 − 7 = 11
35. 15 ÷ 3 × 2 = 10
36. 7 + (3 × 9) = 34
37. 6 + (2 × 4) = 14
38. (4 + 8) ÷ 2 = 6
39. 9 + 9 × 2 = 27
40. 6 × 3 + 4 = 22
41. (9 + 16) ÷ 5 = 5
42. 16 + 18 − 7 = 27
43. (60 ÷ 5) ÷ 4 = 3
44. 36 + (4 × 8) = 68
45. 9 × 9 + 12 = 93
46. 32 ÷ 4 − 3 = 5
47. 12 ÷ 3 × 9 = 36
48. 6 + 9 − 7 = 8
49. 8 × 9 + 7 = 79
50. 8 + 3 × 8 = 32

Success ahoy! Just practice!

Page 97

Equations

Skill: Order of Operations

Name ______________________

Show your work on another sheet. Write your answers here.

Total Problems	50
Problems Correct	______

1. 5 + 6 − 4 = 7
2. 3 × 4 ÷ 3 = 4
3. 32 ÷ 8 + 3 = 7
4. 40 ÷ 8 − 2 = 3
5. 6 + 8 × 3 = 30
6. 14 + 12 − 6 = 20
7. 2 × 9 + 4 = 22
8. 8 × 8 + 6 = 70
9. 5 + 8 ÷ 2 = 9
10. 6 + 6 ÷ 6 = 7
11. 45 ÷ 5 × 3 = 27
12. 9 + 7 − 10 = 6
13. 15 × 2 ÷ 3 = 10
14. 3 × 7 − 1 = 20
15. 18 ÷ 9 × 8 = 16
16. 36 ÷ 9 + 8 = 12
17. 21 ÷ 7 + 6 = 9
18. 7 + 8 − 8 = 7
19. 9 + 6 − 12 = 3
20. 12 + 7 − 8 = 11
21. 56 ÷ 8 + 4 = 11
22. 64 ÷ 8 + 5 = 13
23. 14 + (2 × 8) = 30
24. (7 + 9) ÷ 2 = 8
25. 15 ÷ 3 × 2 = 10
26. (5 + 3) × 3 = 24
27. 15 − 7 + 3 = 11
28. (3 + 7) × 2 ÷ 10 = 2
29. 6 + 8 ÷ 2 = 10
30. 3 × (5 + 6) = 33
31. 12 × 2 + 2 = 26
32. 15 + 3 × 2 = 21
33. 14 − (8 − 2) − 1 = 7
34. 16 − (10 − 4) = 10
35. (14 + 6) ÷ 5 = 4
36. (3 + 2) × (4 + 6) = 50
37. 12 × (3 + 2) = 60
38. 9 × (15 − 7) = 72
39. 6 × (4 + 5) = 54
40. 3 + 6 × 2 + 5 = 20
41. 8 + 4 × 5 = 28
42. 6 × 8 + 2 = 50
43. 30 + 16 × 2 = 62
44. 3 × (9 + 2) = 33
45. 52 − (5 + 3) = 44
46. 64 ÷ 8 × 3 = 24
47. 25 − (3 + 8) = 14
48. 21 ÷ (3 + 4) = 3
49. 12 + 32 ÷ 4 = 20
50. 16 + (4 × 3) = 28

With practice, you can do it!

Page 98

Equations

Skill: Finding Solutions

Name ______________________

Solve these equations using this information: a = 2, b = 3, c = 4. Show your work on another sheet. Write your answers here.

Total Problems	48
Problems Correct	______

1. a + 7 = 9
2. 23 + c = 27
3. 12 ÷ b = 4
4. ab = 6
5. 2a − b = 1
6. 48 ÷ c = 12
7. 15b = 45
8. 5a + 10 = 20
9. b + 13 = 16
10. 6a + c = 16
11. bc = 12
12. 7a − c = 10
13. 3c + −8 = 4
14. ac + 6 = 14
15. 14 ÷ a = 7
16. b + 24 = 27
17. ac = 8
18. 10a + b = 23
19. 6b + 7c = 46
20. 15 − ab = 9
21. 13 + ac = 21
22. 5b + c = 19
23. a + c = 6
24. 36 ÷ b = 12
25. 20 − 4c = 4
26. 62 + a = 64
27. 2a + −6 = −2
28. 21 ÷ (b + c) = 3
29. 9a + 2b = 24
30. 5b + −12 = 3
31. ac + 24 = 32
32. 4a − 5 = 3
33. 8a + 2b = 22
34. bc + a = 14
35. 36 ÷ c = 9
36. 7b + 3c = 33
37. ac + 9 = 17
38. ab + −14 = −8
39. ac + b = 11
40. 4b + −5 = 7
41. 6c − b = 21
42. 14 + ac = 22
43. 20a − b = 37
44. 12c − 17 = 31
45. ab + c = 10
46. a + 27 = 29
47. 3b − c = 5
48. b + −6 = −3

Practice brings success!

Page 99

Equations

Skill: Finding Solutions

Name ______________________

Solve these equations using this information: a = 2, b = 3, x = 4, y = 5. Show your work on another sheet. Write your answers here.

Total Problems	50
Problems Correct	______

1. a + 14 = 16
2. x + 23 = 27
3. 3x − 7 = 5
4. 14 − y = 9
5. 62 + x = 66
6. ab + 3 = 9
7. 48 ÷ x = 12
8. y + ab = 10
9. 6a − 7 = 5
10. 5a + y = 15
11. 7y − 10 = 25
12. 6b ÷ 3 = 6
13. 8x + −9 = 23
14. a^2 + y = 9
15. 17 + b = 20
16. x + 12 = 16
17. y + −16 = −11
18. 3b − 7 = 2
19. 6x ÷ 12 = 2
20. 12 + xy = 32
21. ax + 3 = 11
22. bx − 6 = 6
23. y + −18 = −13
24. ab + xy = 26
25. y + 32 = 37
26. 12a − 14 = 10
27. 3y + −12 = 3
28. 6x − y = 19
29. b^2 + 14 = 23
30. 25 − xy = 5
31. 6x + −2y = 14
32. 16a − xy = 12
33. 10b ÷ y = 6
34. 20 ÷ x = 5
35. 10 + 3x = 22
36. 29 − 3b = 20
37. 60 − ab = 54
38. 16 + b = 19
39. 27 + y = 32
40. 3a + 6x = 30
41. 42 ÷ b = 14
42. 39 + y = 44
43. 32a ÷ 8 = 8
44. ab ÷ 2 = 3
45. 12a − 2b = 18
46. 2a + 18 = 22
47. 81 ÷ b^2 = 9
48. xy + −18 = 2
49. 12 + ax = 20
50. 6b − 7 = 11

Practice! Practice! Practice!

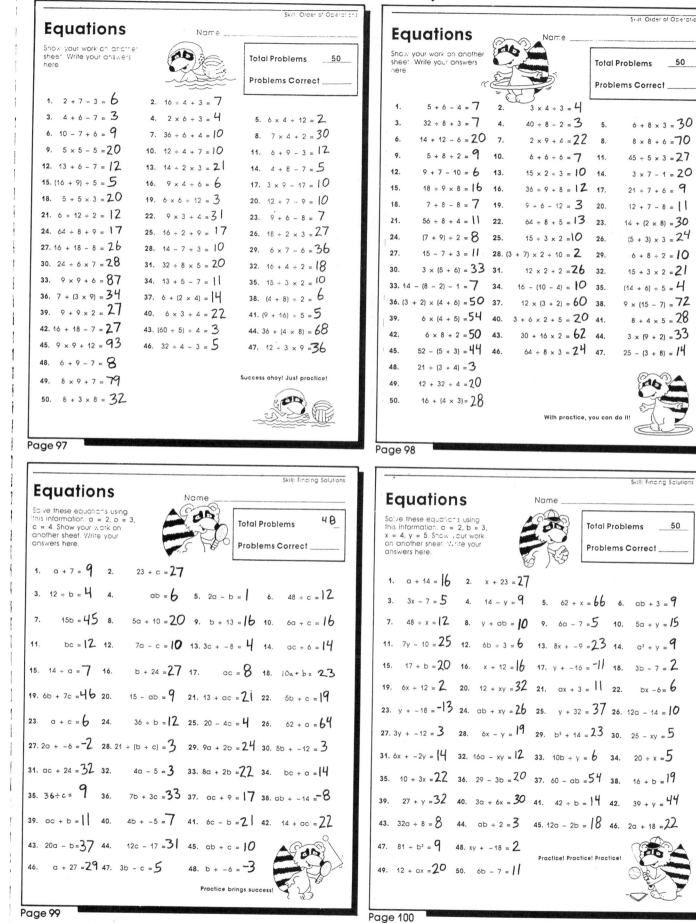

Page 100

Answer Key

Skill: Solving Addition Equations

Equations

Show your work on another sheet. Write your answers here.

Name ______________________

Total Problems 39

Problems Correct ______

1. $d + 7 = 12$ — $d = 5$
2. $a + 8 = 26$ — $a = 18$
3. $17 + a = 34$ — $a = 17$
4. $18 + n = 0$ — $n = -18$
5. $24 + q = 34$ — $q = 10$
6. $a + 3 = 24$ — $a = 21$
7. $15 + m = 31$ — $m = 16$
8. $d + 14 = 37$ — $d = 23$
9. $m + 8 = 21$ — $m = 13$
10. $36 = n + 9$ — $n = 27$
11. $q + 4 = 36$ — $q = 32$
12. $t + 8 = 15$ — $t = 7$
13. $47 + c = 58$ — $c = 11$
14. $43 = m + 17$ — $m = 26$
15. $56 = n + 14$ — $n = 42$
16. $m + 15 = 34$ — $m = 19$
17. $13 + d = 28$ — $d = 15$
18. $28 + n = 47$ — $n = 19$
19. $t + 30 = 43$ — $t = 13$
20. $32 + d = 49$ — $d = 17$
21. $16 + n = 40$ — $n = 24$
22. $2 + m = 14$ — $m = 12$
23. $e + 12 = 43$ — $e = 31$
24. $14 + q = 62$ — $q = 48$
25. $93 = 32 + m$ — $m = 61$
26. $m + 82 = 94$ — $m = 12$
27. $n + 3 = 49$ — $n = 46$
28. $49 = 27 + f$ — $f = 22$
29. $d + 45 = 80$ — $d = 35$
30. $18 = n + 10$ — $n = 8$
31. $60 = n + 29$ — $n = 31$
32. $a + 13 = 17$ — $a = 4$
33. $t + 23 = 40$ — $t = 17$
34. $x + 30 = 54$ — $x = 24$
35. $58 + n = 106$ — $n = 48$
36. $42 + d = 68$ — $d = 26$
37. $15 = y + 15$ — $y = 0$
38. $y + 14 = 36$ — $y = 22$
39. $60 + n = 86$ — $n = 26$

Practice = Success!

Page 101

Skill: Solving Division Equations

Equations

Name ______________________

Show your work on another sheet. Write your answers here.

Total Problems 40

Problems Correct ______

1. $\frac{m}{12} = 3$ — $m = 36$
2. $\frac{n}{6} = 5$ — $n = 30$
3. $\frac{r}{3} = 4$ — $r = 12$
4. $16 = \frac{n}{2}$ — $n = 32$
5. $9 = \frac{n}{9}$ — $n = 81$
6. $9 = \frac{r}{2}$ — $r = 18$
7. $12 = \frac{r}{3}$ — $r = 36$
8. $14 = \frac{n}{3}$ — $n = 42$
9. $\frac{n}{6} = 12$ — $n = 72$
10. $\frac{t}{8} = 4$ — $t = 32$
11. $\frac{x}{5} = 4$ — $x = 20$
12. $\frac{n}{5} = 20$ — $n = 100$
13. $\frac{c}{3} = 8$ — $c = 24$
14. $\frac{d}{5} = 12$ — $d = 60$
15. $\frac{m}{8} = 14$ — $m = 112$
16. $\frac{r}{6} = 7$ — $r = 42$
17. $\frac{r}{12} = 12$ — $r = 144$
18. $\frac{n}{10} = 11$ — $n = 110$
19. $15 = \frac{n}{6}$ — $n = 90$
20. $8 = \frac{r}{11}$ — $r = 88$
21. $12 = \frac{n}{13}$ — $n = 156$
22. $20 = \frac{n}{5}$ — $n = 100$
23. $13 = \frac{r}{7}$ — $r = 91$
24. $\frac{n}{12} = 9$ — $n = 108$
25. $\frac{r}{16} = 3$ — $r = 48$
26. $18 = \frac{d}{4}$ — $d = 72$
27. $\frac{r}{9} = 36$ — $r = 324$
28. $\frac{r}{13} = 3$ — $r = 39$
29. $\frac{n}{6} = 8$ — $n = 48$
30. $\frac{m}{15} = 3$ — $m = 45$
31. $\frac{n}{10} = 18$ — $n = 180$
32. $\frac{m}{15} = 5$ — $m = 75$
33. $\frac{m}{5} = 8$ — $m = 40$
34. $\frac{n}{9} = 27$ — $n = 243$
35. $\frac{m}{6} = 13$ — $m = 78$
36. $\frac{n}{11} = 14$ — $n = 154$
37. $\frac{x}{4} = 9$ — $x = 36$
38. $\frac{d}{5} = 25$ — $d = 125$
39. $\frac{y}{4} = 12$ — $y = 48$
40. $\frac{c}{12} = 6$ — $c = 72$

Through practice you learn!

Page 102